Financial Econometrics

Financial Econometrics

Special Issue Editor
Yiu-Kuen Tse

MDPI • Basel • Beijing • Wuhan • Barcelona • Belgrade

Special Issue Editor
Yiu-Kuen Tse
Singapore Management University
Singapore

Editorial Office
MDPI
St. Alban-Anlage 66
4052 Basel, Switzerland

This is a reprint of articles from the Special Issue published online in the open access journal *Journal of Risk and Financial Management* (ISSN 1911-8074) form 2018 to 2019 (available at: https://www.mdpi.com/journal/jrfm/special_issues/financial_econometrics).

For citation purposes, cite each article independently as indicated on the article page online and as indicated below:

LastName, A.A.; LastName, B.B.; LastName, C.C. Article Title. *Journal Name* **Year**, *Article Number*, Page Range.

ISBN 978-3-03921-626-0 (Pbk)
ISBN 978-3-03921-627-7 (PDF)

© 2019 by the authors. Articles in this book are Open Access and distributed under the Creative Commons Attribution (CC BY) license, which allows users to download, copy and build upon published articles, as long as the author and publisher are properly credited, which ensures maximum dissemination and a wider impact of our publications.

The book as a whole is distributed by MDPI under the terms and conditions of the Creative Commons license CC BY-NC-ND.

Contents

About the Special Issue Editor vii

Yiu-Kuen Tse
Editorial for the Special Issue on Financial Econometrics
Reprinted from: *J. Risk Financial Manag.* **2019**, *12*, 153, doi:10.3390/jrfm12030153 1

Anders Eriksson, Daniel P. A. Preve and Jun Yu
Forecasting Realized Volatility Using a Nonnegative Semiparametric Model
Reprinted from: *J. Risk Financial Manag.* **2019**, *12*, 139, doi:10.3390/jrfm12030139 3

Muhammad Farid Ahmed and Stephen Satchell
Some Dynamic and Steady-State Properties of Threshold Auto-Regressions with Applications to Stationarity and Local Explosivity
Reprinted from: *J. Risk Financial Manag.* **2019**, *12*, 123, doi:10.3390/jrfm12030123 26

Hui Xiao and Yiguo Sun
On Tuning Parameter Selection in Model Selection and Model Averaging: A Monte Carlo Study
Reprinted from: *J. Risk Financial Manag.* **2019**, *12*, 109, doi:10.3390/jrfm12030109 44

Zhongxian Men, Adam W. Kolkiewicz and Tony S. Wirjanto
Threshold Stochastic Conditional Duration Model for Financial Transaction Data
Reprinted from: *J. Risk Financial Manag.* **2019**, *12*, 88, doi:10.3390/jrfm12020088 60

Constantino Hevia and Martin Sola
Bond Risk Premia and Restrictions on Risk Prices [†]
Reprinted from: *J. Risk Financial Manag.* **2018**, *11*, 60, doi:10.3390/jrfm11040060 81

Galyna Grynkiv and Lars Stentoft
Stationary Threshold Vector Autoregressive Models
Reprinted from: *J. Risk Financial Manag.* **2018**, *11*, 45, doi:10.3390/jrfm11030045 103

About the Special Issue Editor

Yiu-Kuen Tse is a Professor of Economics at the Singapore Management University. His research interests are in econometric methodology, financial econometrics, risk management, and actuarial science. He is currently working on a high-frequency estimation of large dimensional covariance matrices, as well as several topics on empirical international finance. He has published a popular textbook entitled "Nonlife Actuarial Models".

Editorial

Editorial for the Special Issue on Financial Econometrics

Yiu-Kuen Tse

School of Economics, Singapore Management University, Singapore 178903, Singapore; yktse@smu.edu.sg

Received: 16 September 2019; Accepted: 17 September 2019; Published: 19 September 2019

Financial econometrics has developed into a very fruitful and vibrant research area in the last two decades. The availability of good data promotes research in this area, specially aided by online data and high-frequency data. These two characteristics of financial data also create challenges for researchers that are different from classical macro-econometric and micro-econometric problems.

This special issue is dedicated to research topics that are relevant for analyzing financial data. We have gathered six articles under this theme. The paper by Eriksson et al. (2019) considers a method to forecast realized volatility using a classical autoregressive model. Two modifications are adopted to make this model suitable for nonnegative valued variables like volatility. First, they apply Tukey's power transformation to their data. Second, they allow the error distribution to be unspecified, resulting in a semiparametric approach. While their model has forecasting volatility as the primary motivation, it can be used for many nonnegative valued variables, thus extending the applicability of their approach.

The empirical study of Eriksson et al. (2019) shows that their method compares very well against some of the most commonly used forecasting models for volatility in terms of post-sample prediction. As mentioned in their concluding remarks, it will be interesting to see how their approach works for intra-day data and multivariate models.

Ahmed and Satchell (2019) consider a threshold autoregressive model with Markovian states. These states may incorporate both explosive and stationary regimes. They investigate the characteristic function of this process and derive analytic formula for their moments. Their approach can be applied to processes for which the moment generating function does not exist. Thus, certain asset pricing models with non-normal errors can be analyzed.

Xiao and Sun (2019) investigate the estimation of the tuning parameter for model selection and averaging. Incorporating the shrinkage averaging estimator method and Mallow's model averaging method, they propose the shrinkage model averaging method, which can be used for averaging high-dimensional sparse models. The method is applicable to a wide range of econometric models, and extends beyond the financial econometrics arena. Their Monte Carlo study shows that their new method performs well against other methods in averaging high-dimensional sparse models.

Men et al. (2019) propose a threshold stochastic conditional duration model that can be used to analyze transaction financial data. They assume a latent AR(1) model, which may switch between two regimes. The regimes are self-excited and are based on the observed duration. The model can be estimated efficiently using a Markov-Chain Monte Carlo approach. Their empirical examples support the desirable performance of their new model in forecasting transaction duration.

Hevia and Sola (2018) examine the effect of imposing over-identifying restrictions on affine term structure models. In particular, they investigate the effects of inappropriate restrictions on some risk measures. They argue that in certain cases, such restrictions may have a significant impact on the estimated risk premium, and it is difficult to ascertain a priori the likely outcome. Due to this uncertainty, they recommend using just-identified models when the purpose is to apply the affine models to compute the risk premium.

Grynkiv and Stentoft (2018) study the multivariate generalization of the threshold autoregressive model. They assume the latent regime driver to follow a dichotomous structure, and one of the regimes may be explosive. They derive conditions under which the overall distribution is stationary. They also derive the unconditional distribution of the process for a special case of the threshold model and show that it follows an infinite mixture-of-normal distribution.

Funding: This research received no external funding.

Conflicts of Interest: The author declares no conflict of interest.

References

Ahmed, Muhammad F., and Stephen Satchell. 2019. Some Dynamic and Steady-State Properties of Threshold Auto-Regressions with Applications to Stationarity and Local Explosivity. *Journal of Financial Risk Management* 12: 123. [CrossRef]

Eriksson, Anders, Daniel P. A. Preve, and Jun Yu. 2019. Forecasting Realized Volatility Using a Nonnegative Semiparametric Model. *Journal of Financial Risk Management* 12: 139. [CrossRef]

Grynkiv, Galyna, and Lars Stentoft. 2018. Stationary Threshold Vector Autoregressive Models. *Journal of Financial Risk Management* 11: 45. [CrossRef]

Hevia, Constantino, and Martin Sola. 2018. Bond Risk Premia and Restrictions on Risk Prices. *Journal of Financial Risk Management* 11: 60. [CrossRef]

Men, Zhongxian, Adam W. Kolkiewicz, and Tony S. Wirjanto. 2019. Threshold Stochastic Conditional Duration Model for Financial Transaction Data. *Journal of Financial Risk Management* 12: 88. [CrossRef]

Xiao, Hui, and Yiguo Sun. 2019. On Tuning Parameter Selection in Model Selection and Model Averaging: A Monte Carlo Study. *Journal of Financial Risk Management* 12: 109. [CrossRef]

© 2019 by the author. Licensee MDPI, Basel, Switzerland. This article is an open access article distributed under the terms and conditions of the Creative Commons Attribution (CC BY) license (http://creativecommons.org/licenses/by/4.0/).

Article

Forecasting Realized Volatility Using a Nonnegative Semiparametric Model

Anders Eriksson [1], Daniel P. A. Preve [2,*] and Jun Yu [2]

1. J.P. Morgan, 25 Bank Street, London E14 5JP, UK
2. School of Economics, Singapore Management University, Singapore 188065, Singapore
* Correspondence: dpreve@smu.edu.sg

Received: 21 June 2019; Accepted: 26 August 2019; Published: 29 August 2019

Abstract: This paper introduces a parsimonious and yet flexible semiparametric model to forecast financial volatility. The new model extends a related linear nonnegative autoregressive model previously used in the volatility literature by way of a power transformation. It is semiparametric in the sense that the distributional and functional form of its error component is partially unspecified. The statistical properties of the model are discussed and a novel estimation method is proposed. Simulation studies validate the new method and suggest that it works reasonably well in finite samples. The out-of-sample forecasting performance of the proposed model is evaluated against a number of standard models, using data on S&P 500 monthly realized volatilities. Some commonly used loss functions are employed to evaluate the predictive accuracy of the alternative models. It is found that the new model generally generates highly competitive forecasts.

Keywords: volatility forecasting; realized volatility; linear programming estimator; Tukey's power transformation; nonlinear nonnegative autoregression; forecast comparisons

JEL Classification: C22; C51; C52; C53; C58

---

1. Introduction

Financial market volatility is an important input for asset allocation, investment, derivative pricing and financial market regulation. Not surprisingly, how to model and forecast financial volatility has been a subject of extensive research. Numerous survey papers are now available on the subject, with hundreds of reviewed research articles. Excellent survey articles on the subject include Bollerslev et al. (1992); Bollerslev et al. (1994); Ghysels et al. (1996); Poon and Granger (2003); and Shephard (2005).

In this vast literature, ARCH and stochastic volatility (SV) models are popular parametric tools. These two classes of models are motivated by the fact that volatilities are time-varying. Moreover, they offer ways to estimate past volatility and forecast future volatility from return data. In recent years, however, many researchers have argued that one could measure latent volatility by realized volatility (RV), see for example Andersen et al. (2001) (ABDL 2001 hereafter) and Barndorff-Nielsen and Shephard (2002), and then build a time series model for volatility forecasting using observed RV, see for example Andersen et al. (2003) (ABDL 2003 hereafter). An advantage of this approach is that "models built for the realized volatility produce forecasts superior to those obtained from less direct methods" (ABDL 2003). In an important study, ABDL (2003) introduced a new Gaussian time series model for logarithmic RV (log-RV) and established its superiority for RV forecasting over some standard methods based on squared returns. Their choice of modeling log-RV rather than raw RV is motivated by the fact that the logarithm of RV, in contrast to RV itself, is approximately normally distributed. Moreover, conditional heteroskedasticity is greatly reduced in log-RV.

Following this line of thought, in this paper we introduce a new time series model for RV. For the S&P 500 monthly RV, we show that although the distribution of log-RV is closer to a normal distribution than that of raw RV, normality is still rejected at all standard significance levels. Moreover, although conditional heteroskedasticity is reduced in log-RV, there is still evidence of remaining conditional heteroskedasticity. These two limitations associated with the logarithmic transformation motivate us to consider a more flexible transformation, that is, the so-called Tukey's power transformation which is closely related to the well-known Box-Cox transformation. In contrast to the logarithmic transformation, Tukey's power transformation or the Box-Cox transformation is generally not compatible with a normal error distribution as the support for the normal distribution covers the entire real line.[1] This well-known truncation problem further motivates us to use nonnegative error distributions. The new model, which we call a Tukey nonnegative type autoregression (TNTAR), is flexible, parsimonious and has a simple forecast expression. Moreover, the numerical estimation of the model is very fast and can easily be implemented using standard computational software.

The new model is closely related to the linear nonnegative models described in Barndorff-Nielsen and Shephard (2001) and Nielsen and Shephard (2003). In particular, it generalizes the discrete time version of the nonnegative Ornstein-Uhlenbeck process of Barndorff-Nielsen and Shephard (2001) by (1) applying a power transformation to volatility; (2) leaving the dependency structure and the distribution of the nonnegative error term unspecified. Our work is also related to Yu et al. (2006) and Gonçalves and Meddahi (2011) where the Box-Cox transformation is applied to stochastic volatility and RV, respectively. The main difference between our model specification and theirs is that an unspecified (marginal) distribution with nonnegative support, instead of the normal distribution, is induced by the transformation. Moreover, our model is loosely related to Higgins and Bera (1992); Hentschel (1995) and Duan (1997) where the Box-Cox transformation is applied to ARCH volatility, and to Fernandes and Grammig (2006) and Chen and Deo (2004). Finally, our model is related to a recent study by Cipollini et al. (2006) where an alternative model with nonnegative errors is used for RV. The main difference here is that the dynamic structure for the transformed RV is linear in our model, whereas the dynamic structure for the RV is nonlinear in theirs.

Our proposed model is estimated using a two-stage estimation method. In the first stage, a nonlinear least squares procedure is applied to a nonstandard objective function. In the second stage a linear programming estimator is applied. The finite sample performance of the proposed estimation method is studied via simulations.

The TNTAR model is used to model and forecast the S&P 500 monthly RV and its out-of-sample performance is compared to a number of standard time series models previously used in the literature, including the exponential smoothing method and two logarithmic long-memory ARFIMA models. Under various loss functions, we find that our parsimonious nonnegative model generally generates highly competitive forecasts. While this paper considers the application of forecasting RV, there are a number of applications beyond financial data for which our model may be useful. For example, modeling and forecasting climatological or telecommunication time series may be interesting alternative applications for our nonnegative model.

While our model is related to several models in the literature, to the best of our knowledge, our specification is new in two ways. First, it is based on Tukey's power transformation. Second, the distribution and functional form of its error component are partially unspecified. Moreover, the estimation method that we propose is new.

The rest of the paper is organized as follows. Section 2 motivates and presents the new model. In Section 3 a novel estimation method is proposed to estimate the parameters of the new model. In Section 4 the finite sample performance of the new method is studied via simulations. Section 5

---

[1] Generally, the distribution of a Box-Cox transformed random variable cannot be normal as its support is bounded either above or below.

describes the S&P 500 realized volatility data and the empirical results. In the same section we also outline the alternative models for volatility forecasting and present the loss functions used to assess their forecast performances. Finally, Section 6 concludes.

2. A Nonnegative Semiparametric Model

Before introducing the new TNTAR model, we first review two related time series models previously used in the volatility literature, namely, a simple nonnegative autoregressive (AR) model and the Box-Cox AR model.

2.1. Related Volatility Models

Barndorff-Nielsen and Shephard (2001) introduced the following continuous time model for financial volatility, $\sigma^2(t)$,

$$d\sigma^2(t) = -\lambda\sigma^2(t)dt + dz(\lambda t), \quad \lambda > 0. \tag{1}$$

In the above z is a Lévy process with independent nonnegative increments, which ensures the positivity of $\sigma^2(t)$ (see Equation (2) in Barndorff-Nielsen and Shephard 2001). Applying the Euler approximation to the continuous time model in (1) yields the following discrete time model

$$\sigma^2_{t+1} = \varphi\sigma^2_t + u_{t+1}, \tag{2}$$

where $\varphi = 1 - \lambda$ and $u_{t+1} = z(\lambda(t+1)) - z(\lambda t)$ is a sequence of independent identically distributed (i.i.d.) random variables whose distribution has a nonnegative support. A well known nonnegative random variable is the generalized inverse Gaussian, whose tails can be quite fat. Barndorff-Nielsen and Shephard (2001) discuss the analytical tractability of this model. In the case when u_{t+1} is exponentially distributed, Nielsen and Shephard (2003) derive the finite sample distribution of a linear programming estimator for φ for the stationary, unit root and explosive cases.[2] Simulated paths from model (2) typically match actual realized volatility data quite well. See, for example, Figure 1c in Barndorff-Nielsen and Shephard (2001). Unfortunately, so far little empirical evidence establishing the usefulness of this model has been reported.

Two restrictions seem to apply to model (2). First, since its errors are independent, conditional heteroskedasticity is not allowed for. The second restriction concerns the ratio of two successive volatilities. More specifically, from (2) it can be seen that $\sigma^2_{t+1}/\sigma^2_t$ is bounded from below by φ, almost surely, implying that σ^2_{t+1} cannot decrease by more than $100(1-\varphi)\%$ compared to σ^2_t. Since the AR parameter φ of the model typically is estimated using linear programming, in practice, this restriction is automatically satisfied. For instance, the full sample estimate of φ in our empirical study is 0.262, implying that σ^2_t cannot decrease by more than 73.8% from one time period to the next. Indeed, 73.8% is the maximum percentage drop in successive monthly volatilities in the sample, which took place on November 1987.

In a discrete time framework, a popular parametric time series model for volatility is the lognormal SV model of Taylor (2007) given by

$$r_t = \sigma_t \varepsilon_t, \tag{3}$$
$$\log \sigma^2_t = (1-\varphi)\mu + \varphi \log \sigma^2_{t-1} + \epsilon_t, \tag{4}$$

where r_t is the return, σ^2_t is the latent volatility, and ε_t and ϵ_t are two independent Gaussian noises. In this specification volatility clustering is modeled as an AR(1) for the log-volatility. The logarithmic transformation in (4) serves three important purposes: First, it ensures the positivity of σ^2_t. Second, it removes heteroskedasticity. Third, it induces normality.

---

[2] See Section 3 for a detailed discussion on the linear programming estimator.

Yu et al. (2006) introduced a closely related SV model by replacing the logarithmic transformation in Taylor's volatility Equation (4) with the more general Box-Cox transformation (Box and Cox 1964),

$$h(\sigma_t^2, \lambda) = (1 - \varphi)\mu + \varphi h(\sigma_{t-1}^2, \lambda) + \epsilon_t, \tag{5}$$

where

$$h(x, \lambda) = \begin{cases} \frac{x^\lambda - 1}{\lambda}, & \lambda \neq 0, \\ \log x, & \lambda = 0. \end{cases} \tag{6}$$

Compared to the logarithmic transformation, the Box-Cox transformation provides a more flexible way to improve normality and reduce heteroskedasticity. A nice feature of the Box-Cox AR model given by (5) and (6) is that it includes several standard specifications as special cases, including the logarithmic transformation ($\lambda = 0$) and a linear specification ($\lambda = 1$). In the context of SV, Yu et al. (2006) find empirical evidence against the logarithmic transformation. Chen and Deo (2004) and Gonçalves and Meddahi (2011) are interested in the optimal power transformation. In the context of RV, Gonçalves and Meddahi (2011) find evidence of non-optimality for the logarithmic transformation. They further report evidence of negative values of λ as the optimal choice for various data generating processes. Our empirical results reinforce this important conclusion, although our approach is very different.

While the above discrete time models have proven useful for modeling volatility, there is little documentation on their usefulness for forecasting volatility. Moreover, the Box-Cox transformation is known to be incompatible with a normal error distribution. This is the well-known truncation problem associated with the Box-Cox transformation in the context of Gaussianity.

2.2. Realized Volatility

In the ARCH or SV models, volatilities are estimated parametrically from returns observed at the same frequency. In recent years, however, it has been argued that one can measure volatility in a model-free framework using an empirical measure of the quadratic variation of the underlying efficient price process, that is, RV. RV has several advantages over ARCH and SV models. First, by treating volatility as directly observable, RV overcomes the well known curse-of-dimensionality problem in the multivariate ARCH or SV models. Second, compared to the squared return, RV provides a more reliable estimate of integrated volatility. This improvement in estimation naturally leads to gains in volatility forecasting.

Let RV_t denote the RV at a lower frequency (say daily or monthly) and $p(t, k)$ denote the log-price at a higher frequency (say intra-day or daily). Then RV_t is defined by

$$RV_t = \sqrt{\sum_{k=2}^{N} [p(t,k) - p(t, k-1)]^2}, \tag{7}$$

where N is the number of higher frequency observations in a lower frequency period.[3]

The theoretical justification for RV as a volatility measure comes from standard stochastic process theory, according to which the empirical quadratic variation converges to integrated variance as the infill sampling frequency tends to zero (ABDL 2001; Barndorff-Nielsen and Shephard 2002; Jacod 2017). The empirical method inspired by this consistency has recently become more popular with the availability of high-frequency data.

---

[3] In ABDL (2003) RV is referred to as the realized variance, $\sum_{k=2}^{N}[p(t,k) - p(t, k-1)]^2$. Although the authors build time series models for the realized variance, they forecast the realized volatility. In contrast, the present paper builds time series models for and forecasts, the realized volatility, which seems more appropriate. Consequently, the bias correction, as described in ABDL (2003), is not required.

In a recent important contribution, ABDL (2003) find that a Gaussian long-memory model for the logarithmic daily realized variance provides more accurate forecasts than the GARCH(1,1) model and the RiskMetrics method of J.P. Morgan (1996). The logarithmic transformation is used since it is found that the distribution of logarithmic realized variance, but not raw realized variance, is approximately normal. In Table 1 we report (to 3 decimals) some summary statistics for monthly RV, log-RV and power-RV for the S&P 500 data in our empirical study over the period Jan 1946–Dec 2004, including the skewness, kurtosis, and p-value of the Jarque-Bera test statistic for normality.[4] For RV, the departure from normality is overwhelming. While the distribution of log-RV is much closer to a normal distribution than that of RV, there is still strong evidence against normality.

Table 1. Summary statistics for S&P 500 monthly RV, log-RV and power-RV over the period Jan 1946–Dec 2004. JB is the p-value of the Jarque-Bera test under the null hypothesis that the data are from a normal distribution.

	Mean	Median	Maximum	Skewness	Kurtosis	JB
RV	0.004	0.003	0.026	3.307	28.791	0.000
log-RV	−5.687	−5.726	−3.666	0.389	3.657	0.000
power-RV	4.894	4.912	6.908	0.032	3.288	0.259

To compare the conditional heteroskedasticities, in Figure 1 we plot squared OLS residuals ($\hat{\epsilon}_{it}^2$, $i = 1, 2, 3$), obtained from AR(1) regressions for RV, log-RV and power-RV, respectively, against each corresponding explanatory variable (lagged RV, log-RV and power-RV). For ease of comparison, superimposed are smooth curves fitted using the LOESS method. It is clear that while the logarithmic transformation reduces the conditional heteroskedasticity there is still evidence of it in the residuals. The power transformation further reduces the conditional heteroskedasticity of RV. While the logarithmic transformation reduces the impact of large observations (extreme deviations from the mean), the second plot of Figure 1 suggests that it is not as effective as anticipated. In contrast, the power transformation with a negative power parameter is able to reduce the impact of large observations further. Thus, the results indicate that there is room for further improvements over the logarithmic transformation. A more detailed analysis of the S&P 500 data is provided in Section 5.

---

[4] The power parameter is −0.278 which is the estimate of λ in our proposed TNTAR model obtained using the entire S&P 500 monthly RV sample. See Sections 3 and 5 for further details.

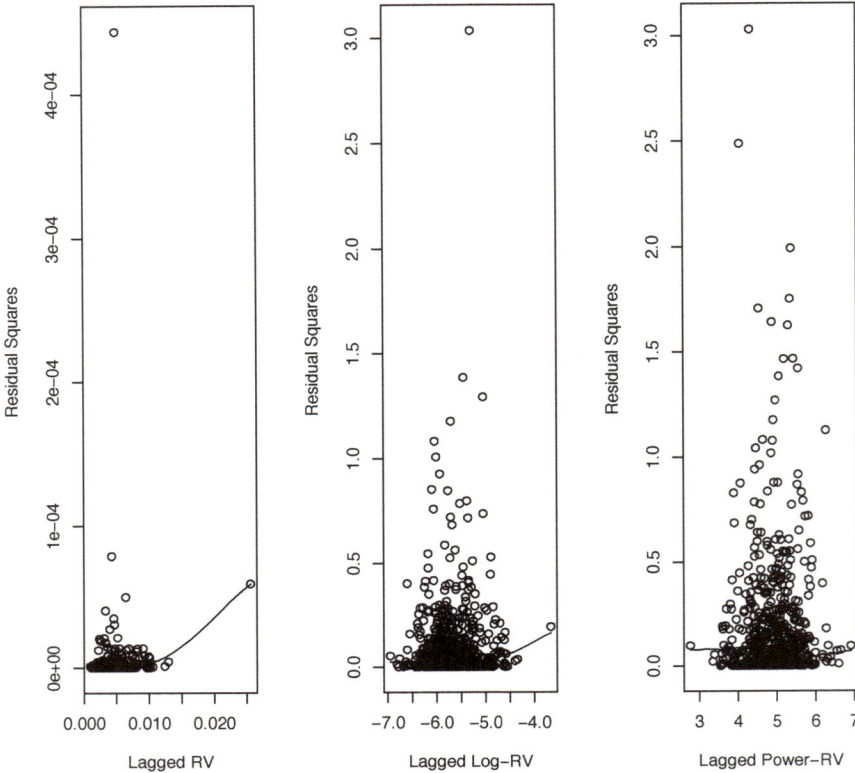

Figure 1. Plots of squared ordinary least squares (OLS) residuals, obtained from AR(1) regressions for RV, log-RV and power-RV, respectively, against each corresponding explanatory variable. Superimposed are smooth curves fitted using the LOESS method.

2.3. The Model

In this paper, our focus is on modeling and forecasting RV. To this end, let us first consider the RV version of model (5),

$$h(RV_t, \lambda) = \alpha + \beta h(RV_{t-1}, \lambda) + \epsilon_t, \tag{8}$$

where ϵ_t is a sequence of independent $N(0, \sigma_\epsilon^2)$ distributed random variables and $h(x, \lambda)$ is given by (6).

If $\lambda \neq 0$, we may rewrite (8) as

$$RV_t^\lambda = (1 + \lambda \alpha) + \beta(RV_{t-1}^\lambda - 1) + \lambda \epsilon_t, \tag{9}$$

where RV_t^λ is a simple power transformation. A special case of (9) is a linear Gaussian AR(1) model, obtained when $\lambda = 1$:

$$RV_t = (1 + \alpha - \beta) + \beta RV_{t-1} + \epsilon_t. \tag{10}$$

If $\lambda = 0$ in (8), we have the log-linear Gaussian AR(1) model previously used in the literature:

$$\log RV_t = \alpha + \beta \log RV_{t-1} + \epsilon_t. \tag{11}$$

While the specification in (8) is more general than the log-linear Gaussian AR(1) model (11), it has a serious drawback. In general, solving for RV_t, the right hand side of (9) has to be nonnegative with probability one or almost surely (a.s.). This requirement is violated since a normal error distribution has a support covering the entire real line.

This drawback motivates us to explore an alternative model specification for RV. Our proposed nonnegative TNTAR model is of the form

$$RV_t^\lambda = \varphi RV_{t-1}^\lambda + u_t, \quad t = 2, 3, \ldots \quad (12)$$

with the power parameter $\lambda \neq 0$, AR parameter $\varphi > 0$ and (a.s.) positive initial value RV_1. The errors u_t driving the model are nonnegative, possibly non-i.i.d., random variables. In the simplest case, u_t is assumed to be a sequence of m-dependent, identically distributed, continuous random variables with nonnegative support $[\eta, \infty)$, for some unknown $\eta \geq 0$.[5] It is assumed that $m \in \mathbf{N}$ is finite and potentially unknown. Hence, the distribution and functional form of u_t is partially unspecified. We expect φRV_{t-1}^λ to be the dominating component in (12) and do not model u_t parametrically.

The power transformation RV_t^λ is closely related to John W. Tukey's ladder of power transformations for linearizing data (Tukey 1977), partially illustrated in (13) below:

$$\frac{1}{x^3} \quad \frac{1}{x^2} \quad \frac{1}{x} \quad \frac{1}{\sqrt{x}} \quad \log x \quad \sqrt{x} \quad x \quad x^2 \quad x^3. \quad (13)$$

The nonnegative restriction on the support of the error distribution ensures the positivity of RV_t^λ. Hence, our model does not suffer from the truncation problem of the classical Box-Cox model (8). As the distribution of u_t is left unspecified, some very flexible tail behavior is allowed for. Consequently, the drawback in the Box-Cox AR model (8) is addressed in the proposed TNTAR model (12).

In the classical Box-Cox model, the transformation parameter λ is required to induce linearity and normality and at the same time eliminate conditional heteroskedasticity. These are too many requirements for a single parameter. In our model, the role of the Tukey-type power transformation is to improve linearity and reduce conditional heteroskedasticity, not to induce normality. To illustrate this, suppose that a square root transformation is applied with $\lambda = 1/2$ in (12), then $RV_t = \varphi^2 RV_{t-1} + 2\varphi \sqrt{RV_{t-1}} u_t + u_t^2$ and the conditional variance of raw RV is time-varying.[6] An intercept in the model is superfluous because the support parameter η can be strictly positive. Our model echoes (8), with the normal distribution replaced by a nonnegative distribution. If $\lambda = 1$ and its errors are i.i.d., our model becomes the discrete time version of Equation (2) in Barndorff-Nielsen and Shephard (2001). In general, the distributional and functional form is not assumed to be known for the error component. Hence, the TNTAR model combines a parametric component for the persistence with a nonparametric component for the error. On the one hand, the new model is highly parsimonious. In particular, there are only two parameters that need to be estimated for the purpose of volatility forecasting, namely φ and λ. On the other hand, the specification is sufficiently flexible for modeling the error.

As mentioned earlier, there exists a lower bound for the percentage change in volatility in model (2). A similar bound applies to our model. It is easy to show that $RV_t/RV_{t-1} \leq \varphi^{1/\lambda}$ if $\lambda < 0$ (upper bound) and $RV_t/RV_{t-1} \geq \varphi^{1/\lambda}$ if $\lambda > 0$ (lower bound). Typical estimated values of φ and λ in (12) for our empirical study are 0.639 and -0.278, respectively, suggesting that RV_t cannot increase by more than 500% from one time period to the next. As we will see later, our proposed estimator for λ depends on the ratios of successive RV's and hence the bound is endogenously determined.

---

[5] Some common m-dependent specifications include $u_t = \epsilon_t + \psi \epsilon_{t-1}$ ($m = 1$) and $u_t = \epsilon_t + \psi \epsilon_{t-1} \epsilon_{t-2}$ ($m = 2$), where ϵ_t is an i.i.d. sequence of random variables.

[6] More generally, suppose that $\lambda = 1/n$ for some natural number n, then $RV_t = \left(\varphi \sqrt[n]{RV_{t-1}} + u_t\right)^n = \sum_{k=0}^{n} \binom{n}{k} \varphi^{n-k} RV_{t-1}^{(n-k)/n} u_t^k$.

3. Robust Estimation and Forecasting

In this section we consider the estimation of the parameters φ and λ and a one-step-ahead forecast expression, for the TNTAR model. First, we consider the special case when λ is assumed to be known. Some common power transformations include $\lambda = 1/n$ (the nth root transformation) and its reciprocal, $\lambda = -1/n$. Second, we consider the more general case when both φ and λ are unknown and need to be estimated. We then examine the finite sample performance of the proposed estimation method via simulations.

3.1. Robust Estimation of φ

If the true value of the power transformation parameter is known, a natural estimator for φ in (12) given the sample $RV_1, \ldots, RV_T$ of size T and the nonnegativity of the errors is

$$\widehat{\varphi}_T = \min\left\{\frac{RV_2^\lambda}{RV_1^\lambda}, \ldots, \frac{RV_T^\lambda}{RV_{T-1}^\lambda}\right\} = \varphi + \min\left\{\frac{u_2}{RV_1^\lambda}, \ldots, \frac{u_T}{RV_{T-1}^\lambda}\right\}. \qquad (14)$$

The estimator $\widehat{\varphi}_T$ in (14) can be viewed as the solution to a linear programming problem. Because of this, we will refer to it as a linear programming estimator (LPE). This estimator is also the conditional (on RV_1) maximum likelihood estimator (MLE) of φ when the errors in (12) are i.i.d. exponentially distributed random variables, cf. Nielsen and Shephard (2003). Interestingly, the LPE is strongly consistent for more general error specifications, including heteroskedasticity and m-dependence. It is robust in the sense that its consistency conditions allow for certain model misspecifications in u_t. For example, the order of m-dependence in the error sequence and the conditional distribution of RV_t may be incorrectly specified. Moreover, the LPE is strongly consistent even under quite general forms of heteroskedasticity and structural breaks. For a more detailed account of the properties of the LPE, see Preve (2015).

Like the ordinary least squares (OLS) estimator for φ, the LPE is distribution-free in the sense that its consistency does not rely on a particular distributional assumption for the error component. However, the LPE is in many ways superior to the OLS estimator. For example, its rate of convergence can be faster than $O_p(T^{-1/2})$ even for $\varphi < 1$, whereas the rate of covergence for the OLS estimator is faster than $O_p(T^{-1/2})$ only for $\varphi \geq 1$, see Phillips (1987). Furthermore, unlike the OLS estimator the consistency conditions for the LPE do not involve the existence of any higher order moments.

Under additional technical conditions, Davis and McCormick (1989) and Feigin and Resnick (1992) obtain the limiting distribution of a LPE for which (14) appear as a special case when $\lambda = 1$ and the errors are i.i.d.. The authors show that the accuracy of the LPE depends on the index of regular variation at zero (or infinity) of the error distribution function. For example, for standard exponential errors, the index of regular variation at zero is 1 and the LPE converges to φ at the rate of $O_p(T^{-1})$. In general, a difficulty in the application of the limiting distribution is that the index of regular variation at zero appears both in a normalizing constant and in the limit. Datta and McCormick (1995) avoid this difficulty by establishing the asymptotic validity of a bootstrap scheme based on the LPE.

It is readily verified that the LPE in (14) is positively biased and stochastically decreasing in T, that is, $\varphi < \widehat{\varphi}_{T_2} \leq \widehat{\varphi}_{T_1}$ a.s. for any $T_1 < T_2$.[7] Hence, the accuracy of the LPE either remains the same or improves as the sample size increases (cf. Figure 2).

To illustrate the robustness of the LPE, consider a covariance stationary AR(1) model

$$RV_t = \varphi RV_{t-1} + u_t, \quad t = 0, \pm 1, \pm 2, \ldots,$$

---

[7] Whenever necessary we use the subscript T to emphasize on the sample size.

under the possible misspecification

$$u_t = \epsilon_t + \sum_{i=1}^{m} \psi_i \epsilon_{t-i},$$

where ϵ_t is a sequence of non-zero mean i.i.d. random variables. For $m > 0$ the (identically distributed) errors u_t are serially correlated. In this setting the OLS estimator for φ is inconsistent while the LPE remains consistent. In the first panel of Figure 2 we plot 100 observations simulated from the nonnegative ARMA(1,1) model, $RV_t = \varphi RV_{t-1} + \epsilon_t + \psi \epsilon_{t-1}$ with $\varphi = 0.5$, $\psi = 0.75$ and standard exponential noise. In the second panel of Figure 2 we plot the sample paths of the recursive LPEs and OLS estimates for φ obtained from the simulated data. In each iteration, a new observation is added to the sample used for estimation. It can be seen that the LPEs quickly approach the true value φ, whereas the OLS estimates do not. Moreover, the OLS estimates fluctuate much more than the LPEs when the sample size is small, suggesting that the LPE is less sensitive to extreme deviations from the mean than the OLS estimator in small samples.

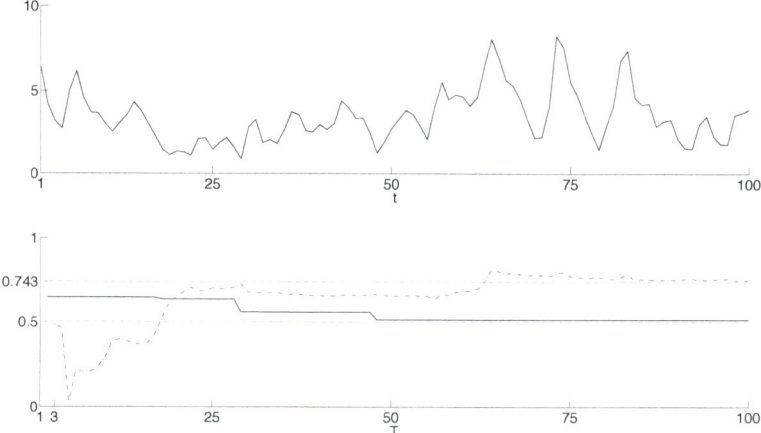

Figure 2. The top panel displays a time series plot of data simulated from the nonnegative ARMA(1,1) process $RV_t = \varphi RV_{t-1} + \epsilon_t + \psi \epsilon_{t-1}$ with $\varphi = 0.5$, $\psi = 0.75$ and i.i.d. standard exponential noise ϵ_t. The bottom panel displays the sample paths of the recursive LPEs and OLS estimates for φ in the *misspecified* AR(1) model $RV_t = \varphi RV_{t-1} + u_t$, obtained from the sample $RV_1, \ldots, RV_T$ for $T = 3, \ldots, 100$. The solid line represents the LPEs and the dash-dotted line the OLS estimates.

We now list simple assumptions under which the consistency of the LPE in (14) holds. More general assumptions, allowing for an unknown number of unknown breaks in the error mean and variance, under which the LPE converges to φ for a known λ are given in Preve (2015).

Assumption 1. *The power transformation parameter $\lambda \neq 0$ in (12) is known. The AR parameter $\varphi > 0$, and the initial value RV_1 is a.s. positive. The errors u_t driving the autoregression form a sequence of m-dependent, identically distributed, nonnegative continuous random variables. The order, m, of the dependence is finite.*

Assumption 1 allows for various kinds of m-dependent error specifications, with $m \in \mathbf{N}$ potentially unknown. For example, serially correlated finite-order MA specifications. Since the functional form and distribution of u_t are taken to be unknown, the formulation is nonparametric.

Assumption 2. *The error component in (12) satisfies $P(c_1 < u_t < c_2) < 1$ for all $0 < c_1 < c_2 < \infty$.*

It is important to point out that Assumption 2 is satisfied for any error distribution with unbounded nonnegative support.

Theorem 1. *Suppose that Assumptions 1 and 2 hold. Then the LPE in (14) is strongly consistent for φ in (12). That is, $\widehat{\varphi}_T$ converges to φ a.s. as T tends to infinity.*

The convergence of $\widehat{\varphi}_T$ is almost surely (and, hence, also in probability). Our interest is in forecasting raw RV, not the power transformation of RV in (12). Let $\widehat{RV}_{T+1}$ denote a forecast of RV_{T+1} made at time T. A simple approximation to the optimal mean squared error, one-step-ahead, forecast of RV_{T+1} at time T is given by the sample average

$$\widehat{RV}_{T+1} = \frac{1}{T-1} \sum_{i=2}^{T} \left(\widehat{\varphi}_T RV_T^\lambda + \widehat{u}_i \right)^{1/\lambda},$$

where $\widehat{u}_i = RV_i^\lambda - \widehat{\varphi}_T RV_{i-1}^\lambda$ converges to u_i in distribution as T tends to infinity under Assumptions 1 and 2.

3.2. Estimation of φ and λ

In practice, we usually do not know the true value of λ. In this section we propose an LPE based two-stage estimation method for φ and λ in the TNTAR model (12). In doing so, we also establish a general expression for its one-step-ahead forecast. The estimators are easily computable using standard computational software such as MATLAB.

Joint estimation of φ and λ is non-trivial, even under certain parametric and simplifying assumptions for u_t. For example, even in the simple case when u_t is a sequence of independent exponentially distributed random variables it appears that the MLEs of φ and λ are inconsistent. Because of this we propose an estimation method based on the LPE for φ.

In our LPE based two-stage estimation method, we first choose $\widehat{\lambda}_T$ to minimize the sum of squared one-step-ahead prediction errors:

$$\widehat{\lambda}_T = \min_l \frac{1}{T-1} \sum_{t=2}^{T} \left[RV_t - \widehat{RV}_t(l) \right]^2, \tag{15}$$

where

$$\widehat{RV}_t(l) = \frac{1}{T-1} \sum_{i=2}^{T} \left[\widehat{\varphi}_T(l) RV_{t-1}^l + \widehat{u}_i(l) \right]^{1/l},$$

with

$$\widehat{\varphi}_T(l) = \min \left\{ \frac{RV_t^l}{RV_{t-1}^l} \right\}_{t=2}^{T} \quad \text{and} \quad \widehat{u}_i(l) = RV_i^l - \widehat{\varphi}_T(l) RV_{i-1}^l,$$

respectively. Although our estimator for λ looks like the standard nonlinear least squares (NLS) estimator of Jennrich (1969), the two approaches are quite different because in our model an explicit expression for $E(RV_t \mid RV_{t-1})$ is not available. In fact, the NLS estimators of λ and φ, that minimizes $\sum_{t=2}^{T}(RV_t^l - pRV_{t-1}^l)^2$, always take values of 0 and 1, respectively and hence are inconsistent.

The intuition behind the proposed estimation method is that we expect $\widehat{RV}_t(\widehat{\lambda}_T)$ to be close to $E(RV_t \mid RV_{t-1})$ for large values of T. This is not surprising since the TNTAR model (12) implies that

$$RV_t = \left(\varphi RV_{t-1}^\lambda + u_t \right)^{1/\lambda},$$

and hence

$$E(RV_t \mid RV_{t-1}) = E\left[\left(\varphi RV_{t-1}^\lambda + u_t \right)^{1/\lambda} \mid RV_{t-1} \right].$$

In the second stage, we use the LPE to estimate φ. More specifically,

$$\widehat{\varphi}_T = \widehat{\varphi}_T(\widehat{\lambda}_T) = \min \left\{ \frac{RV_t^{\widehat{\lambda}_T}}{RV_{t-1}^{\widehat{\lambda}_T}} \right\}_{t=2}^{T}. \tag{16}$$

while we minimize the sum of squared one-step-ahead prediction errors when estimating λ, other criteria, such as minimizing the sum of absolute one-step-ahead prediction errors, can be used. We have experimented with absolute prediction errors using the S&P 500 data and found that our out-of-sample forecasting results for the TNTAR model are quite insensitive to the choice of the objective function in the estimation stage. However, the objective function with squared prediction errors performs better in simulations.

It is beyond the scope of this paper to derive asymptotic properties for the two-stage estimators. However, under primitive assumptions, the consistency of $\widehat{\lambda}_T$ and $\widehat{\varphi}_T$ can be established using the fundamental consistency result for extremum estimators. Moreover, under high-level assumptions, the martingale central limit theorem can be used to establish the asymptotic distribution of $\widehat{\lambda}_T$.

With an estimated λ and φ, a general one-step-ahead semiparametric forecast expression for the TNTAR model is given by

$$\widehat{RV}_{T+1} = \frac{1}{T-1} \sum_{i=2}^{T} \left(\widehat{\varphi}_T RV_T^{\widehat{\lambda}_T} + \widehat{u}_i \right)^{1/\widehat{\lambda}_T},$$

where $\widehat{u}_i = RV_i^{\widehat{\lambda}_T} - \widehat{\varphi}_T RV_{i-1}^{\widehat{\lambda}_T}$ is the residual at time i. Of course, in line with Granger and Newbold (1976), several forecasts of RV_{T+1} may be considered. For example, one could base a forecast on the well known approximation $E[h(y)] \approx h[E(y)]$ using $h(y) = y^{1/\lambda}$. However, this approximation does not take into account the nonlinearity of $h(y)$.[8]

4. Monte Carlo Studies

We now examine the performance of our estimation method via simulations. We consider two experiments in which data are generated by the nonnegative model

$$RV_t^\lambda = \varphi RV_{t-1}^\lambda + u_t$$
$$u_t = \epsilon_t + \psi \epsilon_{t-1},$$

with i.i.d. standard exponential driving noise ϵ_t.

In the first Monte Carlo experiment λ is assumed to be known and we only estimate φ using the LPE in (14). In this case the consistency is robust to the first-order moving average specification of u_t. Hence, we simulate data from the model with the value of ψ being different from zero. Specifically, the parameter values are set to $\lambda = -0.25$ and $\psi = 0.75$. The values of φ considered are 0.25, 0.5 and 0.75, respectively. In the second experiment λ is assumed to be unknown and is estimated together with φ using the proposed two-stage method. The parameter values are $\lambda = -0.5$ and -0.25, $\varphi = 0.5$ and 0.75, and $\psi = 0$.

The values chosen for λ and φ in the two experiments are empirically realistic (cf. the results of Section 5). We consider sample sizes of $T = 200, 400$ and 800 in both experiments. The sample size of 400 is close to the smallest sample size used for estimation in our empirical study, while the sample size of 800 is close to the largest sample size in the study. Simulation results based on 100,000 Monte Carlo replications are reported in Tables 2 and 3. Several interesting results emerge from the tables.

---

[8] For instance, if $y \sim N(0, \sigma^2)$ and $h(y) = y^2$ then $E[h(y)] = \sigma^2 \neq h[E(y)] = 0$.

First, the smaller the value of T, the greater the empirical bias in $\widehat{\varphi}_T$ in the first experiment and in $\widehat{\lambda}_T$ and $\widehat{\varphi}_T$ in the second experiment. Second, as T increases, the empirical mean squared error of $\widehat{\varphi}_T$ in the first experiment, and those of $\widehat{\lambda}_T$ and $\widehat{\varphi}_T$ in the second experiment, decreases. It may be surprising to see that the bias of $\widehat{\varphi}_T$ can be negative in the second experiment. Here the negative bias arises because λ is estimated. In sum, it seems that the proposed estimation method works well, especially when T is reasonably large.

Table 2. Simulation results for the LPE method. Summary statistics for $\widehat{\varphi}_T$ based on data generated by the nonnegative process $RV_t^{-0.25} = \varphi RV_{t-1}^{-0.25} + \epsilon_t + 0.75\epsilon_{t-1}$ with i.i.d. standard exponential noise ϵ_t. The values of φ considered are 0.25, 0.50 and 0.75, respectively. Bias and MSE denotes the empirical bias and mean squared error, respectively. Results based on 100,000 Monte Carlo replications.

		$T = 200$		$T = 400$		$T = 800$	
Parameter	Estimator	Bias	MSE	Bias	MSE	Bias	MSE
$\varphi = 0.25$	$\widehat{\varphi}_T$	0.047	0.003	0.033	0.001	0.023	0.001
$\varphi = 0.50$	$\widehat{\varphi}_T$	0.028	0.001	0.020	0.001	0.014	0.000
$\varphi = 0.75$	$\widehat{\varphi}_T$	0.013	0.000	0.009	0.000	0.006	0.000

Table 3. Simulation results for the proposed two-stage estimation method. Summary statistics for $\widehat{\lambda}_T$ and $\widehat{\varphi}_T$ based on data generated by the nonnegative process $RV_t^\lambda = \varphi RV_{t-1}^\lambda + \epsilon_t$ with i.i.d. standard exponential noise ϵ_t. Bias and MSE denotes the empirical bias and mean squared error, respectively. Results based on 100,000 Monte Carlo replications.

		$T = 200$		$T = 400$		$T = 800$	
Parameter	Estimator	Bias	MSE	Bias	MSE	Bias	MSE
$\lambda = -0.50$	$\widehat{\lambda}_T$	−0.197	0.126	−0.113	0.069	−0.060	0.047
$\varphi = 0.50$	$\widehat{\varphi}_T$	−0.106	0.028	−0.069	0.018	−0.043	0.012
$\lambda = -0.50$	$\widehat{\lambda}_T$	−0.139	0.106	−0.062	0.067	−0.014	0.052
$\varphi = 0.75$	$\widehat{\varphi}_T$	−0.064	0.012	−0.038	0.006	−0.021	0.004
$\lambda = -0.25$	$\widehat{\lambda}_T$	−0.195	0.064	−0.136	0.033	−0.098	0.019
$\varphi = 0.75$	$\widehat{\varphi}_T$	−0.144	0.030	−0.106	0.017	−0.080	0.011

5. An Empirical Study

We also study the performance of the proposed model for forecasting actual RV relative to popular existing models. Before we report empirical results, we first review some alternative models and criteria to evaluate the performance of different models.

5.1. Alternative Models

Numerous models and methods have been applied to forecast stock market volatility. For example, ARCH-type models are popular in academic publications and RiskMetrics is widely used in practice. Both methods use returns to forecast volatility at the same frequency. However, since the squared return is a noisy estimator of volatility ABDL (2003) instead consider RV and present strong evidence to support time series models based directly on RV in terms of forecast accuracy. Motivated by their empirical findings, we compare the forecast accuracy of the TNTAR model against four alternative models, all based on RV: (1) the linear Gaussian AR(1) model (AR); (2) the log-linear Gaussian AR(1) model (log-AR); (3) the logarithmic autoregressive fractionally integrated moving average (ARFIMA) model; (4) the heterogeneous autoregressive (HAR) model. We also compare the performance of our model against the exponential smoothing method, a RV version of RiskMetrics. The AR and log-AR models are defined by (10) and (11), respectively. We now review the exponential smoothing method, the ARFIMA model, and the HAR model.

5.1.1. Exponential Smoothing

Exponential smoothing (ES) is a simple method of forecasting, where the one-step-ahead forecast of RV_{T+1} at time T is given by

$$\widehat{RV}_{T+1} = (1-\alpha)RV_T + \alpha\widehat{RV}_T = (1-\alpha)\sum_{i=0}^{T-1}\alpha^i RV_{T-i}, \qquad (17)$$

with $0 < \alpha < 1$.

The exponential smoothing formula can be understood as the RV version of RiskMetrics, where the squared return, r_T^2, is replaced by RV_T. Under the assumption of conditional normality of the return distribution, r_t^2 is an unbiased estimator of σ_t^2. RiskMetrics recommends $\alpha = 0.94$ for daily data and $\alpha = 0.97$ for monthly data.

To see why the squared return is a noisy estimator of volatility even under the assumption of conditional normality of the return distribution, suppose that r_t follows (3). Conditional on σ_t, it is easy to show that (Lopez 2001)

$$P\left(r_t^2 \in \left[\frac{1}{2}\sigma_t^2, \frac{3}{2}\sigma_t^2\right]\right) = 0.259. \qquad (18)$$

This implies that with a probability close to 0.74 the squared return is at least 50% greater, or at most 50% smaller, than the true volatility. Not surprisingly, Andersen and Bollerslev (1998) find that RiskMetrics is dominated by models based directly on RV. For this reason, we do not use RiskMetrics directly. Instead, we use (17) with $\alpha = 0.97$, which assigns a weight of 3% to the most recently observed RV. We remark that the forecasting results of Section 5 were qualitatively left unchanged when other values for α were used.

5.1.2. ARFIMA(p, d, q)

Long range dependence is a well documented stylized fact for volatility of many financial time series. Fractional integration has previously been used to model the long range dependence in volatility and log-volatility. The autoregressive fractionally integrated moving average (ARFIMA) was considered as a model for logarithmic RV in ABDL (2003) and Deo et al. (2006), among others. In this paper, we consider two parsimonious ARFIMA models for log-RV, namely, an ARFIMA($0, d, 0$) and an ARFIMA($1, d, 0$).

The ARFIMA($p, d, 0$) model for log-RV is defined by

$$(1 - \beta_1 B - \cdots - \beta_p B^p)(1-B)^d(\log RV_t - \mu) = \varepsilon_t,$$

where the parameters $\mu, \beta_1, \ldots, \beta_p$ and the memory parameter d are real valued, and ε_t is a sequence of independent $N(0, \sigma_\varepsilon^2)$ distributed random variables.

Following a suggestion of a referee, we estimate all the parameters of the ARFIMA model using an approximate ML method by minimizing the sum of squared one-step-ahead prediction errors. See Beran (1995), Chung and Baillie (1993), and Doornik and Ooms (2004) for detailed discussions about the method and for Monte Carlo evidence supporting it. Compared to the exact ML method of Sowell (1992), there are two advantages to the approximate ML method. First, it does not require d to be less than 0.5. Second, it has smaller finite sample bias. Compared to the semi-parametric methods, it is also more efficient.[9] The one-step-ahead forecast of RV_{T+1} at time T of an ARFIMA$(p, d, 0)$ for log-RV with $p = 0$ is given by

$$\widehat{RV}_{T+1} = \exp\left\{\widehat{\mu} - \sum_{j=0}^{T-1} \widehat{\pi}_j \left(\log RV_{T-j} - \widehat{\mu}\right) + \frac{\widehat{\sigma}_\epsilon^2}{2}\right\},$$

and with $p = 1$ by

$$\widehat{RV}_{T+1} = \exp\left\{\widehat{\mu} + \widehat{\beta}\left(\log RV_T - \widehat{\mu}\right) + \sum_{j=1}^{T-1} \widehat{\pi}_j \left[\widehat{\beta}\left(\log RV_{T-j} - \widehat{\mu}\right) - \left(\log RV_{T-j+1} - \widehat{\mu}\right)\right] + \frac{\widehat{\sigma}_\epsilon^2}{2}\right\},$$

where

$$\widehat{\pi}_j = \frac{\Gamma(j - \widehat{d})}{\Gamma(j+1)\Gamma(-\widehat{d})},$$

and $\Gamma(\cdot)$ denotes the gamma function.

5.1.3. HAR

The HAR model proposed by Corsi (2009) is one of the most popular models for forecasting volatility. Given that we will forecast monthly RV in the empirical study, we modify the original HAR model with monthly, quarterly and yearly components. The original HAR model was proposed to model daily RV. We apply the modified model to raw RV (HAR) and to log-RV (log-HAR). The model for raw RV can be expressed as

$$RV_t = \beta_0 + \beta_1 RV_{t-1}^m + \beta_2 RV_{t-1}^q + \beta_3 RV_{t-1}^y + \epsilon_t, \tag{19}$$

where the parameters $\beta_0, \ldots, \beta_3$ are real valued, RV_t is the realized volatility of month t, and $RV_{t-1}^m = RV_{t-1}$, $RV_{t-1}^q = \frac{1}{3}\sum_{i=1}^{3} RV_{t-i}$, $RV_{t-1}^y = \frac{1}{12}\sum_{i=1}^{12} RV_{t-i}$ denote the monthly, quarterly and yearly lagged RV components, respectively. This specification of RV parsimoniously captures the high persistence observed in our empirical study. The one-step-ahead forecast of RV_{T+1} at time T is given by

$$\widehat{RV}_{T+1} = \widehat{\beta}_0 + \widehat{\beta}_1 RV_T + \frac{\widehat{\beta}_2}{3}\sum_{i=1}^{3} RV_{T+1-i} + \frac{\widehat{\beta}_3}{12}\sum_{i=1}^{12} RV_{T+1-i}.$$

The corresponding forecast of the HAR model in (19) for log-RV is

$$\widehat{RV}_{T+1} = \exp\left\{\widehat{\beta}_0 + \widehat{\beta}_1 \log RV_T + \frac{\widehat{\beta}_2}{3}\sum_{i=1}^{3} \log RV_{T+1-i} + \frac{\widehat{\beta}_3}{12}\sum_{i=1}^{12} \log RV_{T+1-i} + \frac{\widehat{\sigma}_\epsilon^2}{2}\right\},$$

where $\widehat{\sigma}_\epsilon^2$ is the estimated variance of the independent $N(0, \sigma_\epsilon^2)$ distributed errors ϵ_t.

5.2. Forecast Accuracy Measures

It is not obvious which accuracy measure is more appropriate for the evaluation of the out-of-sample performance of alternative time series models. Rather than making a single choice, we use four measures to evaluate forecast accuracy, namely, the mean absolute error (MAE), the mean absolute percentage error (MAPE), the mean square error (MSE) and the mean square percentage error (MSPE). Let $\widehat{RV}_{it}$ denote the one-step-ahead forecast of RV_t at time $t-1$ of model i and define

---

[9] We also applied the exact ML method of Sowell (1992) and the exact local Whittle estimator of Shimotsu and Phillips (2005) in our empirical study and found that the forecasts remained essentially unchanged.

the accompanying forecast error by $e_{it} = RV_t - \widehat{RV}_{it}$. The four accuracy measures are defined, respectively, by

$$\text{MAE} = \frac{1}{P}\sum_{t=1}^{P}|e_{it}|, \quad \text{MAPE} = \frac{100}{P}\sum_{t=1}^{P}\left|\frac{e_{it}}{RV_t}\right|, \quad \text{MSE} = \frac{1}{P}\sum_{t=1}^{P}e_{it}^2, \quad \text{MSPE} = \frac{100}{P}\sum_{t=1}^{P}\left(\frac{e_{it}}{RV_t}\right)^2,$$

where P is the length of the forecast evaluation period.

An advantage of using MAE instead of MSE is that it has the same scale as the data. The MAPE and the MSPE are scale independent measures. For a comprehensive survey on these and other forecast accuracy measures see Hyndman and Koehler (2006).

When calculating the forecast error, it is implicitly assumed that RV_t is the true volatility at time t. However, in reality the volatility proxy RV_t is different from the true, latent, volatility. Several recent papers discuss the implications of using noisy volatility proxies when comparing volatility forecasts under certain loss functions. See, for example, Andersen and Bollerslev (1998); Hansen and Lunde (2006) and Patton (2011). The impact is found to be particularly large when the squared return is used as a proxy for the true volatility, but diminishes with the approximation error. In this paper, the true (monthly) volatility is approximated by the RV using 22 (daily) squared returns. As a result, the approximation error is expected to be considerably smaller than in the case of using a single squared return.

5.3. Data

The data used in this paper consists of daily closing prices for the S&P 500 index over the period 2 January 1946–31 December 2004, covering 708 months and 15,054 trading days. We measure the monthly volatility using realized volatility calculated from daily data. Denote the log-closing price on the k'th trading day in month t by $p(t,k)$. Assuming there are T_t trading days in month t, we define the monthly RV as

$$RV_t = \sqrt{\frac{1}{T_t}\sum_{k=2}^{T_t}\left[p(t,k) - p(t,k-1)\right]^2}, \quad t = 1,\ldots,708$$

where $1/T_t$ serves the purpose of standardization.

In order to compare the out-of-sample predictive accuracy of the alternative models, we split the time series of monthly RV into two subsamples. The first time period is used for the initial estimation. The second period is the hold-back sample used for forecast evaluation. When computing the forecasts we use a recursive scheme, where the size of the sample used for parameter estimation successively increases as new forecasts are made. The time series plot of monthly RV for the entire sample is shown in Figure 3, where the vertical dashed line indicates the end of the initial sample period used for estimation in our first forecasting exercise.

Table 4 shows the sample mean, maximum, skewness, kurtosis, the p-value of the JB test statistic for normality, and the first three sample autocorrelations of the entire sample for RV and log-RV. For RV, the sample maximum is 0.026 which occurred in October 1987. The sample kurtosis is 28.791 indicating that the distribution of RV is non-Gaussian. In contrast, log-RV has a much smaller kurtosis (3.657) and is less skewed (0.389). It is for this reason that we include Gaussian time series models for log-RV in the exercise. However, a formal test for normality via the JB statistic rejects the null hypothesis of normality of log-RV, suggesting that further improvements over log-linear Gaussian approaches are possible.

Higher order sample autocorrelations are in general slowly decreasing and not statistically negligible, indicating that RV and log-RV are predictable. To test for possible unit roots, augmented Dickey-Fuller (ADF) test statistics were calculated. The ADF statistic for the sample from 1946 to 2004 is -5.69 for RV and -5.43 for log-RV, which is smaller than -2.57, the critical value at the 10% significance level. Hence, we reject the null hypothesis that RV or log-RV has a unit root.

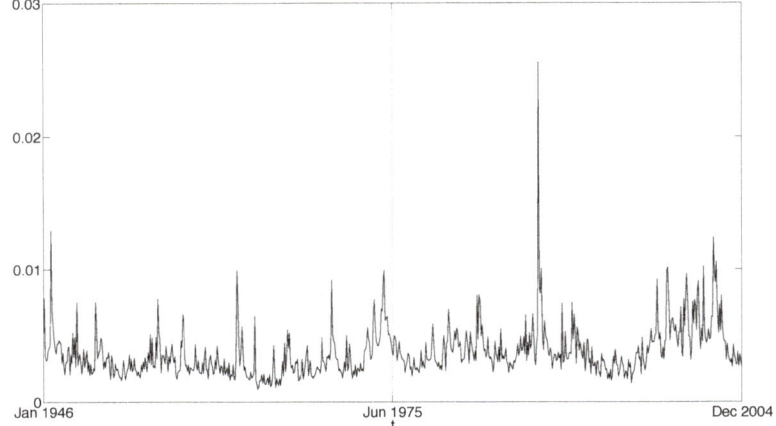

Figure 3. S&P 500 monthly realized volatilities, Jan 1946-Dec 2004. The vertical dashed line indicates the end of the initial sample period used for parameter estimation in our first out-of-sample forecasting exercise.

Table 4. Summary statistics for the S&P 500 monthly RV data. JB is the p-value of the Jarque-Bera test under the null hypothesis that the data are from a normal distribution, $\hat{\rho}_i$ is the ith sample autocorrelation.

	Mean	Maximum	Skewness	Kurtosis	JB	$\hat{\rho}_1$	$\hat{\rho}_2$	$\hat{\rho}_3$
RV	0.004	0.026	3.307	28.791	0.000	0.576	0.477	0.408
log-RV	−5.687	−3.666	0.389	3.657	0.000	0.683	0.595	0.511

5.4. Empirical Results

Each alternative model was fitted to the in-sample RV data and used to generate one-step-ahead out-of-sample forecasts.[10] Following a suggestion of a referee, we also included a standard GARCH(1,1) (sGARCH) and a realized GARCH(1,1) with a log-linear specification (realGARCH), Hansen et al. (2012).[11] Since a forecast frequency of one month is sufficiently important in practical applications, we focus on one-step-ahead forecasts in this paper. However, multi-step-ahead forecasts can be obtained in a similar manner.

We perform two out-of-sample forecasting exercises. In both exercises, we use the recursive scheme, where the size of the sample used to estimate the alternative models grows as we make forecasts for successive observations.[12] More precisely, in the first exercise, we first estimate all the alternative models with data from the period January 1946–June 1975 and use the estimated models to forecast the RV of July 1975. We then estimate all models with data from January 1946–July 1975 and use the model estimates to forecast the RV of August 1975. This process (an expanding window of initial size 354) is repeated until, finally, we estimate the models with data from January 1946–November 2004. The final model estimates are used to forecast the RV of December 2004, the last observation in the sample.

---

[10] The Ox language of Doornik (2009) was used to estimate the two ARFIMA models. MATLAB code and data used in this paper can be downloaded from http://www.mysmu.edu/faculty/yujun/research.html.
[11] The sGARCH and realGARCH models were estimated using monthly log-returns and the rugarch R package of Ghalanos (2019).
[12] While we consider the recursive forecasting scheme one could, of course, also consider the rolling or fixed scheme.

5.4.1. Sample including the 1987 Crash

In the first exercise, the first month for which an out-of-sample volatility forecast is obtained is July 1975. In total 354 monthly volatilities are forecasted, including the volatility of October 1987 when the stock market crashed and the RV is 0.026.

In Figure 4, we plot the monthly RV and the corresponding one-month-ahead TNTAR forecasts for the out-of-sample period, July 1975 to December 2004. It seems that the TNTAR model captures the overall movements in RV reasonably well. The numerical computation of the 354 forecasts is fast and takes less than five minutes on a standard desktop computer.

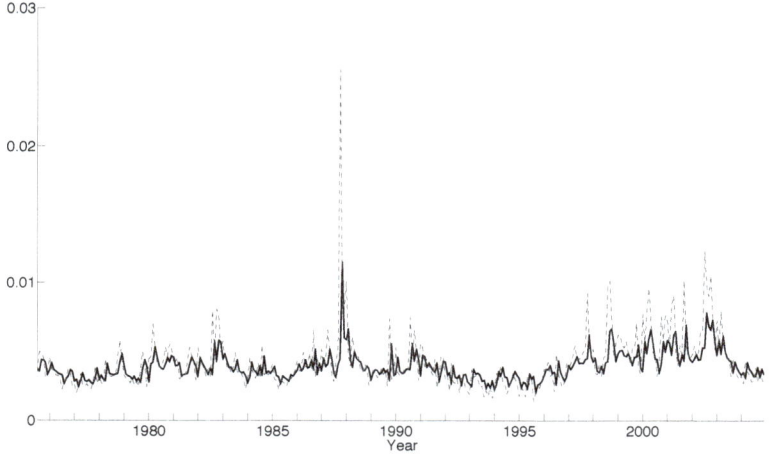

Figure 4. Realized volatility and out-of-sample TNTAR forecasts for the period Jul 1975–Dec 2004. *Dashed line:* S&P 500 monthly realized volatility. *Solid line:* one-step-ahead TNTAR forecasts.

In Figure 5, we plot the recursive estimates, $\widehat{\lambda}_T$ and $\widehat{\varphi}_T$. While $\widehat{\lambda}_T$ takes values from -0.45 to -0.28, $\widehat{\varphi}_T$ ranges between 0.58 and 0.64. It may be surprising to see that the path of $\widehat{\varphi}_T$ is non-monotonic. This is because the estimates of the power transformation parameter, λ, are varying over time. Our empirical estimates of λ seem to corroborate well with the optimal value of λ obtained by Gonçalves and Meddahi (2011) using simulations in the context of a GARCH diffusion and a two factor SV model. While $\widehat{\varphi}_T$ is quite stable, $\widehat{\lambda}_T$ jumps in October 1987.

For comparison, we also consider a TNTAR model with λ taken to be known. Visual inspection, see Figure 6, shows that a power transformation with $\lambda = -1/2$ improves linearity considerably.[13] We denote the corresponding TNTAR model TNTAR*, and employ the LPE based forecasting scheme proposed in Preve (2015): We first fit the TNTAR model

$$\frac{1}{\sqrt{RV_t}} = \frac{\varphi}{\sqrt{RV_{t-1}}} + u_t,$$

using the LPE and calculate LP residuals

$$\widehat{u}_t = \frac{1}{\sqrt{RV_t}} - \frac{\widehat{\varphi}_T}{\sqrt{RV_{t-1}}}.$$

---

[13] We explored all non-zero λ-values on Tukey's ladder of power transformations in (13) and found that $\lambda = -1/2$ produced the strongest linear relationship (an increase in R^2 from 0.341 to 0.410).

Due to the robustness of the LPE, simple semiparametric forecasts in the (possible) presence of structural breaks are then obtained by applying a one-sided moving median. More specifically, as a simple one-month-ahead forecast we take $\widehat{RV}_{T+1} = m_T$, where m_T is the sample median of

$$\left(\frac{\widehat{\varphi}_T}{\sqrt{RV_T}} + \widehat{u}_{T-11} \right)^{-2}, \ldots, \left(\frac{\widehat{\varphi}_T}{\sqrt{RV_T}} + \widehat{u}_T \right)^{-2},$$

the reciprocals of the by $\widehat{\varphi}_T / \sqrt{RV_T}$ shifted, squared last 12 LP residuals.

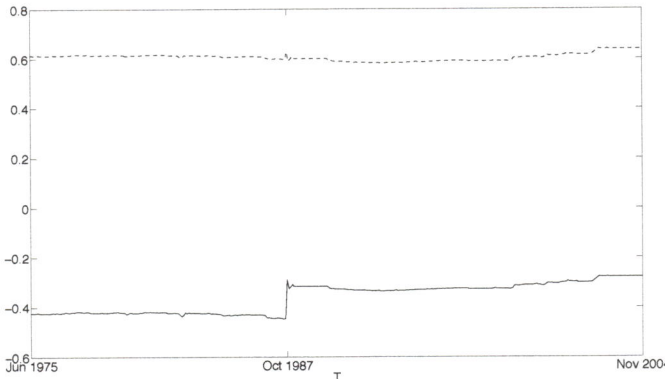

Figure 5. Recursive TNTAR parameter estimates for the first out-of-sample forecasting exercise. *Solid line:* path of $\widehat{\lambda}_T$. *Dashed line:* path of $\widehat{\varphi}_T$.

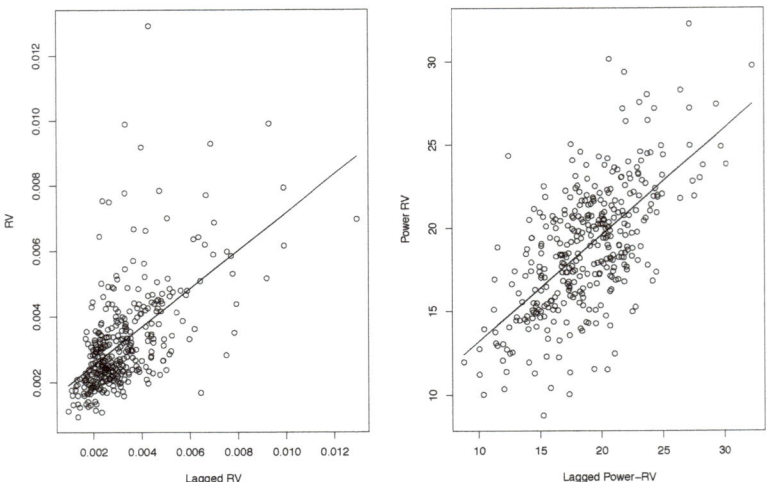

Figure 6. The left panel displays a plot of the target variable against the explanatory variable in the AR model (10). The right panel displays a similar plot for the TNTAR model (12), with power transformation parameter $\lambda = -1/2$. Superimposed are simple linear regression lines. Data for the period January 1946-June 1975.

Table 5 reports the forecasting performance of the alternative models under the four forecast accuracy measures of Section 5.2. Several results emerge from the table. First, the relative performances of the alternative models are sensitive to the forecast accuracy measures. Under the MSE measure, the two ARFIMA models rank as the best, followed by the log-HAR and TNTAR* models. ABDL (2003) found that their ARFIMA models perform well in terms of R^2 in the Mincer-Zarnomitz regression. Since the MSE is closely related to the R^2 in the Mincer-Zarnomitz regression, our results reinforce their findings. However, the rankings obtained under MSE are very different from those obtained under the other three accuracy measures. The MAPE and the MSPE, for example, rank the TNTAR* model the first and the TNTAR model the fourth. Second, the performances of the two ARFIMA models are very similar under all measures. To understand why, we plotted the sample autocorrelation functions of the ARFIMA$(0, d, 0)$ residuals for the entire sample and found that fractional differencing alone successfully removes the serial dependence in log-RV. Third, the improvement of ARFIMA$(0, d, 0)$ over TNTAR is 7.4% in terms of MSE. On the other hand, the improvement of TNTAR over ARFIMA$(0, d, 0)$ is 0.8%, 5.9% and 6.0% in terms of MAE, MAPE and MSPE, respectively. These improvements are striking as we expect ARFIMA models to be hard to beat. Fourth, ES performs the worst in all cases.

Table 5. Forecasting performance of the alternative models under four different accuracy measures. Results based on 354 one-step-ahead forecasts for the period *Jul 1975–Dec 2004*.

	MAE $\times 10^3$		MAPE		MSE $\times 10^6$		MSPE	
	Value	Rank	Value	Rank	Value	Rank	Value	Rank
ES	1.268	9	31.04	11	3.862	11	15.30	9
AR	0.975	6	20.93	6	3.312	9	7.80	5
HAR	0.945	2	20.75	3	3.018	5	7.29	2
log-AR	0.954	4	20.74	2	3.076	8	7.56	4
log-HAR	0.937	1	20.90	5	2.866	3	7.33	3
sGARCH	1.101	8	27.23	9	3.344	10	12.43	7
realGARCH	1.089	7	28.05	10	3.026	6	12.93	8
log-ARFIMA$(0, d, 0)$	0.961	5	22.09	8	2.847	1	8.04	6
log-ARFIMA$(1, d, 0)$	0.961	5	22.08	7	2.851	2	8.04	6
TNTAR	0.954	4	20.78	4	3.075	7	7.56	4
TNTAR*	0.948	3	20.47	1	2.911	4	6.96	1

Table 6 reports *p*-values of the Diebold and Mariano (1995) test for equal predictive accuracy of different models in Table 5 with respect to the benchmark TNTAR model. We compare forecast differences using four different loss functions. Under absolute loss (MAE), the TNTAR delivers superior forecasts in three cases. In six cases, the forecasts are not statistically different. For MAPE, the TNTAR delivers superior forecasts in five cases. The forecasts are not statistically different in four cases. Under square loss (MSE), the TNTAR delivers superior forecasts in two cases, the forecasts are not statistically different in four cases and in three cases alternative models have the best performance. Finally, for MSPE, the TNTAR delivers superior forecasts in three cases. In six cases, the forecasts are not statistically different.

Table 6. *p*-values of the Diebold-Mariano test for equal predictive accuracy of different models with respect to the benchmark TNTAR model under four different loss functions. Results based on 354 one-step-ahead forecasts for the period *Jul 1975–Dec 2004*.

	MAE	MAPE	MSE	MSPE
ES	0.000	0.000	0.001	0.001
AR	0.275	0.680	0.208	0.431
HAR	0.660	0.961	0.607	0.480
log-AR	0.898	0.754	0.973	0.968
log-HAR	0.418	0.824	0.003	0.482
sGARCH	0.001	0.000	0.057	0.000
realGARCH	0.001	0.000	0.709	0.000
log-ARFIMA$(0, d, 0)$	0.728	0.034	0.008	0.188
log-ARFIMA$(1, d, 0)$	0.725	0.035	0.008	0.184

5.4.2. Sample Post the 1987 Crash

To examine the sensitivity of our results with respect to the 1987 crash and the 1997 crash due to the Asian financial crisis, we redo the forecasting exercise so that the first month for which an out-of-sample volatility forecast is obtained is January 1988 and the last month is September 1997.

In Figure 7, we plot the monthly RV and the corresponding one-month-ahead TNTAR forecasts for the out-of-sample period, January 1988-September 1997. As before, forecasts from the TNTAR model captures the overall movements in RV reasonably well. Table 7 reports the forecasting performance of the alternative models under the four forecast accuracy measures. Since the RVs are smaller in this subsample, as expected, the MAE and the MSE are smaller than before. However, the relative performances of the alternative models obtained for the subsample are similar to those obtained for the entire sample, although the HAR and log-HAR models now outperform the ARFIMA models also in MSE. The TNTAR* model once again performs the best overall.

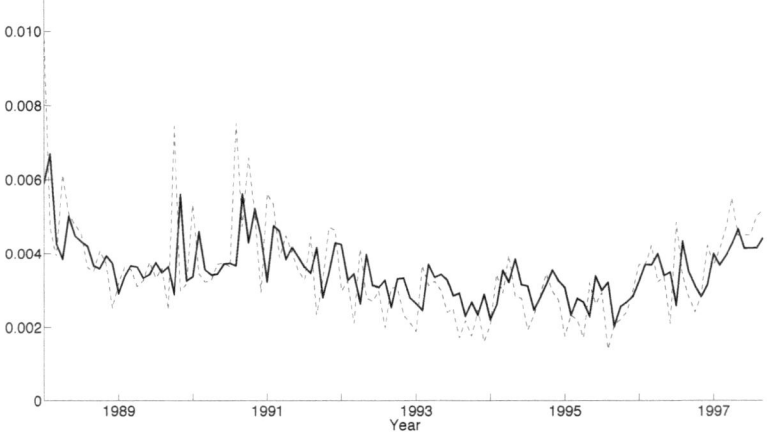

Figure 7. Realized volatility and out-of-sample TNTAR forecasts for the period Jan 1988–Sep 1997. *Dashed line:* S&P 500 monthly realized volatility. *Solid line:* one-month-ahead TNTAR forecasts.

Table 7. Forecasting performance of the alternative models under four different accuracy measures. Results based on 117 one-step-ahead forecasts for the period *Jan 1988–Sep 1997*.

	MAE × 10^3		MAPE		MSE × 10^6		MSPE	
	Value	Rank	Value	Rank	Value	Rank	Value	Rank
ES	1.077	10	35.38	11	1.707	11	20.18	11
AR	0.783	7	23.88	8	1.258	6	10.73	8
HAR	0.749	2	22.68	3	1.079	1	9.28	2
log-AR	0.779	6	23.38	4	1.272	8	10.53	6
log-HAR	0.750	3	22.45	2	1.123	2	9.37	3
sGARCH	0.963	8	32.90	9	1.387	9	18.77	9
realGARCH	0.991	9	33.73	10	1.480	10	19.51	10
log-ARFIMA$(0, d, 0)$	0.779	6	23.65	7	1.160	3	10.24	5
log-ARFIMA$(1, d, 0)$	0.778	5	23.61	6	1.162	4	10.22	4
TNTAR	0.777	4	23.45	5	1.260	7	10.58	7
TNTAR*	0.744	1	21.27	1	1.163	5	8.18	1

6. Concluding Remarks

In this paper, a simple time series model is introduced to model and forecast RV. The new TNTAR model combines a nonnegative valued process for the error term with the flexibility of Tukey's power transformation. The transformation is used to improve linearity and reduce heteroskedasticity while the nonnegative support of the error distribution overcomes the truncation problem in the classical Box-Cox setup. The model is semiparametric as the order of m-dependence, support parameter η and functional form of its error term are left unspecified. Consequently, the proposed model is highly parsimonious, having only two parameters that need to be estimated for the purpose of forecasting. A two-stage estimation method is proposed to estimate the parameters of the new model. Simulation studies validate the new estimation method and suggest that it works reasonably well in finite samples.

We empirically examine the forecasting performance of the proposed model relative to a number of existing models, using monthly S&P 500 RV data. The out-of-sample performances were evaluated under four different forecast accuracy measures (MAE, MAPE, MSE and MSPE). We found empirical evidence that our nonnegative model generates highly competitive volatility forecasts.

Why does the simple nonnegative model generate such competitive forecasts? Firstly, as shown in Section 2.2, the logarithmic transformation may not reduce heteroskedasticity and improve normality as well as anticipated. A more general transformation may be required. Secondly, the nonnegative model is highly parsimonious. This new approach is in sharp contrast to the traditional approach which aims to find a model that removes all the dynamics in the original data. When the dynamics are complex, a model with a rich parametrization is called for. This approach may come with the cost of over-fitting and hence may not necessarily lead to superior forecasts. By combining a parametric component for the persistence and a nonparametric error component, our approach presents an effective utilization of more recent information.

Although we only examine the performance of the proposed model for predicting S&P 500 realized volatility one month ahead, the technique itself is quite general and can be applied in many other contexts. First, the method requires no modification when applied to intra-day data to forecast daily RV. In this context, it would be interesting to compare our method to the preferred method in ABDL (2003). Second, our model can easily be extended into a multivariate context by constructing a nonnegative vector autoregressive model. Third, while we focus on stock market volatility in this paper, other financial assets and financial volatility from other financial markets can be treated in the same fashion. Fourth, as two alternative nonnegative models, it would be interesting to compare the performance of our model with that of Cipollini et al. (2006). Finally, it would be interesting to examine the usefulness of the proposed model for multi-step-ahead forecasting. These extensions will be considered in later work.

Author Contributions: All authors contributed equally to all parts of the paper.

Funding: The authors gratefully acknowledge research support from the Jan Wallander and Tom Hedelius Research Foundation (grant P 2006-0166:1), and the Singapore MOE AcRF Tier 2 fund (grant T206B4301-RS) and are thankful to the Sim Kee Boon Institute for Financial Economics at Singapore Management University for partial research support.

Acknowledgments: The authors would like to thank two anonymous referees, Torben Andersen, Federico Bandi, Frank Diebold, Marcelo Medeiros, Bent Nielsen and Neil Shephard for their helpful comments and suggestions. The views expressed in this paper are those of the authors and are not those of J.P. Morgan. All remaining errors are our own.

Conflicts of Interest: The authors declare no conflict of interest.

References

Andersen, Torben G., and Tim Bollerslev. 1998. Answering the skeptics: Yes, standard volatility models do provide accurate forecasts. *International Economic Review* 39: 885–905. [CrossRef]

Andersen, Torben G., Tim Bollerslev, Francis X. Diebold, and Paul Labys. 2001. The distribution of realized exchange rate volatility. *Journal of the American Statistical Association* 96: 42–55. [CrossRef]

Andersen, Torben G., Tim Bollerslev, Francis X. Diebold, and Paul Labys. 2003. Modeling and forecasting realized volatility. *Econometrica* 71: 579–625. [CrossRef]

Barndorff-Nielsen, Ole E., and Neil Shephard. 2001. Non-Gaussian Ornstein-Uhlenbeck-based models and some of their uses in financial economics. *Journal of the Royal Statistical Society. Series B (Statistical Methodology)* 63: 167–241. [CrossRef]

Barndorff-Nielsen, Ole E., and Neil Shephard. 2002. Econometric analysis of realized volatility and its use in estimating stochastic volatility models. *Journal of the Royal Statistical Society: Series B (Statistical Methodology)* 64: 253–80. [CrossRef]

Beran, Jan. 1995. Maximum likelihood estimation of the differencing parameter for invertible short and long memory autoregressive integrated moving average models. *Journal of the Royal Statistical Society. Series B (Methodological)* 57: 659–72. [CrossRef]

Bollerslev, Tim, Ray Y. Chou, and Kenneth F. Kroner. 1992. ARCH modeling in finance: A review of the theory and empirical evidence. *Journal of Econometrics* 52: 5–59. [CrossRef]

Bollerslev, Tim, Robert F. Engle, and Daniel B. Nelson. 1994. Chapter 49 ARCH models. *Handbook of Econometrics* 4: 2959–3038.

Box, George E. P., and David R. Cox. 1964. An analysis of transformations. *Journal of the Royal Statistical Society: Series B (Methodological)* 26: 211–43. [CrossRef]

Chen, Willa W., and Rohit S. Deo. 2004. Power transformations to induce normality and their applications. *Journal of the Royal Statistical Society: Series B (Statistical Methodology)* 66: 117–30. [CrossRef]

Chung, Ching-Fan, and Richard T. Baillie. 1993. Small sample bias in conditional sum-of-squares estimators of fractionally integrated ARMA models. *Empirical Economics* 18: 791–806. [CrossRef]

Cipollini, Fabrizio, Robert F. Engle, and Giampiero M. Gallo. 2006. Vector Multiplicative Error Models: Representation and Inference. Working Paper 12690. Cambridge, UK: National Bureau of Economic Research.

Corsi, Fulvio. 2009. A simple approximate long-memory model of realized volatility. *Journal of Financial Econometrics* 7: 174–96. [CrossRef]

Datta, Somnath, and William P. McCormick. 1995. Bootstrap inference for a first-order autoregression with positive innovations. *Journal of the American Statistical Association* 90: 1289–300. [CrossRef]

Davis, Richard A., and William P. McCormick. 1989. Estimation for first-order autoregressive processes with positive or bounded innovations. *Stochastic Processes and their Applications* 31: 237–50. [CrossRef]

Deo, Rohit, Clifford Hurvich, and Yi Lu. 2006. Forecasting realized volatility using a long-memory stochastic volatility model: Estimation, prediction and seasonal adjustment. *Journal of Econometrics* 131: 29–58. [CrossRef]

Diebold, Francis X., and Roberto S. Mariano. 1995. Comparing predictive accuracy. *Journal of Business & Economic Statistics* 13: 253–63.

Doornik, Jurgen A. 2009. *An Object-Oriented Matrix Programming Language Ox 6*. London: Timberlake Consultants Press.

Doornik, Jurgen A., and Marius Ooms. 2004. Inference and forecasting for ARFIMA models with an application to US and UK inflation. *Studies in Nonlinear Dynamics & Econometrics* 8. [CrossRef]

Duan, Jin-Chuan. 1997. Augmented GARCH(p,q) process and its diffusion limit. *Journal of Econometrics* 79: 97–127. [CrossRef]

Feigin, Paul D., and Sidney I. Resnick. 1992. Estimation for autoregressive processes with positive innovations. *Communications in Statistics. Stochastic Models* 8: 685–717. [CrossRef]

Fernandes, Marcelo, and Joachim Grammig. 2006. A family of autoregressive conditional duration models. *Journal of Econometrics* 130: 1–23. [CrossRef]

Ghalanos, Alexios. 2019. Rugarch: Univariate GARCH Models. R Package Version 1.4-1. Available online: https://cran.r-project.org/web/packages/rugarch/index.html (accessed on 4 August 2019).

Ghysels, Eric, Andrew C. Harvey, and Eric Renault. 1996. Stochastic volatility. In *Statistical Methods in Finance*. Handbook of Statistics. Amsterdam: Elsevier, vol. 14, pp. 119–91.

Gonçalves, Sílvia, and Nour Meddahi. 2011. Box-Cox transforms for realized volatility. *Journal of Econometrics* 160: 129–44. [CrossRef]

Granger, Clive W. J., and Paul Newbold. 1976. Forecasting transformed series. *Journal of the Royal Statistical Society. Series B (Methodological)* 38: 189–203. [CrossRef]

Hansen, Peter Reinhard, and Asger Lunde. 2006. Consistent ranking of volatility models. *Journal of Econometrics* 131: 97–121. [CrossRef]

Hansen, Peter Reinhard, Zhuo Huang, and Howard Howan Shek. 2012. Realized GARCH: A joint model for returns and realized measures of volatility. *Journal of Applied Econometrics* 27: 877–906. [CrossRef]

Hentschel, Ludger. 1995. All in the family: Nesting symmetric and asymmetric GARCH models. *Journal of Financial Economics* 39: 71–104. [CrossRef]

Higgins, Matthew L., and Anil K. Bera. 1992. A class of nonlinear ARCH models. *International Economic Review* 33: 137–58. [CrossRef]

Hyndman, Rob J., and Anne B. Koehler. 2006. Another look at measures of forecast accuracy. *International Journal of Forecasting* 22: 679–88. [CrossRef]

Jacod, Jean. 2017. Limit of random measures associated with the increments of a Brownian semimartingale. *Journal of Financial Econometrics* 16: 526–69. [CrossRef]

Jennrich, Robert I. 1969. Asymptotic properties of non-linear least squares estimators. *The Annals of Mathematical Statistics* 40: 633–43. [CrossRef]

J.P. Morgan. 1996. *RiskMetrics^{TM}–Technical Document*. London: J.P. Morgan.

Lopez, Jose A. 2001. Evaluating the predictive accuracy of volatility models. *Journal of Forecasting* 20: 87–109. [CrossRef]

Nielsen, Bent, and Neil Shephard. 2003. Likelihood analysis of a first-order autoregressive model with exponential innovations. *Journal of Time Series Analysis* 24: 337–44. [CrossRef]

Patton, Andrew J. 2011. Volatility forecast comparison using imperfect volatility proxies. *Journal of Econometrics* 160: 246–56. [CrossRef]

Phillips, Peter C.B. 1987. Time series regression with a unit root. *Econometrica* 55: 277–301. [CrossRef]

Poon, Ser-Huang, and Clive W. J. Granger. 2003. Forecasting volatility in financial markets: A review. *Journal of Economic Literature* 41: 478–539. [CrossRef]

Preve, Daniel P. A. 2015. Linear programming-based estimators in nonnegative autoregression. *Journal of Banking & Finance* 61: 225–34.

Shephard, Neil. 2005. *Stochastic Volatility: Selected Readings*. Oxford: Oxford University Press.

Shimotsu, Katsumi, and Peter C. B. Phillips. 2005. Exact local Whittle estimation of fractional integration. *The Annals of Statistics* 33: 1890–933. [CrossRef]

Sowell, Fallaw. 1992. Maximum likelihood estimation of stationary univariate fractionally integrated time series models. *Journal of Econometrics* 53: 165–88. [CrossRef]

Taylor, Stephen J. 2007. *Modelling Financial Time Series*, 2nd ed. Singapore: World Scientific.

Tukey, John W. 1977. *Exploratory Data Analysis*. Boston: Addison-Wesley.

Yu, Jun, Zhenlin Yang, and Xibin Zhang. 2006. A class of nonlinear stochastic volatility models and its implications for pricing currency options. *Computational Statistics & Data Analysis* 51: 2218–231.

© 2019 by the authors. Licensee MDPI, Basel, Switzerland. This article is an open access article distributed under the terms and conditions of the Creative Commons Attribution (CC BY) license (http://creativecommons.org/licenses/by/4.0/).

Article

Some Dynamic and Steady-State Properties of Threshold Auto-Regressions with Applications to Stationarity and Local Explosivity

Muhammad Farid Ahmed [1,2,3,*] and Stephen Satchell [4,5]

1. Cambridge INET, Faculty of Economics, University of Cambridge, Cambridge CB3 9DD, UK
2. Magdalene College, University of Cambridge, Cambridge CB3 0AG, UK
3. Department of Economics, Lahore University of Management Sciences, Lahore 54000, Pakistan
4. The University of Sydney Business School, The University of Sydney, Sydney, NSW 2006, Australia
5. Trinity College, University of Cambridge, Cambridge CB2 1TQ, UK
* Correspondence: faridahm@gmail.com or mfa30@cam.ac.uk

Received: 13 June 2019; Accepted: 18 July 2019; Published: 22 July 2019

Abstract: The purpose of this paper is to investigate the dynamics and steady-state properties of threshold autoregressive models with exogenous states that follow Markovian processes. Markovian processes are widely used in applied economics although their statistical properties have not been explored in detail. We use characteristic functions to carry out the analysis, and this allows us to describe limiting distributions for processes not considered in the literature previously. We also calculate analytical expressions for some moments. Furthermore, we see that we can have locally explosive processes that are explosive in one regime whilst being strongly stationary overall. This is explored through simulation analysis, where we also show how the distribution changes when the explosive state becomes more frequent although the overall process remains stationary. In doing so, we are able to relate our analysis to asset prices which exhibit similar distributional properties.

Keywords: threshold auto-regression; Markov process; stationarity

JEL Classification: C22; C32; C53

1. Introduction

The purpose of this paper is to investigate the dynamics and steady-state properties of threshold autoregressive models with exogenous states that follow Markovian processes. These models fall within the class of regime-switching models, which have become increasingly popular in applied economics and finance. Initially introduced by Goldfeld and Quandt (1973) and Tong (1978), regime-switching models have been used in economics and finance for a wide variety of applications including forecasting exchange rates (Engel 1994), understanding price transmission (Goodwin and Harper 2000), detecting bubbles in the art market (Knight et al. 2014), and providing a metric of market efficiency (Ahmed and Satchell 2018). Hansen (2011) provides a concise summary of threshold autoregressive processes and their applications.

Hamilton (1989, 1990, 2010) has made seminal contributions to the theory and application of regime-switching models. As outlined above, this article discusses a particular class of regime-switching models. The problems we discuss appear to have much in common with Markov switching models, and Timmermann (2000) has provided a detailed analysis of moments and autocorrelations, which would include our model as "MSIII" in his terminology. However, his analysis does not address non-moment distributional properties or the non-existence of moment-generating functions (mgfs).

Indeed, Timmermann states in Appendix 1, page 103, that "The expressions for the cases where ε_t follows a t-distribution or a normal distribution are based on the moment-generating distributions for these distributions", and this is confusing as it is known that the t-distribution does not have a moment-generating function. We therefore re-examine this model, allowing for the non-existence of moment-generating functions, and use the characteristic function (which will always exist) to derive various properties of the model.

Whilst we could carry out a similar analysis for the other models described in Timmermann (2000), our focus is on threshold auto-regression and the elusive search for explicit steady-state distributions. Prior to this article, Gonzalo and Gonzalez-Rozada (1997) described statistical properties of Threshold Autoregressive models of order 1 (TAR(1)) models. However, their analysis was restricted to a mixture of stationary and unit roots, whereas our analysis considers non-stationary roots as well. Another important contribution relevant to our work is Pourahmadi (1988). In Theorem 3.1 in his article, Pourahmadi (ibid.) discussed the covariance stationarity of a process similar to the threshold autoregressive process we consider in Section 4, in that he analyzed processes with a unit root and a zero root. However, the results derived in Section 2 below and the processes considered in Section 4 are applicable to a more general setting and we do not restrict ourselves to covariance stationarity. We acknowledge Pourahmadi's contributions while deriving our results in Section 2.

Caner and Hansen (2001) and Kapetanios and Shin (2006) also considered similar processes, but their objective was to derive the distribution of unit root test statistics in the threshold autoregressive framework rather than the distribution of the underlying process. Our results build upon the results of Knight and Satchell (2011) and Ahmed and Satchell (2018): Both articles discussed theoretical moments for threshold autoregressive models with exogenous triggers. While Ahmed and Satchell (2018) only considered moments when the exogenous variable is independently and identically distributed, Knight and Satchell (2011) also considered a Markovian exogenous variable.

In addition to deriving theoretical moments, we also use simulation analysis to show how the distributions of threshold autoregressive models change when the process's two states consist of one stationary state and an explosive state. Our analysis focuses on these models for two reasons. Firstly, we are able to derive a characteristic function for this case, thereby adding to the literature on analytical results for threshold autoregressive models. We believe this is a significant contribution to the statistical literature. Secondly, this class of models is of interest in the financial literature concerned with explosive roots. In particular, Theorem 6 in Section 2 specifically refers to a special case that is of interest to researchers working on asset pricing with some non-stationarity. The latter is what we consider for our simulation analysis, and thus we consider it the most important contribution of the current article. We also believe that these models can prove to be useful in the applied macroeconomic literature. The simulation analysis presented in this article will help the reader appreciate how these models can be useful in practice.

In applied Macroeconomics, for instance, Dynamic Stochastic General Equilibrium (DSGE) models often model shocks as AR(1) processes (see Schmitt-Grohe and Uribe 2004). The literature came under particular scrutiny after the financial crisis for its inability to simulate and thereby predict conditions and outcomes that were observed during the crisis. In addition to the absence of financial markets, such models are also restricted by their reliance on a stationary AR(1) model as a shock process, as these processes can rarely be used to study the kind of macroeconomic shocks that led to the financial crisis. On the other hand, these models will not have analytical or numerical solutions if the process is non-stationary.

We postulate that using a TAR(1) shock process which is stationary but nevertheless can exhibit locally non-stationary behavior can improve these models. Our work will enable calculation of moments for such shocks (where such moments exist), allowing the user to work with analytical solutions, or, if the user is deriving a numerical solution, ensuring that such a solution will exist. Indeed, some work has already started relying on Markov-switching DSGE models (Foerster et al. 2016). This paper complements the proposed methodology by enabling researchers to control and simulate shocks of specific variances.

There are further applications in the finance literature where TAR models have become popular. The applications may extend to forecasting oil prices through threshold models or in modelling exchange rate fluctuations. There are many areas where a TAR model and the characteristic functions we derive can provide more depth to the underlying analysis. To use one recent example, Aleem and Lahiani (2014) estimated a TAR model of exchange-rate pass through for Mexico. Their analysis was limited to an estimation of the threshold above which the pass through is greater. The characteristic functions from our article would have allowed them to estimate the volatility of exchange rates in their model, improving both their model and the resulting predictions. Similarly, in Ahmed and Satchell (2018), the empirical application relied on a Markovian exogenous trigger. The results from this article would have allowed them to derive moments of their empirical TAR(1). Corollary 2 in Section 2 offers one example of how the results of this article may contribute to applied and empirical work in finance.

The rest of the article is organized as follows. In Section 2, we present the derivation and formulae for characteristic functions of threshold autoregressive (1) models with exogenous Markovian triggers. Section 3 outlines the simulation methodology. A separate section is necessary since obtaining a sample from the steady-state distribution of a TAR model with a Markov-switching exogenous trigger is a non-trivial exercise. Section 4 presents and discusses simulation results and Section 5 concludes.

2. Moment-Generating Functions of TAR(1) Models with Exogenous Markov-Triggers

In this section, we introduce the threshold autoregressive model with a Markov-switching exogenous trigger. After introducing the model, we derive the moment-generating functions for this model and present some interesting results. We shift to characteristic functions after Theorem 3, where we do not have to assume the existence of all moments so that moment-generating functions for such processes need not exist. Characteristic functions on the other hand will always exist (Stuart and Ord 1994, chps. 3 and 4). Such processes are often used to model prices (particularly in finance), therefore, we refer to our model as a price process indicated by p_t.

The price process has a switching AR(1) form:

$$p_t = \alpha_{t-1} + \beta_{t-1} p_{t-1} + \sigma_{t-1} \eta_t \tag{1}$$

where α_{t-1} is a switching drift, β_{t-1} is a switching coefficient term, and σ_{t-1} is a switching variance term for the error process. Let:

$$\alpha_{t-1} = \langle \alpha, z_{t-1} \rangle \ \beta_{t-1} = \langle \beta, z_{t-1} \rangle \ \sigma_{t-1} = \langle \sigma, z_{t-1} \rangle$$

where α is a vector containing all drift terms, β is a vector of coefficients, and σ is a vector of error standard deviations. In general, all the above vectors are $k \times 1$, but we illustrate them when $k = 3$ for notational convenience. We assume that z_t is Markovian and follows a multinomial distribution, and that η_t has a moment-generating function $\psi(u)$ which is assumed to be location-scale. z_t determines what state α_{t-1} and β_{t-1} are in. In particular,

$$\alpha = (\alpha_1, \alpha_2, \alpha_3)' \ \beta = (\beta_1, \beta_2, \beta_3)' \ \sigma = (\sigma_1, \sigma_2, \sigma_3)' \ \eta_t \sim iid(0,1)$$

$$z_t \in \{e_1, e_2, e_3\} \ e_1 = \begin{pmatrix} 1 \\ 0 \\ 0 \end{pmatrix} e_2 = \begin{pmatrix} 0 \\ 1 \\ 0 \end{pmatrix} e_3 = \begin{pmatrix} 0 \\ 0 \\ 1 \end{pmatrix}$$

$E[z_t | z_{t-1}] = P z_{t-1}$, where P represents the Transition Matrix for the Markovian state variable z_t. For econometric purposes, we envisage an exogenous continuous random variable Z_t and constants $\vartheta_0, \ldots, \vartheta_3$, so that $z_t = e_j$ if $\vartheta_{j-1} \leq Z_t < \vartheta_j$, i.e., when the continuous random variable Z_t is between thresholds ϑ_{j-1} and ϑ_j, and the value of the Markovian variable z_t is equal to e_j. The nature of Z_t determines P and the kind of regime-switching model Z_t is.

Here, $P = \begin{pmatrix} p_{11} & p_{12} & p_{13} \\ p_{21} & p_{22} & p_{23} \\ p_{31} & p_{32} & p_{33} \end{pmatrix}$ is the transition matrix, which describes the probability of switching states. Note that $i'P = i'$, where i is a vector of ones, and $P\pi = \pi$ where π is the vector of stationary (steady-state) probabilities and $i'\pi = 1$.

$$p_{ji} = P(z_{t+1} = e_j | z_t = e_i) = P(z_1 = e_j | z_0 = e_i) \; 1 \leq i, j \leq 3$$

so that the Markov Chain is stationary. Whilst we can estimate P by counting frequencies, we can also hypothesize a Markov process for Z_t and then integrate over the appropriate rectangle of the probability density function of (Z_t, Z_{t+1}).

We now consider $\exp(up_t)$ in order to derive the moment-generating function for p_t. Here, $u \in \mathbb{R}$. The moment-generating function of p_t is defined by $\phi_t(u) = E[\exp(up_t)]$. Our aim is to determine a recursion for $\phi_t(u) \in R$.

Now,
$$z_t = Pz_{t-1} + v_t \in R^3 \tag{2}$$

where,
$$E[v_t | z_{t-1}] = \begin{pmatrix} 0 \\ 0 \\ 0 \end{pmatrix} = 0 \in R^3.$$

From (1), we have that:

$$\exp(up_t) = \exp[u\langle \alpha, z_{t-1} \rangle] \exp[u \langle \beta, z_{t-1} \rangle p_{t-1}] \exp(u\langle \sigma, z_{t-1} \rangle \eta_t)$$

Using iterated expectations, we find that the moment-generating function for p_t is:

$$\phi_t(u) = E(E(\exp[u\langle \alpha, z_{t-1} \rangle] \exp[u \langle \beta, z_{t-1} \rangle p_{t-1}] \exp(u\langle \sigma, z_{t-1} \rangle \eta_t | z_{t-1}))$$

For functions $F(p_{t-1}, Z_{t-1})$, we note that:

$$E(F(p_{t-1}, Z_{t-1})) = E\left(\sum_{j=1}^{k} F(p_{t-1}, e_j) \pi_j\right)$$

by the law of total probability.

Thus,
$$\phi_t(u) = \sum_{j=1}^{k} \pi_j \left(\exp[u\langle \alpha, e_j \rangle]\right) \phi_{t-1}\left[\langle \beta, e_j \rangle u\right] \psi(\langle \sigma, e_j \rangle u) \tag{3}$$

is a dynamic recursion for the moment-generating function of p_t.

Steady-State Distribution under Markovian States

The above discussion leads to the following result.

Theorem 1. *Assuming a steady state for prices, denote $E(\exp(up_t)) = \phi(u)$ and $E(\exp(u\eta_t)) = \psi(u)$ as the appropriate mgfs (or characteristic functions with a trivial definitional change). Then,*

$$\phi(u) = \sum_{j=1}^{k} \exp(u\alpha_j) \phi(\beta_j u) \pi_j \psi(\sigma_j u) \tag{4}$$

is the steady-state relationship.

We can use Theorem 1 to arrive at analytical expressions for different moments of the process, p_t.

Define:
$$\mu_B = \sum_{j=1}^{k} \pi_j \beta_j \; ; \; \mu_{2B} = \sum_{j=1}^{k} \pi_j \beta_j^2 \; ; \; \sigma_B^2 = \mu_{2B} - (\mu_B)^2$$
$$\mu_\alpha = \sum_{j=1}^{k} \pi_j \alpha_j \; ; \; \mu_\sigma = \sum_{j=1}^{k} \pi_j \sigma_j; \; \mu_{\alpha B} = \sum_{j=1}^{k} \pi_j \beta_j \alpha_j \; \text{etc.}$$

We differentiate (4) once to obtain the first moment of p_t, and we get:

$$E(p_t) = \frac{\mu_\alpha + \mu_\sigma E(\eta_t)}{1 - \mu_B}$$

Differentiating the mgf a second time gives us the second moment of p_t:

$$E(p_t^2) = \frac{\mu_{2\alpha} + 2\mu_{\alpha B} E(p_t) + 2\mu_{\sigma B} E(\eta_t) E(p_t) + 2\mu_{\alpha\sigma} E(\eta_t) + \mu_{2\sigma} E(\eta_t^2)}{1 - \mu_{2B}}.$$

Further calculations and simplifications lead to an expression for the variance of p_t:

$$Var(p_t) = E(p_t^2) - (E(p_t))^2$$
$$Var(p_t) = \frac{\mu_{2\alpha} + 2\mu_{\alpha B} E(p_t) + 2\mu_{\sigma B} E(\eta_t) E(p_t) + 2\mu_{\alpha\sigma} E(\eta_t) + \mu_{2\sigma} E(\eta_t^2)}{1 - \mu_{2B}} - \left(\frac{\mu_\alpha + \mu_\sigma E(\eta_t)}{1 - \mu_B}\right)^2$$

Various interesting results can be derived from Theorem 1 for plausible parameter values. We list one case below, but other results can be regarded as special cases. Here, we are concerned with the case where $k = 2$, $\alpha_j = 0$, $\beta_1 = \beta$, $\beta_2 = 0$, and $\sigma_2 = 0$, so that the mgf function becomes:

$$\phi(u) = \phi(\beta u)(\pi + (1 - \pi)\psi(u)) \quad (5)$$

Corollary 1. *If $\psi(u)$ is the moment-generating function of a negative exponential with parameter λ, and $\alpha_j = 0, \sigma_1 = \sigma, \sigma_2 = 0$, and $\pi = \beta$ where $\beta_1 = \beta_2 = \beta$ which is less than 1, then $\phi(u) = \frac{\lambda}{\lambda - u}$, i.e., a negative exponential random variable with parameter λ.*

Proof. To show that Equation (5) has a solution for some $\psi(u)$, we consider the negative exponential function, i.e., we assume that the disturbance term is distributed as a negative exponential with parameter λ. The corresponding moment-generating function, $\phi(u)$, for this disturbance term is $\frac{\lambda}{\lambda - u}$ if we further assume that $\beta = \pi$ and that $0 \leq \beta < 1$. Note that Equation (5) corresponds to the situation where the β coefficient does not move across states, but the standard deviation of the disturbance term does, i.e., $\sigma_1 = \sigma$ and $\sigma_2 = 0$. Our result implies that $\sigma = \frac{1}{\lambda}$. □

For our distributional assumption regarding the disturbance, the corresponding moment-generating function is (taking into consideration the two states):

$$(\pi + (1 - \pi)\psi(u)) = \pi + \frac{(1-\pi)\lambda}{\lambda - u}$$

Substituting this in (5) and using the trial solution, $\phi(u) = \frac{\lambda}{\lambda - u}$, we have:

$$\frac{\lambda}{\lambda - u} = \left(\frac{\lambda}{\lambda - \beta u}\right)\left(\pi + \frac{(1-\pi)\lambda}{\lambda - u}\right)$$

If we further assume that $\beta = \pi$, the LHS and RHS are equal, thereby proving our result.

We recognize the solution as being a negative exponential auto-regression of degree 1 (NEAR(1)). These models were investigated in detail by Gaver and Lewis (1980), which also included earlier references to related models. We note that the same arguments could be applied to Gamma random variables with integer degrees of freedom.

The attractiveness of these models is that they are AR(1) models where the underlying process is always positive, and hence, can be used to model equity or bond prices in finance. Our version is a slight extension of existing NEAR(1) models, in that Corollary 2 will be consistent with a Markov process for the state process rather than an i.i.d. process, as in the current NEAR(1) literature.

Furthermore, if Z_{t-1} is Markovian with transition matrix P such that $\pi = P\pi$, then:

$$\pi_j = \sum_{m=1}^{k} \pi_m P_{jm},$$

and

$$\phi(u) = \sum_{j=1}^{k} \exp(u\alpha_j)\, \phi(\beta_j u)\, \psi(\sigma_j u) \sum_{m=1}^{k} P_{jm}\, \pi_m$$

Alternatively,

$$\phi(u) = \langle \exp(u\alpha)\phi(\beta u)\, \psi(\sigma u),\ P\pi \rangle \qquad (6)$$

There are a number of observations relevant to (4) and (6) which we present below:

Theorem 2. *Since $\pi = P\pi$ has multiple solutions for P given π, these different P's do not change the solution to Equation (6). As an example, for $k = 2$, suppose $\pi = 0.5$. It then follows that $P_{11} = P_{22}$, but if $P_{11} = 0.2$ or 0.8 in this context, the steady-state distribution will be unaffected except through a change in position.*

The steady-state values are equal (i.e., 0.5), and thus, such changes in the structure of the transition matrix should not influence steady-state values. Note, however, that this does not say anything about the speed at which the two processes in this example converge to the steady state. For more on speed of convergence, refer to Rosenthal (1995). Since the processes converge to the steady state through different paths, simulating the steady state becomes a non-trivial procedure, as explained in Section 3.

Theorem 3. *Suppose that in Equation (6), α is zero, and $\phi(u)$ and $\psi(u)$ are infinitely differentiable moment-generating functions and that the variance of the error process is constant.*

Theorem 4. *If $\phi(u)$ is symmetric, then $\psi(u)$ is symmetric. The proof is trivial.*

Theorem 5. *If $\psi(u)$ is symmetric, then $\phi(u)$ is symmetric (proof by induction on Taylors series terms). We shall prove that all odd moments are zero:*

Proof.

$$\phi(u) = \left(\sum_{j=1}^{k} \phi(\beta_j u)\, \pi_j\, \psi(u) \right)$$

The coefficient of u^n for $\phi(u)$,

$$\phi_n = \sum_{j=1}^{k} \pi_j \sum_{s=0}^{n} \phi_{n-s} \beta_j^{n-s} \psi_s \qquad (7)$$

$\psi_1 = 0$ implies that $\phi_1 = 0$. We now suppose that $\psi_{2j+1} = 0$, which implies that $\phi_{2j+1} = 0$ for $j = 0, \ldots, k$ and consider ϕ_{2j+3}. From (7), the inductive hypothesis and the properties of products of odd and even numbers, the result follows. □

Theorem 6. *Suppose that $\alpha_j = 0$, the variance of the error term is constant, and that we treat*

$$\phi(u) = \left(\sum_{j=1}^{k} \phi(\beta_j u) \pi_j\, \psi(u) \right) \qquad (8)$$

as a statement about characteristic functions. Then, if at least one of the β_j's is greater than 1 and all of them are non-negative, for some n, the nth moment will not exist. The proof follows from using (7) again and noting that ϕ_n (the nth differential of $\phi(u)$), which is proportional to the nth moment (if it exists), can be expressed as:

$$\phi_n\left(1 - \sum_{j=1}^{k} \pi_j \beta_j^n\right) = \sum_{j=1}^{k} \pi_j \sum_{s=1}^{n} \phi_{n-s} \beta_j^{n-s} \psi_s$$

The requirement for the existence of ϕ_n is that $\sum_{j=1}^{k} \pi_j \beta_j^n < 1$, which cannot hold for a large enough n under the assumptions of Theorem 6. This result links local explosivity to fat tails. Thus, processes with locally explosive states will cease to have moments once n becomes sufficiently large.

Ahmed and Satchell (2018) derived similar conditions for the existence of a mean and variance for a TAR(1) process with an independently distributed exogenous trigger for state switching. We have generalized the result for the nth moment and for an exogenous trigger that is Markovian. Pourahmadi (1988) arrived at a similar result in Section 2 of his article (see Equations (2.3)–(2.5) in Pourahmadi (ibid.)), but he carried out his derivation in the context of doubly stochastic processes, as opposed to the specific case of a threshold autoregressive process that we consider. Secondly, Pourahmadi was mainly interested in second-order stationarity, while we present results for the existence of all moments. Thus, we substantially improve upon the results contained in Pourahmadi (1988) and Ahmed and Satchell (2018). Below, we consider a special case which will be of particular interest to finance practitioners.

Corollary 2. *Assume that $\alpha_j = 0$, and the variance of the error term is constant, i.e., $\sigma_1 = \sigma_2 = \sigma$.*

Consider now the special case $k = 2$, $\beta_1 = 1$, and $\beta_2 = 0$. This is an important special case as it gives us a random walk in one regime and white noise in the other. Substituting into (8), we see that:

$$\phi(u) = (\phi(u)\pi + 1 - \pi)\psi(u)$$

This can be re-arranged to yield:

$$\phi(u) = \frac{(1-\pi)\psi(u)}{(1-\pi\psi(u))}$$

Since $|\psi(u)| \leq 1$, $\pi|\psi(u)| < 1$ and $\phi(u)$ can be represented in terms of a valid series expansion which can be analyzed term by term. Indeed,

$$\phi(u) = (1-\pi) \sum_{j=0}^{\infty} \pi^j \psi(u)^{j+1} \qquad (9)$$

The right-hand side is uniformly and absolutely convergent because of the Weirstrass M-test, and thus we can integrate term by term. Pourahmadi (1988) also considered this as a special case in his article and derives conditions for the existence of a variance and covariance (see Sections 3 and 4 in his article).

We can now consider different choices for $\psi(u)$.

Suppose we have a normally distributed error term with a mean of zero and a variance of σ^2, i.e., $\psi(u) = \exp\left(-\frac{\sigma^2 u^2}{2}\right)$. Then, $\psi(u)^{j+1}$ represents a normal random variable with a mean of zero and a variance of $(j+1)\sigma^2$. We can identify the distribution of p_t as an infinite weighted sum of normal random variables of increasing variances, but whose relative importance declines with a power of π. This process was analyzed in Knight and Satchell (2011) and extended in Grynkiv and Stentoft (2018).

Likewise, assume the variance of the error is constant. If we consider a mean corrected Poisson so that $\psi(u) = \exp(\theta(\exp(iu) - 1 - iu))$ with mean parameter θ, we can identify the distribution of p_t as an infinite weighted sum of Poisson random variables of increasing means $(j+1)\theta$, but whose relative importance declines with a power of π.

This case can be extended to include intercepts, in which case,

$$\phi(u) = (\exp(i\alpha_1 u)\phi(u)\pi + (\exp(i\alpha_2 u)(1-\pi))\psi(u)$$
$$\phi(u) = \frac{\exp(i\alpha_2 u)(1-\pi)\psi(u)}{1-\exp(i\alpha_1 u)\pi\psi(u)}$$

Since $\left|\exp(i\alpha_1 u)\pi\psi(u)\right| < 1$, the analysis proceeds as before, and:

$$\phi(u) = (1-\pi)\exp(i\alpha_2 u)\sum_{j=0}^{\infty}\pi^j\psi(u)^{j+1}\exp(ij\alpha_1 u)$$

We see that the jth component is as above, but has a mean augmented by $j\alpha_1 + \alpha_2$. For other examples, we refer the interested reader to Pourahmadi (1988) Section 4, who derived marginal distributions for different processes.

The results can be generalized to Vector threshold auto-regressions. These results are not presented here but are available upon request. The interested reader may also refer to Grynkiv and Stentoft (2018) for some discussion.

3. A Caveat on Simulating the Steady State

Simulating the steady state for processes similar to those considered in Section 2 is not as straight forward as it may appear at first glance and warrants further consideration, which this section seeks to provide. Generating a discrete Markov chain, which is essentially a variable that takes discrete integer values of 0 or 1 depending on the transition matrix P, does not generate a steady-state Markov chain, but rather a path to the steady state. It is common in this literature to simulate steady-state paths rather than a steady-state Markov chain. Indeed, in our earlier work, we worked with paths and not steady states, as did Timmerman in his article (see Figures 1–6 in his articles for example). While simulating steady-state paths sufficed for our earlier work, we need to simulate the steady state in order to corroborate our results from Section 2. Otherwise, the underlying moments of the simulated series can be different even if they converge to the same steady state.

This path is dependent upon the transition matrix P. If states are persistent, as determined by the transition probabilities of the process staying in the prevailing state (p_{ii}), this path may diverge significantly from the steady state. On the opposite spectrum is a transition matrix with frequent state switches, due to higher switching probabilities, which will take a different path to the steady state. Although the steady-state probabilities of both paths are identical, the dynamics vary due to the different paths taken by the processes.

We need to consider how discrete Markov chains converge to their steady states. The usual definition is based on total variation distance, and considers the supremum, taken over measurable subsets A, of the absolute difference between $v(A)$ and $u(A)$, where $v()$ and $u()$ are the two probability measures (see Rosenthal 1995). Whilst our process will converge in this sense, it will almost surely not converge along a sample path. Intuitively, it keeps moving from state to state.

We illustrate this by considering two different transition matrices that correspond to the steady-state probability vector $\begin{bmatrix} 0.5 \\ 0.5 \end{bmatrix}$. We consider a transition matrix with highly persistent states $P_1 = \begin{pmatrix} 0.9 & 0.1 \\ 0.1 & 0.9 \end{pmatrix}$ and a transition matrix with frequent state switches $P_2 = \begin{pmatrix} 0.5 & 0.5 \\ 0.5 & 0.5 \end{pmatrix}$. While both processes approach the same steady states, the simulated series have different probability distributions. Specifically, persistence of the non-stationary process, corresponding to $\beta_j > 1$, causes the path to diverge far from the steady-state values, resulting in a process that has extreme values with significant probability, which also obtains very high kurtosis. With frequent state switches, the simulated series comes closer to a normally distributed process.

To remedy this, each of the above paths was simulated for 10,000 periods and the process was repeated 2000 times. The parameter values in the two switching states are 0 in state 1 and 1 in state 2. We also carried out simulations when the switching states corresponded to values of 0.1 in state 1 and 1.1 in state 2. We recorded the average of the first four moments of both paths in Table 1. As mentioned previously, the persistent path obtains a much higher kurtosis and standard deviation than the more frequently switching path, even though both paths continue to be symmetrically distributed. An alternative approach would be to write out the solution to Equation (1) and simulate directly by taking long samples of the error term and the exogenous process. From Table 1, we observe that the highest 2nd and 4th moments are obtained for the persistent state when $\beta_1 = 0.1$ and $\beta_2 = 1.1$. This is despite the fact that this process also converges to a steady-state vector $[0.50\ 0.50]$. The moments are significantly different for the alternative paths corresponding to P_2.

Table 1. Moments of TAR(1) with Markov-switching exogenous variables.

Steady State Vector	Transition Matrix	δ	Mean	Stdev	Skewness	Kurtosis
[0.50 0.50]	$P_1 = \begin{pmatrix} 0.9 & 0.1 \\ 0.1 & 0.9 \end{pmatrix}$	0	0.0004	2.450	0.00289	8.786
[0.50 0.50]	$P_1 = \begin{pmatrix} 0.9 & 0.1 \\ 0.1 & 0.9 \end{pmatrix}$	0.10	−0.170	78.17	0.2761	424.7
[0.50 0.50]	$P_2 = \begin{pmatrix} 0.5 & 0.5 \\ 0.5 & 0.5 \end{pmatrix}$	0	−0.0001	1.4139	−0.0004	4.480
[0.50 0.50]	$P_2 = \begin{pmatrix} 0.5 & 0.5 \\ 0.5 & 0.5 \end{pmatrix}$	0.10	0.0000	1.6014	−0.0012	6.837

Table 1 reports the first four moments of simulated threshold autoregressive series with Markov-switching exogenous variables. Each series is 10,000 observations long, and 2000 series were simulated for each set of values. P represents the transition matrix and delta represents a parameter that determines the values of β_j in the two states; $\beta_1 = \delta$, $\beta_2 = 1 + \delta$.

Figures 1 and 2 below highlight the different distributions that result from the different paths, along with cumulative probabilities corresponding to the normal probability density function's quintile values. Tail probabilities are much higher for the more persistent path, which also has more extreme values, especially when the non-stationary state becomes explosive. Tail probabilities are 28.7% and 30.8% for $\delta = 0$ and $\delta = 0.10$, respectively, in Figure 1, which correspond to the more persistent transition matrix, P_1. In fact, the distribution corresponding to $\delta = 0.10$ appears like a horizontal line instead of a bell-shaped curve.

On the other hand, the distributions of simulated series corresponding to the more frequently switching path (transition matrix P_2) have lower tail probabilities and distributions that are closer to the standard normal distribution. Figure 2 contrasts the distribution for the series corresponding to path P_2 to a standard normal. While this simulated distribution has heavier tails, as evident from the higher probabilities corresponding to normal quintiles, its 2nd and 4th moments are much closer to the normal than to the simulated series for path P_1. Similarly, for the distributions in Figure 2, corresponding to $\beta_1 = 0.10$ and $\beta_2 = 1.10$, path P_2 look much closer to a normal distribution than to their P_1 counterparts in Figure 1.

Thus, we need a different approach to generate the steady-state distribution of the threshold autoregressive process with Markovian triggers that are independent of the transition matrix, subject to the same steady state. It is important to understand that the results derived in the section above correspond to the steady state itself and not to the path of the process tending to a steady state, which, as we have shown in this section, depends on the transition matrix. We describe how we simulate the steady-state distribution in the next section.

$$P_1 = \begin{pmatrix} 0.90 & 0.10 \\ 0.10 & 0.90 \end{pmatrix}, \pi = \begin{bmatrix} 0.50 \\ 0.50 \end{bmatrix}, \delta = 0.10, \beta_1 = \delta, \beta_2 = 1 + \delta$$

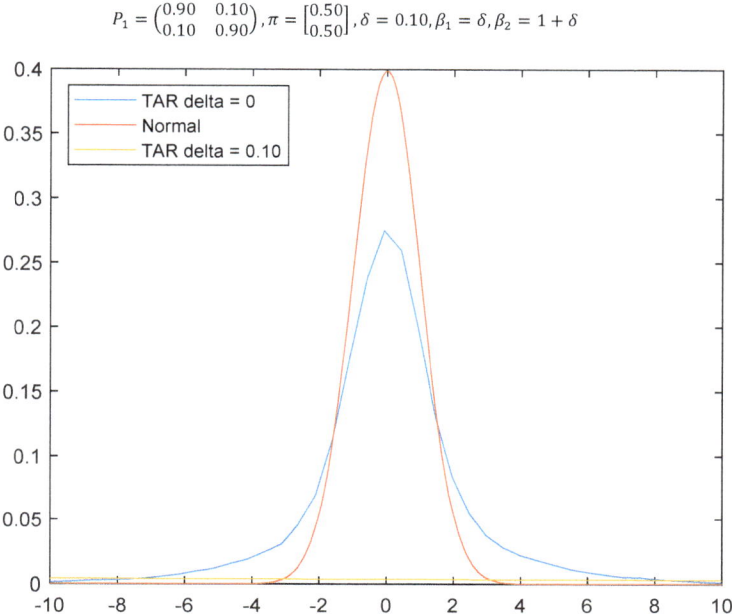

Figure 1. Simulated Distributions for TAR(1) with P_1 as the transition matrix.

$$P_2 = \begin{pmatrix} 0.50 & 0.50 \\ 0.50 & 0.50 \end{pmatrix}, \pi = \begin{bmatrix} 0.50 \\ 0.50 \end{bmatrix}, \delta = 0.10, \beta_1 = \delta, \beta_2 = 1 + \delta$$

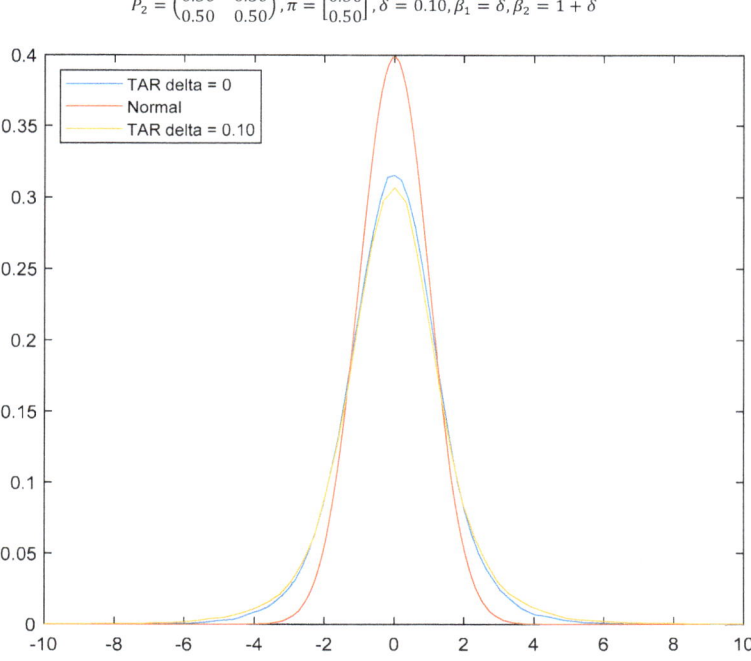

Figure 2. Simulated Distributions for TAR(1) with P_2 as the transition matrix.

4. Simulation Results

In order to simulate a distribution for the steady state, we observed the Markov chain 10,000 times. However, each observation was 1000 time periods or steps apart. Thus, the Markov chain we simulated was 10,000,000 periods long, and the steady-state simulation was 10,000 observations in length. We verified that each series simulated this way converges to the steady-state probability vector while at the same time being independent of the transition matrix, P. We did this by simulating steady states for different transition matrices P that shared the same steady states.[1] Thus, the analysis considered in this section depends only on the steady-state vector and not on the transition matrices. The steady-state chain was then used to simulate the following threshold model:

$$y_t = \alpha + \beta_{it} y_{t-1} + \eta_t$$

where β_{it} depends on the value taken by the exogenous discrete Markov state variable z_i. Our simulations assumed that $\eta_t \sim N(0,1)$ and that $\alpha = 0$. In order for our simulated series to have a steady-state stationary distribution, we required that the criterion $\sum_{i=1}^{2} \pi_i \ln|\beta_i| < 0$ be satisfied. Since we considered a two-state process, the criterion can alternatively be written as $\beta_1^\pi \beta_2^{1-\pi} < 1$. The criterion is trivially satisfied when $\beta_1 = 0$ as $\ln(0) = -\infty$. When $\beta_1 = \delta$ and $\beta_2 = (1+\delta)$, the criterion becomes $\delta^\pi (1+\delta)^{1-\pi} < 1$. Note, that the expression $\delta^\pi (1+\delta)^{1-\pi}$ is maximized for $\pi = 0$.

We considered a maximum δ of 0.10, and checked that the criterion was satisfied for all our simulations and that a steady-state distribution does exist. For exposition, we included the value taken by the criterion function for each set of simulations in column 7 of Table 2 below.

Steady-state distributions obtained this way can be analyzed through the results derived in Section 2. For each set of steady-state vectors in Table 2, we simulated threshold autoregressive series (as described above) 2000 times. The parameter values in the two switching states are δ in state 1 and $1 + \delta$ in state 2. Thus, the first state is always stationary, while the second state is either a random walk or explosive.

Some patterns are exhibited clearly. The distributions of the series appear to be centered on zero, and statistically their skewness (column 5) is not significantly different from zero, which follows from Theorem 3. Since the disturbance term has an even distribution, it follows that the distribution of our simulated series will also be even, symmetric, and centered on zero, i.e., $\psi(u) = \psi(-u)$ implies that $\phi(u) = \phi(-u)$.

The standard deviation (column 2), however, does appear to be much larger than the standard deviation of the error process driving the threshold process. The series have excess kurtosis (column 6), which should not come as a surprise since the series display non-stationary behavior when $\beta_i \geq 1$. This state leads to excess kurtosis and higher standard deviation. As we deviate from our base case, ($\delta = 0$), we note a clear pattern in the 2nd and 4th moments of the series. Both the standard deviation and kurtosis start to increase, since this behavior is caused by the non-stationary state becoming increasingly more explosive ($\beta_i = 1 + \delta$, when $\delta > 0$). The pattern is repeated irrespective of the steady-state vector chosen.

Unsurprisingly, the higher the steady-state probability of the stationary state ($\beta_i = \delta$), the closer the process's distribution is to a normal distribution. This is reflected in the first four moments. For instance, when the stationary state occurs 90% of the time (as in rows 2–6 of Table 2), the standard deviation and kurtosis are both lower compared to corresponding cases (i.e., same δ) when the stationary state occurs less than 90% of the time. When $\delta = 0.05$, the standard deviation and kurtosis respectively are 1.061 and 3.362 for $\pi = 0.90$, 1.134 and 3.762 for $\pi = 0.80$, 1.339 and 4.660 for $\pi = 0.60$, and 1.494 and 5.302 for $\pi = 0.5$. While all distributions appear symmetric and centered on 0, they become increasingly leptokurtic as π falls.

---

[1] These results have not been included but are available upon request.

Table 2. Average moments of TAR(1) with changing Steady State Vectors.

Steady State Vector [π 1−π]	δ	Mean	Stdev	Skewness	Kurtosis	Criteria = $\sum_{i=1}^{2}\pi_i \ln|\beta_i|$
[0.90 0.10]	0	0.0001	1.0544	−0.0012	3.306	−∞
[0.90 0.10]	0.01	−0.0007	1.0552	0.0004	3.311	−4.1437
[0.90 0.10]	0.03	0.0001	1.0583	−0.0008	3.336	−3.1529
[0.90 0.10]	0.05	0.0007	1.0608	−0.0006	3.362	−2.6913
[0.90 0.10]	0.10	0.0007	1.0714	−0.0007	3.442	−2.0628
[0.80 0.20]	0	0.0004	1.118	−0.002	3.597	−∞
[0.80 0.20]	0.01	−0.0000	1.121	−0.0007	3.630	−3.6821
[0.80 0.20]	0.03	0.0001	1.128	−0.0016	3.705	−2.7993
[0.80 0.20]	0.05	0.0005	1.134	0.003	3.762	−2.3868
[0.80 0.20]	0.10	0.0001	1.152	0.0003	3.967	−1.8230
[0.60 0.40]	0	0.0004	1.291	−0.003	4.195	−∞
[0.60 0.40]	0.01	−0.0011	1.300	−0.001	4.277	−2.7591
[0.60 0.40]	0.03	−0.0001	1.316	−0.005	4.421	−2.0921
[0.60 0.40]	0.05	−0.0007	1.339	−0.002	4.660	−1.7779
[0.60 0.40]	0.10	−0.0004	1.400	0.002	5.410	−1.3434
[0.50 0.50]	0	0.0017	1.413	0.0026	4.470	−∞
[0.50 0.50]	0.01	−0.0004	1.428	−0.0042	4.612	−2.2976
[0.50 0.50]	0.03	−0.0006	1.460	−0.0001	4.915	−1.7385
[0.50 0.50]	0.05	−0.0004	1.494	−0.0021	5.302	−1.4735
[0.50 0.50]	0.10	0.001	1.601	0.0227	6.720	−1.1036

Table 2 reports the first four moments of the simulated series along with the stationary criterion. Each row corresponds to 2000 threshold autoregressive simulations with Markov triggers, 10,000 observations long; columns 3–6 report average moments.

We also plotted sample distributions for $\delta = 0$ and $\delta = 0.10$ for each set of steady-state vectors (Figures 3–6) and carried out quintile analysis by calculating the weights in the distribution corresponding to the quintile values of a normal distribution, i.e., we found $P(y_t) < q_1$, $q_1 < P(y_t) < q_2$, $q_2 < P(y_t) < q_3$, $q_3 < P(y_t) < q_4$, and $P(y_t) > q_4$, where q_i corresponds to the normal distribution's quintile values. We note that tail probabilities, i.e., those corresponding to the 1st and 5th normal quintile values, go up as the steady-state probabilities for the non-stationary state go up. They are also dependent on the value of δ, and as we increase explosivity in the non-stationary state (by increasing δ), tail probabilities increase and the distributions moves farther away from a normal. The symmetry of the distribution is also reflected in these probabilities.

The results above depend only on the steady-state vector $\begin{bmatrix} \pi \\ 1-\pi \end{bmatrix}$ and not on the transition matrix (the dynamic path) that generates this steady-state vector. We note that all series generated this way have excess kurtosis due to the presence of a non-stationary state.[2] Below, we simulate probability density functions for some of the cases considered in Table 2. The graphs only report the distribution for $\delta = 0$ and $\delta = 0.10$, so we can analyze how far the distribution moves from a normal as we increase δ and increase the probability of the non-stationary part of the distribution. We also draw a comparison with a normal distribution for illustrative purposes.

It is worth mentioning at this point that $\delta = 0.10$ may not present as interesting an empirical case as say $\delta = 0.01$ or $\delta = 0.03$. In empirical work (e.g., Ahmed and Satchell 2018), estimates have suggested that even with an explosive state in a threshold autoregressive model, the δ of the explosive state from the random walk state does not extend beyond 0.03. Our analysis is thus meant to provide a graphical view of how the distribution evolves as δ is varied, and this is most obvious when considering the two extreme values. Distributional analysis for other values was also considered and is available upon

---

[2] We have checked that the kurtosis exist by verifying that $1 - \sum_{j=1}^{2} \pi_j \beta_j^4 < 0$. Indeed, for our most extreme case ($\pi_1 = 0.5$, $pi_2 = 0.5$, $\beta_1 = 0.10$, $\beta_2 = 1.1$), the kurtosis does exist as the criterion for its existence is satisfied: $1 - \sum_{j=1}^{2} \pi_j \beta_j^4 = 0.7321$.

request. While results for other values of δ follow in the same direction as those considered here, the differences are less stark as would be expected. For researchers interested in modelling non-stationary behavior using threshold auto-regressions, a value of δ < 0.03 may be more appropriate.

From Figure 3a,b, we can see that when the stationary state is dominant ($\pi = 0.90$), the distribution appears very close to a normal distribution, even if δ is increased from 0 to 0.10. Contrast this distribution with Figure 6a,b, where the stationary and non-stationary states occur with equal probability. The distributions in Figure 6a,b are significantly leptokurtic, with tail probabilities of 25.2% and 26.2%, respectively, as opposed to tail probabilities of 20.8% and 21% in Figure 3a,b, respectively.

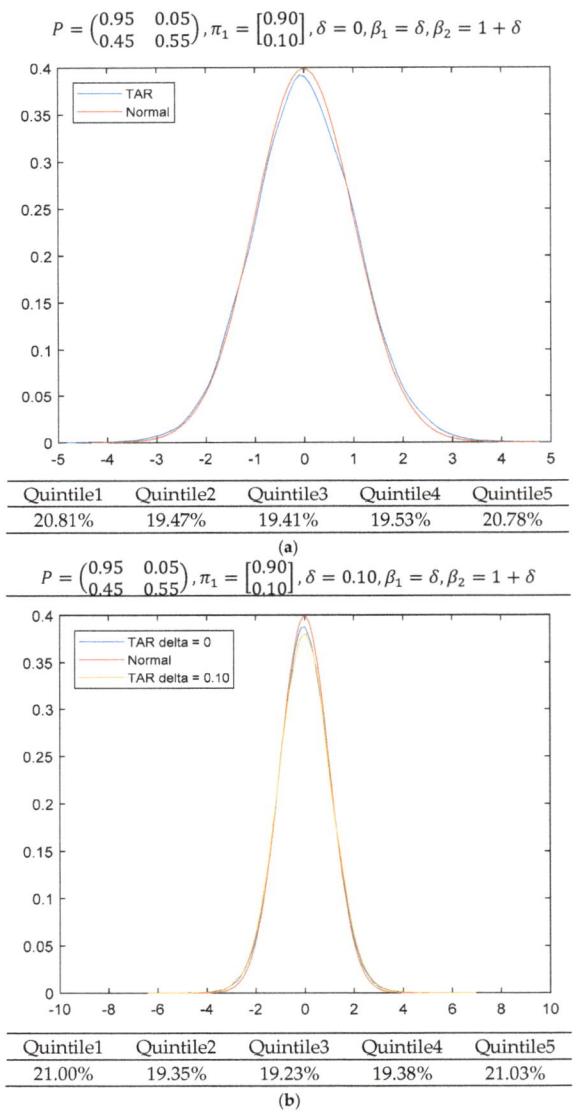

Figure 3. (a) Simulated Distributions for TAR(1) with π_1 as the steady state vector and $\delta = 0$. (b) Simulated Distributions for TAR(1) with π_1 as the steady state vector and $\delta = 0.10$.

These results are interesting, particularly for those relying on DSGE models. In finance, asset prices often exhibit locally non-stationary behavior, which leads to leptokurtosis in the series. Similarly, macroeconomists often consider different shock mechanisms in DSGE models. The results in this article will assist macroeconomists in considering shock processes that follow threshold auto-regressions with a non-stationary state. Since we have outlined a procedure for deriving analytical expressions, this would enable macroeconomists to analyze locally explosive shock processes which nevertheless are stationary overall and facilitate the implementation of numerical solutions.

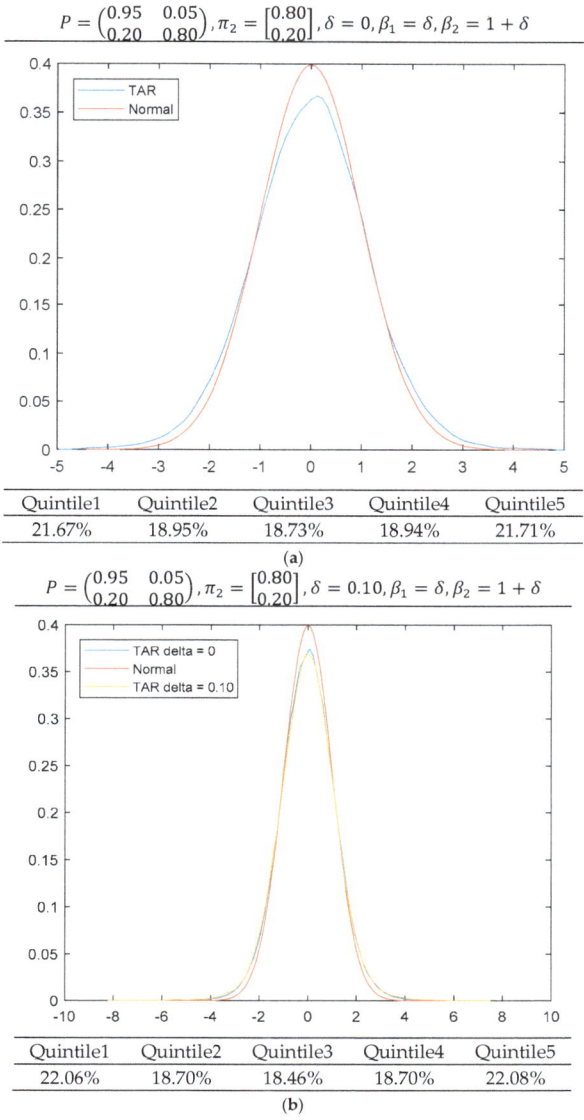

Figure 4. (a) Simulated Distributions for TAR(1) with π_2 as the steady state vector and $\delta = 0$. (b) Simulated Distributions for TAR(1) with π_2 as the steady state vector and $\delta = 0.10$.

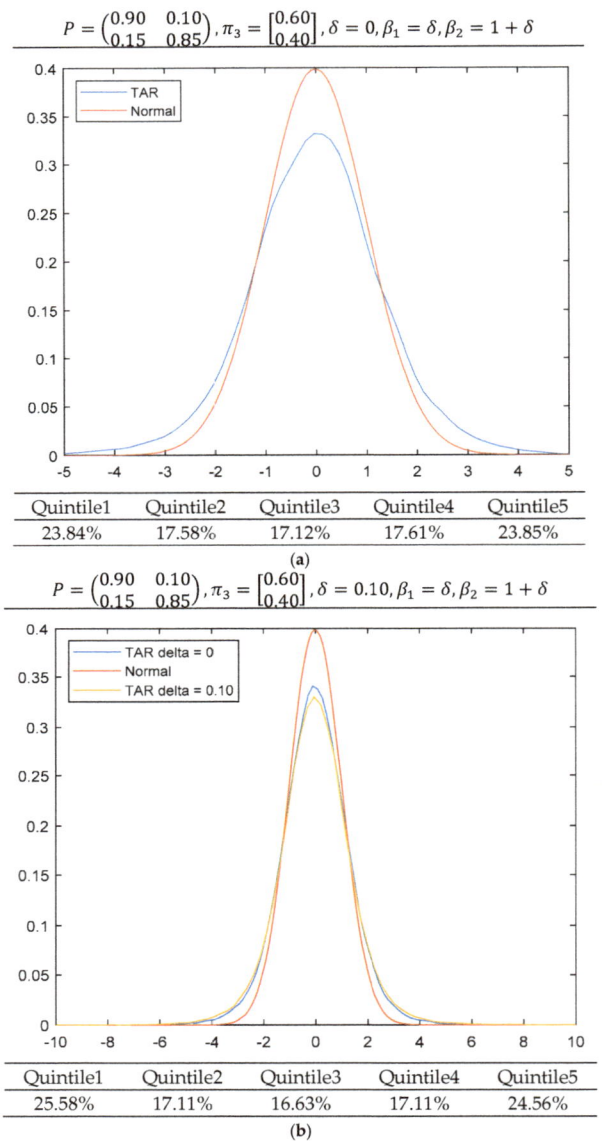

Figure 5. (**a**) Simulated Distributions for TAR(1) with π_3 as the steady state vector and $\delta = 0$. (**b**) Simulated Distributions for TAR(1) with π_3 as the steady state vector and $\delta = 0.10$.

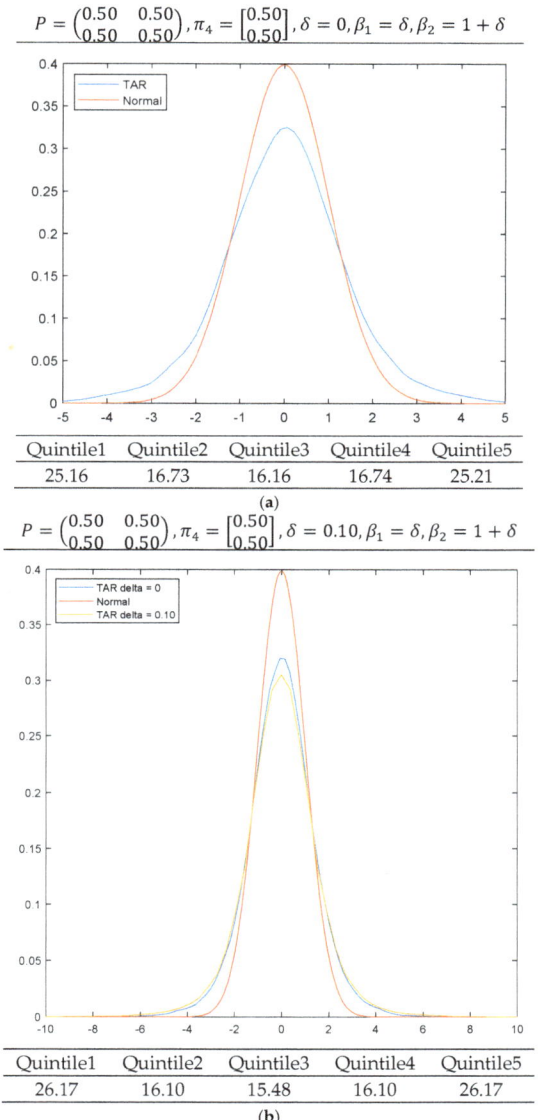

Figure 6. (a) Simulated Distributions for TAR(1) with π_4 as the steady state vector and $\delta = 0$. (b) Simulated Distributions for TAR(1) with π_4 as the steady state vector and $\delta = 0.10$.

5. Conclusions

In this article, we have derived formulae for characteristic functions for threshold autoregressive models of order 1, which have a Markovian state-switching variable. In doing so, we have not only improved the results first considered in Timmermann (2000), but have also generalized the formulae to a great degree. These formulae will allow readers, if they are so inclined, to derive analytical moments for TAR models in this class for a range of different error specifications. We believe that these will have applications in both finance and applied macroeconomics, given increasing interest in these models.

Considering a special case of interest, we have also shown using simulation analysis that the existence of a non-stationary state in a TAR model can cause the distribution of a particular series to deviate significantly from normality. The further away the non-stationary state moves from a random walk, the farther away the distribution is from that of a normal. Models for asset prices often consider a mixture of stationary and non-stationary states, and we believe that this simulation analysis will aid researchers in better understanding the behavior of asset prices that go through locally explosive states. In Sections 1 and 2, we have further outlined how our results may be applicable to applied macroeconomic and finance literatures.

Indeed, articles like Ahmed and Satchell (2018) would have found these results useful. While Ahmed and Satchell (2018) provided an empirical example to estimate market efficiency using a threshold autoregressive model, they were unable to calculate means and variances for their series. Through the results in our article, they would have been able to compare the two asset price series using well-known metrics in finance, such as Sharpe ratios. Similarly, any researchers modelling asset prices through threshold autoregressive models with a Markov-switching variable will be able to calculate moments and provide a more holistic narrative.

Furthermore, the contributions in the article will allow researchers to consider non-normal distributions for asset price series. Normality or log-normality is often assumed in the asset pricing literature to allow derivation of analytical expressions at the cost of accuracy. As we have shown, not only are threshold autoregressive models better at capturing asset pricing-like behavior, but they also allow for analytical solutions that can be useful in helping us better understand asset pricing behavior.

Another avenue worth considering from a statistical point of view will be to consider relevant moment-generating functions for the error process, and analyzing the resulting distributions for the underlying process, which we have referred to as the price process. Whilst we have considered the standard normal and Poisson distributions, future research could consider other distributions, which may inform future Finance and Economics research.

Thus, our article makes significant contributions to the existing literature on TAR models and offers insights into how such models may be used in applied economics and finance.

Author Contributions: S.S. conceptualized the article and derived the theoretical results contained in the article. M.F.A. carried out all simulation analysis following on from the theoretical results and wrote the article. Some results were the result of discussions between the co-authors.

Funding: This research received no external funding.

Acknowledgments: The authors would like to thank Robert Elliot, Mike Tehranchi and Alan Timmermann for helpful comments. Farid Ahmed would like to thank Cambridge INET for their generous support.

Conflicts of Interest: The authors declare no conflict of interest.

References

Ahmed, Muhammad Farid, and Stephen E. Satchell. 2018. What Proportion of Time is a Particular Market Inefficient? ... A Method for Analysing the Frequency of Market Efficiency when Equity Prices follow Threshold Autoregression. *Journal of Time Series Econometrics* 10. [CrossRef]

Aleem, Abdul, and Amine Lahiani. 2014. A Threshold Vector Auto-regression Model of Exchange-rate pass-through in Mexico. *Research in International Business and Finance* 30. [CrossRef]

Caner, Mehmet, and Bruce E. Hansen. 2001. Threshold Autoregression with a Unit Root. *Econometrica* 69: 1555–96. Available online: http://www.jstor.org/stable/2692267 (accessed on 10 December 2018).

Engel, Charles. 1994. Can the Markov switching model forecast exchange rates? *Journal of International Economics* 36: 151–65. [CrossRef]

Foerster, Andrew, Juan Rubio-Ramirez, Daniel F. Waggoner, and Tao Zha. 2016. Perturbation methods for Markov-Switching DSGE Models. *Quantitative Economics* 7: 637–69. [CrossRef]

Gaver, Donald P., and P. A. W. Lewis. 1980. First-Order Autoregressive Gamma sequences and Point Processes. *Advanced Applied Probability* 12: 727–45. [CrossRef]

Goldfeld, S. M., and R. E. Quandt. 1973. A Markov Model for Switching Regressions. *Journal of Econometrics* 1: 3–16. [CrossRef]

Gonzalo, Jesus, and Martin Gonzalez-Rozada. 1997. *Threshold Unit Root Models. DES—Working Papers. Statistics and Econometrics. WS*. Madrid: Universidad Carlos III de Madrid.

Goodwin, Barry K., and Daniel C. Harper. 2000. Price Transmission, threshold behaviour and asymmetric adjustment in the U.S. pork sector. *Journal of Agricultural and Applied Economics* 32: 543–53. [CrossRef]

Grynkiv, Galyna, and Lars Stentoft. 2018. Stationary Threshold Vector Autoregressive Models. *Journal of Risk and Financial Management* 11: 45. [CrossRef]

Hamilton, J. D. 1989. A New Approach to the Economic Analysis of Nonstationary Time Series and the Business Cycle. *Econometrica* 57: 319–52. [CrossRef]

Hamilton, James D. 1990. Analysis of Time Series Subject to Regime Changes. *Journal of Econometrics* 45: 39–70. [CrossRef]

Hamilton, James D. 2010. Regime switching models. In *Macroeconometrics and Time Series Analysis*. Edited by Steven N. Durlauf and Lawrence E. Blume. London: Palgrave Macmillan.

Hansen, Bruce E. 2011. Threshold autoregression in Economics. *Statistics and Its Interface* 4: 123–7. [CrossRef]

Kapetanios, George, and Yongcheol Shin. 2006. Unit root tests in three-regime SETAR models. *The Econometrics Journal* 9: 252–78. [CrossRef]

Knight, John, and Stephen E. Satchell. 2011. Some New Results for Threshold AR(1) Models. *Journal of Time Series Econometrics* 3. [CrossRef]

Knight, John, Stephen E. Satchell, and Nandini Srivastava. 2014. Steady State Distributions for Models of Locally Explosive Regimes: Existence and Econometric Implications. *Economic Modelling* 41: 281–8. [CrossRef]

Pourahmadi, Mohsen. 1988. Stationarity of the solution of $X_t = A_t X_{t-1} + \Sigma_t$ and analysis of non-Gaussian dependent random variable. *Journal of Time Series Analysis* 9: 225–30. [CrossRef]

Rosenthal, Jeffrey S. 1995. Convergence Rates for Markov Chains. *SIAM Review* 37: 387–405. [CrossRef]

Schmitt-Grohe, Stephanie, and Martin Uribe. 2004. Solving Dynamic General Equilibrium Models using a Second-order approximation to the Policy Function. *Journal of Economic Dynamics and Control* 28. [CrossRef]

Stuart, Alan, and Keith Ord. 1994. *Kendall's Advanced Theory of Statistics: Distribution Theory: 1*, 6th ed. London: Wiley-Blackwell, chps. 3–4.

Timmermann, Allan. 2000. Moments of Markov Switching Models. *Journal of Econometrics* 96: 75–111. [CrossRef]

Tong, Howell. 1978. On a Threshold Model. In *Pattern Recognition and Signal Processing*. Edited by Chun Hsien Chen. Amsterdam: Tijhthoff and Noordhoff.

© 2019 by the authors. Licensee MDPI, Basel, Switzerland. This article is an open access article distributed under the terms and conditions of the Creative Commons Attribution (CC BY) license (http://creativecommons.org/licenses/by/4.0/).

Article

On Tuning Parameter Selection in Model Selection and Model Averaging: A Monte Carlo Study

Hui Xiao and Yiguo Sun *

Department of Economics and Finance, University of Guelph, Guelph, ON N1G 2W1, Canada
* Correspondence: yisun@uoguelph.ca

Received: 24 May 2019; Accepted: 24 June 2019; Published: 26 June 2019

Abstract: Model selection and model averaging are popular approaches for handling modeling uncertainties. The existing literature offers a unified framework for variable selection via penalized likelihood and the tuning parameter selection is vital for consistent selection and optimal estimation. Few studies have explored the finite sample performances of the class of ordinary least squares (OLS) post-selection estimators with the tuning parameter determined by different selection approaches. We aim to supplement the literature by studying the class of OLS post-selection estimators. Inspired by the shrinkage averaging estimator (SAE) and the Mallows model averaging (MMA) estimator, we further propose a shrinkage MMA (SMMA) estimator for averaging high-dimensional sparse models. Our Monte Carlo design features an expanding sparse parameter space and further considers the effect of the effective sample size and the degree of model sparsity on the finite sample performances of estimators. We find that the OLS post-smoothly clipped absolute deviation (SCAD) estimator with the tuning parameter selected by the Bayesian information criterion (BIC) in finite sample outperforms most penalized estimators and that the SMMA performs better when averaging high-dimensional sparse models.

Keywords: Mallows criterion; model averaging; model selection; shrinkage; tuning parameter choice

---

1. Introduction

Model selection and model averaging have long been the competing approaches in dealing with modeling uncertainties in practice. Model selection estimators help us search for the most relevant variables, especially when we suspect that the true model is likely to be sparse. On the other hand, model averaging aims to smooth over a set of candidate models so as to reduce risks relative to committing to a single model.

Uncovering the most relevant variables is one of the fundamental tasks of statistical learning, which is more difficult if modeling uncertainty is present. The class of penalized least squares estimators have been developed to handle modeling uncertainty. Fan and Li (2006) laid out a unified framework for variable selection via penalized likelihood.

Tuning parameter selection is vital in the optimization of the penalized least squares estimators for achieving consistent selection and optimal estimation. To select the proper tuning parameter, the existing literature offers two frequently applied approaches, which are the cross-validation (CV) approach and the information criterion (IC)-based approach. Shi and Tsai (2002) have shown that the Bayesian information criterion (BIC), under certain conditions, can consistently identify the true model when the number of parameters and the size of the true model are both finite. Wang et al. (2009) further proposed a modified BIC for tuning parameter selection when the number of parameters diverges with the increase in the sample size.

Although most of the penalized least squares estimators such as the adaptive least absolute shrinkage and selection operator (AdaLASSO) by Zou (2006), the smoothly clipped absolute deviation penalty (SCAD) estimator by Fan and Li (2001), and the minimax concave penalty (MCP) estimator by Zhang (2010) have been researched with well-documented finite sample performances, few studies have focused on the finite sample performances of the class of ordinary least squares (OLS) post-selection estimators with the tuning parameter choice determined by different tuning parameter selection approaches.

Despite decent selection performance from the current penalized least squares estimators, there is not yet a unified approach in estimating the distribution of such estimators, due to the complicated constraints and penalty functions. Knight and Fu (2000), Pötscher and Leeb (2009) and Pötscher and Schneider (2009) investigated the distributions of LASSO-type and SCAD estimators and concluded that they tend to be highly non-normal. Hansen (2014) stated that the distribution for model selection and model averaging estimators are highly non-normal but routinely ignored. This ushered in the development of the class of post-selection estimators such as the OLS post-LASSO estimator by Belloni and Chernozhukov (2013). Such a class of OLS post-selection estimators avoids the complicated constraints and penalty functions when building inferences.

Model averaging is applied to hedge against the risks stemming from the possible specification errors of a single model. For this paper, we attempt to combine the model selection and model averaging approaches to deal with modeling uncertainty. Therefore, inspired by the shrinkage averaging estimator (SAE) by Schomaker (2012) and the Mallows model averaging (MMA) criterion by Hansen (2007), we further propose a shrinkage Mallows model averaging (SMMA) estimator to reduce the asymptotic risks in high-dimensional sparse models from possible specification errors. Briefly, the existing model averaging methods lack a systematic rule in selecting candidate models, while penalty estimation methods are sensitive to the choice of tuning parameters. The shortcomings of these two methods motivate us to propose our SMMA estimator, which effectively combines these two methods to address such weaknesses. That is, our estimator provides a data-driven approach to select the candidate models for averaging, while at the same time, the usage of a set of data-driven tuning parameters relieves the sensitivity problem of the shrinkage estimators. Finite sample performances from the SMMA will be compared with some of the existing model averaging estimators.

The Monte Carlo design is similar to that of Wang et al. (2009), which features an expanding sparse parameter space as the sample size increases. Our Monte Carlo design further considers the effect of changes in the effective sample size and the degree of model sparsity on the finite sample performances of model selection and model averaging estimators. We find that the OLS post-SCAD(BIC) estimator in finite samples outperforms most of the current penalized least squares estimators. In addition, the SMMA performs better given sparser models. This supports the use of the SMMA estimator when averaging high dimensional sparse models.

The rest of the paper is organized as follows. Section 2 gives a brief review of the existing model selection and model averaging estimators in the literature. Section 3 introduces our proposed SMMA estimator. Section 4 reports the finite sample performances of the OLS post-selection estimators and compares the finite sample performance of the SMMA with those of the existing model averaging estimators. Section 5 concludes.

2. Literature Review

In this section, we will review some of the frequently applied model selection and model averaging estimators in the existing literature. We start by defining a simple linear model from which the corresponding model selection and model averaging estimators will be defined, respectively, in the following subsections. Consider a simple linear model given by

$$y_i = X_i^T \beta + \varepsilon_i, \quad \forall i = 1, 2, \ldots, n, \quad (1)$$

where X_i is a $p \times 1$ vector of exogenous regressors, and β is a $p \times 1$ parameter vector with only p_0 number of nonzero parameters. We further assume that $p_0 < p$ and that the error term $\varepsilon_i \sim i.i.d\ (0, \sigma^2)$.

The literature on model selection and model averaging is large and continues to grow with time. Our review below is limited to the most frequently used model selection and model averaging estimators.

2.1. Model Selection

The traditional best subsets approach predating the class of penalized least squares estimators is generally computationally costly and highly unstable due to the discrete nature of the selection algorithm, as pointed out in Fan and Li (2001). The subsequent stepwise approach, which is essentially a variation of the best subsets approach, frequently fails to generate a solution path that leads to the global minimum. In addition, both approaches assume all variables are relevant, even if the underlying true model might have a sparse representation. Then came the class of penalized least squares estimators, which minimize the loss function subjected to some forms of penalty. Some of the frequently applied penalized least squares estimators include the ridge estimator, the LASSO-type estimators, the SCAD estimator, and the MCP estimator.

Hoerl and Kennard (1970) introduced the original ridge estimator with an l_2 penalty. The ridge estimator is defined as

$$\widehat{\beta}^{ridge} = \underset{\beta}{\mathrm{argmin}} \|y - X\beta\|^2 + \lambda \sum_{k=1}^{p} \beta_k^2, \qquad (2)$$

where λ is the so-called tuning parameter.

Tibshirani (1996) introduced an l_1-penalty and constructed the LASSO estimator as follows:

$$\widehat{\beta}^{LASSO} = \underset{\beta}{\mathrm{argmin}} \|y - X\beta\|^2 + \lambda \sum_{k=1}^{p} |\beta_k|. \qquad (3)$$

Compared to the best subsets approach, where all possible subsets need to be evaluated for variable selection, both of the ridge and LASSO estimators conduct the selection and estimation of the parameters simultaneously, thus gaining computational savings. However, both estimators fail to satisfy the oracle properties, due to inconsistent selection and asymptotic bias. The oracle properties describe the ability of an estimator to perform the same asymptotically, as if we knew the true specification of the model beforehand. In the high-dimensional parametric estimation literature, an oracle efficient estimator is therefore able to simultaneously identify the nonzero parameters and achieve optimal estimation of the nonzero parameters. However, Fan and Li (2001) and Zou (2006), among others, questioned whether the LASSO satisfies the oracle properties.

Thus, various LASSO-type estimators have been developed since then to overcome the selection bias of the original ridge and LASSO estimator. Zou and Hastie (2005) introduced the elastic net estimator by averaging between the l_1 penalty and l_2 penalty. Specifically, the elastic net estimator is defined as

$$\widehat{\beta}^{ElasticNet} = \underset{\beta}{\mathrm{argmin}} \|y - X\beta\|^2 + \lambda_1 \sum_{k=1}^{p} |\beta_k| + \lambda_2 \sum_{k=1}^{p} \beta_k^2, \qquad (4)$$

where depending on the choices of the two tuning parameters, λ_1 and λ_2, the elastic net estimator combines the properties of the ridge estimator and the LASSO estimator and enjoys the oracle properties.

Zou (2006) further introduced a LASSO-type estimator, namely the adaptive LASSO estimator, which is defined as

$$\widehat{\beta}^{AdaLASSO} = \underset{\beta}{\mathrm{argmin}} \|y - X\beta\|^2 + \lambda \sum_{k=1}^{p} \widehat{w}_k |\beta_k|, \qquad (5)$$

where the adaptive weights $\widehat{w}_k = |\widehat{\beta}_k^*|^{-\gamma}$ with $\gamma > 0$, and $\widehat{\beta}^*$ denotes any root-n consistent estimator for β. The adaptive LASSO estimator also fulfills the oracle properties.

Fan and Li (2001) proposed the smoothly clipped absolute deviation (SCAD) penalty estimator, which features a symmetric non-concave penalty function that leads to sparse solutions. The SCAD estimator is defined as

$$\hat{\beta}^{SCAD} = \underset{\beta}{\operatorname{argmin}} \|y - X\beta\|^2 + \sum_{k=1}^{p} F(|\beta_k|; \lambda, \gamma), \tag{6}$$

where the continuously differentiable penalty function $F(|\beta|; \lambda, \gamma)$ is defined as

$$F(|\beta|; \lambda, \gamma) = \begin{cases} \lambda|\beta| & \text{if } |\beta| \leq \lambda \\ \frac{2\gamma\lambda|\beta| - |\beta|^2 - \lambda^2}{2\gamma - 1} & \text{if } \gamma\lambda > |\beta| > \lambda , \\ \frac{\lambda^2(\gamma+1)}{2} & \text{if } |\beta| \geq \gamma\lambda \end{cases} \tag{7}$$

and γ defaults to 3.7 following the recommendation from Fan and Li (2001).

Zhang (2010) introduced the minimax concave penalty (MCP) estimator, which produces nearly unbiased variable selection. The MCP estimator is defined as

$$\hat{\beta}^{MCP} = \underset{\beta}{\operatorname{argmin}} \|y - X\beta\|^2 + \sum_{k=1}^{p} F(|\beta_k|; \lambda, \gamma), \tag{8}$$

where the continuously differentiable penalty function $F(|\beta|; \lambda, \gamma)$ is defined as

$$F(|\beta|; \lambda, \gamma) = \begin{cases} \lambda|\beta| - \frac{|\beta|^2}{2\gamma}, & \text{if } |\beta| \leq \lambda\gamma \\ \frac{1}{2}\gamma\lambda^2, & \text{if } |\beta| > \lambda\gamma \end{cases}, \tag{9}$$

and γ defaults to 3, as suggested by Breheny and Huang (2011).

2.1.1. Choice of Tuning Parameter

Tuning parameters play a crucial role in the optimization problem for the aforementioned penalized least squares estimators to achieve consistent selection and optimal estimation. There exists an extensive debate in the model selection literature regarding the proper choice for the tuning parameter. Two of the frequently applied approaches used to select the tuning parameter are the n-fold cross-validation (CV), or the generalized cross-validation (GCV) approach, and the information criterion (IC)-based approach. In practice, the CV approach could also be computationally costly for big datasets.

The traditional IC approaches have been modified for the selection of the tuning parameters in the penalized least squares framework. Shi and Tsai (2002) have shown that the BIC, under certain conditions, can consistently identify the true model when the number of parameters and the size of the true model are finite. For scenarios where the number of parameters diverges with the increase in the sample size, Wang et al. (2009) proposed a modified BIC for the selection of the tuning parameter. This criterion yields consistent selection and reduces asymptotic risks. Fan and Tang (2013) further introduced a generalized information criterion (GIC) for determining the optimal tuning parameters in penalty estimators. They proved that the tuning parameters selected by such a GIC produce consistent variable selection and generate computational savings.

Regarding the generation of the candidate tuning parameters in the penalized likelihood framework, Tibshirani et al. (2010) first introduced the cyclical coordinate descent algorithm to compute the solution path for generalized linear models with convex penalties such as LASSO and Elastic Net. This algorithm helps generate a set of candidate tuning parameters to facilitate the selection of the optimal tuning parameter. Breheny and Huang (2011) further applied this algorithm to calculate the solution path for non-convex penalty estimators such as the SCAD and MCP estimators. They compared the performances of some of the popular penalty estimators such as the LASSO, SCAD, and MCP estimators for variable selection in sparse models. Their simulation study and data examples indicated that the choice of the tuning parameter greatly affects the outcome of the variable selection.

2.1.2. Post-Selection Estimators

Despite decent selection performance from the current mainstream penalized least squares estimators, there is not yet a unified approach in estimating the distribution of such estimators, due to the complicated constraints and penalty functions. Knight and Fu (2000), Pötscher and Leeb (2009) and Pötscher and Schneider (2009), among others, investigated the distributions of LASSO-type and SCAD estimators and concluded that they tend to be highly non-normal. This ushered in the burgeoning development in post-model-selection inferential methods. Hansen (2014) stated that the distributions for the model selection and model averaging estimators are highly non-normal but routinely ignored in practice. Belloni and Chernozhukov (2013) proposed the OLS post-LASSO estimator, which, under certain assumptions, outperforms the LASSO estimator in reducing asymptotic risks associated with high-dimensional sparse models. The OLS post-LASSO estimator utilizes the LASSO estimator as a variable selection operator in the first step and reverts back to the OLS estimator to produce parameter estimates for the selected model in the second step. Such an estimator avoids the complicated penalty functions in estimating the distribution of the estimator in the second step and thus yields easier access to inference that is solely based on the OLS estimator. Inspired by the OLS post-LASSO estimator, other post-selection estimators could be constructed with the tuning parameters in the penalty function selected by either the BIC or GCV approach.

For example, an OLS post-SCAD(BIC) estimator can be constructed with the tuning parameter in the penalty function selected by the BIC approach. More specifically, let $\Lambda = \{\lambda^1, \ldots, \lambda^q\}$ be the set of candidate tuning parameters and $|\Lambda| = q$ with $q \in \mathbb{Z}^+$.

Given any $\lambda \in \Lambda$ and γ defaulting to 3.7, the SCAD estimator from Equation (6) evaluated at λ gives

$$\widehat{\beta}^\lambda = \underset{\beta}{\operatorname{argmin}} \|y - X\beta\|^2 + \sum_{k=1}^{p} F(|\beta_k|; \lambda). \tag{10}$$

The BIC evaluated at this λ is defined as BIC_λ, which is given by

$$BIC_\lambda = \log\left(\frac{\left\|y - X\widehat{\beta}^\lambda\right\|^2}{n}\right) + |S_\lambda|\frac{\log(n)}{n}C_n, \tag{11}$$

where the values for λ originate from an exponentially decaying grid as in Tibshirani et al. (2010). Let S_λ denote the set of nonzero parameters of the model when evaluated at λ, and more specifically, $S_\lambda = \{k : \widehat{\beta}_k^\lambda \neq 0\}$. For any set $\mathbb{S}$, let $|\mathbb{S}|$ represent its cardinality. Then, $|S_\lambda|$ gives the number of nonzero parameters of the model when evaluated at λ, and C_n is a constant. Shi and Tsai (2002) have shown that the above BIC with $C_n = 1$ consistently identifies the true model when both p and p_0 are finite.

The estimate of the optimal tuning parameter is denoted by $\widehat{\lambda}^{BIC}$, which is the solution to the following problem:

$$\widehat{\lambda}^{BIC} = \underset{\lambda \in \{\lambda^1, \ldots, \lambda^q\}}{\operatorname{argmin}} BIC_\lambda. \tag{12}$$

Consequently, $\widehat{\beta}^{\widehat{\lambda}^{BIC}}$ minimizes the SCAD penalized objective function given by Equation (6); i.e.,

$$\widehat{\beta}^{\widehat{\lambda}^{BIC}} = \underset{\beta}{\operatorname{argmin}} \|y - X\beta\|^2 + \sum_{k=1}^{p} F(|\beta_k|, \widehat{\lambda}^{BIC}). \tag{13}$$

Denoting $S_{\hat{\lambda}^{BIC}} = \{k : \hat{\beta}_k^{\hat{\lambda}^{BIC}} \neq 0\}$, we define the OLS post-SCAD(BIC) estimator as

$$\hat{\beta}^{BIC} = \underset{\beta}{\operatorname{argmin}} \left\| y - \sum_{l \in S_{\hat{\lambda}^{BIC}}} X_l \beta_l \right\|^2, \qquad (14)$$

where X_l is an $n \times 1$ vector, which is the lth column of the predictor matrix X, and β_l is the lth parameter.

In the same vein, other OLS post-selection estimators such as the OLS post-MCP (BIC or GCV) estimator could also be constructed for comparing the finite sample performances. The OLS post-MCP (BIC or GCV) estimator minimizes, respectively, the BIC and the GCV in the estimation for the optimal tuning parameter. It is worth pointing out that for the penalized estimators that are already oracle efficient, post-selection estimators such as the OLS post-SCAD estimator do not outperform the SCAD estimator asymptotically. That being said, there could be differences in the finite sample performances between the penalized least squares estimators and the OLS post-selection estimators. Even for the same estimator, different tuning parameter selection approaches could also yield different selection outcomes.

2.1.3. Measures of Selection and Estimation Accuracy

To evaluate the performance of the shrinkage estimators, various measures for variable selection and estimation accuracy have been introduced in the literature. Wang et al. (2009) used the model size (MS), the percentage of the correctly identified true model (CM), and the median of relative model error (MRME) to evaluate the finite sample performances of the adaptive LASSO and SCAD estimators with tuning parameters selected either by the GCV or BIC approach.

The model size, MS, for the true model is defined as the number of nonzero parameters or $|S_0| = p_0$, where p_0 is the dimension for the nonzero parameters. For any model selection procedure, ideally, the estimated model size $|\hat{S}| = \hat{p}_0$ should tend to p_0 asymptotically, and $\hat{S} = \{k : \hat{\beta}_k \neq 0\}$. This measure evaluates the precision with which the said selection procedure estimates the number of nonzero parameters from the data. In the context of Monte Carlo simulations, the average is taken over all of the estimated MSs, which are generated per each round of simulation.

The correct model CM is revealed as the true model if the said model selection procedure accurately yields the right nonzero parameters. The CM measure is defined as

$$CM = \left\{ \hat{\beta}_k \neq 0 : k \in S_0, \hat{\beta}_k = 0 : k \in S_0^c \right\}. \qquad (15)$$

An estimation of the model is only considered correct if the above criterion is satisfied, where all of the non-zero and zero parameters are correctly identified. The higher the correction rate over a number of simulation runs, the better the performance for an estimator.

The model prediction error (ME) for a model selection procedure is defined as

$$ME = (\hat{\beta} - \beta)^T E[X^T X] (\hat{\beta} - \beta), \qquad (16)$$

where $\hat{\beta}$ represents any estimator such as a penalized least squares estimator. The relative model error (RME) is the ratio of the model prediction error to that of the naive OLS estimator of the model given by Equation (1). For example, the RME for the SCAD estimator is given by

$$RME = \frac{(\hat{\beta}^{SCAD} - \beta)^T E[X^T X] ((\hat{\beta}^{SCAD} - \beta)}{(\hat{\beta}^{OLS} - \beta)^T E[X^T X] ((\hat{\beta}^{OLS} - \beta)}. \qquad (17)$$

For a given number of Monte Carlo replications, the median of the RME (MRME) is used to evaluate the finite sample performance of the said model selection estimator.

2.2. Model Averaging

On the other hand, an alternative to model selection in handling modeling uncertainties is model averaging. In general, the model averaging estimator is defined as

$$\widehat{\beta}_{MA} = \sum_{s=1}^{S} w_s \widehat{\beta}_s, \qquad (18)$$

where w_s represents the weight assigned to the sth model of an $\mathcal{S}$ number of candidate models, and $w = [w_1, w_2 \ldots, w_S]$ is a weight vector in the unit simplex in $\mathbb{R}^\mathcal{S}$ with $\mathcal{S} \in \mathbb{Z}^+$, such that

$$\mathcal{H}_\mathcal{S} = \left\{ w \in [0,1]^\mathcal{S} : \sum_{s=1}^{S} w_s = 1 \right\}. \qquad (19)$$

Over time, various estimators have been proposed for estimating the weight vector, w, for averaging the candidate models. Buckland et al. (1997) proposed the smoothed information criterion model averaging estimator, where the weight for the sth model, w_s, can be estimated as

$$\widehat{w}_s^{IC} = \frac{exp(-I_s/2)}{\sum_{s=1}^{S} exp(-I_s/2)}, \qquad (20)$$

where I_s, the information criterion evaluated at the sth model, is defined as

$$I_s = -2log(\widehat{L}_s) + P_s, \qquad (21)$$

with $\widehat{L}_s$ being the maximized likelihood value and P_s being the penalty term that takes the form of $2p_s$ for the smoothed Akaike information criterion (S-AIC) and $ln(n)p_s$ for the smoothed BIC (S-BIC).

Hansen (2007) proposed a Mallows model averaging (MMA) estimator whose weight choice is estimated as

$$\widehat{w}^{MMA} = \underset{w \in \mathcal{H}_\mathcal{S}}{\operatorname{argmin}} \left(y - \widehat{\mu}(w)\right)^T \left(y - \widehat{\mu}(w)\right) + 2\sigma^2 k(w), \qquad (22)$$

where the model averaging estimator $\widehat{\mu}(w)$ is defined as

$$\widehat{\mu}(w) = \sum_{s=1}^{S} w_s P_s y = P(w)y, \qquad (23)$$

and the projection matrix for model s is defined as

$$P_s = X_s \left(X_s^T X_s\right)^{-1} X_s^T. \qquad (24)$$

Moreover, the effective number of parameters, $k(w)$, is defined as

$$k(w) = \sum_{s=1}^{S} w_s k_s, \qquad (25)$$

where k_s equals the number of parameters in model s. The σ^2 term can be estimated using the variance of a larger model in the set of the candidate models according to Hansen (2007).

Under certain assumptions, Hansen (2007) showed that the MMA minimizes the mean squared prediction error (MSPE), and Gao et al. (2016) showed that the MMA can produce smaller mean squared errors (MSEs) than the OLS estimator. Wan et al. (2010) further relaxed the assumptions of discrete weights and nested regression models that are required by the asymptotic optimality conditions for the MMA to continuous weights without imposing ordering on the predictors.

Hansen and Racine (2012) proposed the heteroskedasticity-consistent jackknife model averaging (JMA) estimator. The weight choice for the JMA estimator is defined as

$$\widehat{w}^{JMA} = \underset{w \in \mathcal{H}_S}{\operatorname{argmin}} \frac{1}{n} \tilde{\varepsilon}(w)^T \tilde{\varepsilon}(w), \tag{26}$$

where $\tilde{\varepsilon}(w) = \sum_{s=1}^{S} w_s \tilde{\varepsilon}_s$ with $\tilde{\varepsilon}_s$ being the leave-one-out residual vector from the sth model.

Schomaker (2012) further explored the role of the tuning parameters in the shrinkage averaging estimator (SAE) post model selection. The SAE estimates β by averaging over a set of candidate shrinkage estimators, $\widehat{\beta}_\lambda$, which are calculated with a sequence of tuning parameters. For example, an SAE that averages over an $\mathcal{S}$ number of candidate $\widehat{\beta}_{\lambda_s}^{LASSO}$ from an $\mathcal{S}$-fold cross-validation procedure can be defined as

$$\widehat{\beta}_{SAE} = \sum_{s=1}^{S} w_{\lambda_s} \widehat{\beta}_{\lambda_s}^{LASSO}, \tag{27}$$

where $\lambda_s \in \{\lambda_1, \ldots, \lambda_S\}$ as one of the $\mathcal{S}$ competing tuning parameters. The weights for the SAE are calculated as follows:

$$\widehat{w}^{SAE} = \underset{w \in \mathcal{H}_S}{\operatorname{argmin}} \frac{1}{n} \tilde{\varepsilon}(w)^T \tilde{\varepsilon}(w), \tag{28}$$

where $\tilde{\varepsilon}(w) = \sum_{s=1}^{S} w_{\lambda_s} \tilde{\varepsilon}_s(\lambda_s)$ with $\tilde{\varepsilon}_s(\lambda_s)$ being the residual vector for the sth cross-validation.

In this paper, we aim to explore the possibility of combining the model selection and model averaging methods in dealing with modeling uncertainty. We expect that the specifications of the candidate models guided by the appropriate choice of tuning parameter could significantly reduce modeling uncertainty given sparse models.

3. The Shrinkage MMA Estimator

Inspired by the shrinkage averaging estimator (SAE) and the Mallows model averaging (MMA) estimator, we further propose a shrinkage Mallows model averaging (SMMA) estimator to hedge against the possible specification errors from model selection. The SMMA estimator is a two-stage estimator. In the first stage, by applying different penalty estimators introduced in Section 2 with optimal tuning parameters selected via the GCV or BIC method, we obtain a sequence of candidate models. In the second stage, we apply the MMA to estimate β. The SMMA estimator compliments the class of penalty estimators by allowing for more than one model selection outcome rather than committing to a single model. In addition, this estimator also extends the current MMA framework by introducing a reasonable way to select the set of candidate models to be averaged. The SMMA is especially helpful for averaging high-dimensional candidate models when the generation of such a set of candidate models would be computationally costly if not done via shrinkage approaches. It would be difficult for the traditional MMA to exhaust all possible subsets of candidate models for a high-dimensional dataset. This estimator also builds on the SAE by incorporating the tuning parameter optimization problem, which is crucial to the variable selection process for each candidate model. This estimator is essentially a variation of the MMA estimator, so the asymptotic properties should be similar to those of the MMA.

Lehrer and Xie (2017) briefly mentioned the possibility of having a set of candidate models first shrunk by the LASSO before applying MMA. There is a clear distinction between Lehrer and Xie (2017) and our idea, since the candidate models for averaging are subjectively chosen in Lehrer and Xie (2017), which is the same as the traditional literature on the MMA estimator. However, the SMMA starts with a general, large model and applies different penalty methods to select the candidate models for averaging.

Below we explain the SMMA estimator in detail. Let Λ^{Opt} be the set of optimal tuning parameters selected either by the BIC or GCV for the model selection procedures introduced in Section 2, and a typical element in Λ^{Opt} is denoted as $\widehat{\lambda}_s^{Opt}$. Therefore Λ^{Opt} is defined as

$$\Lambda^{Opt} = \{\widehat{\lambda}_1^{Opt}, \ldots, \widehat{\lambda}_s^{Opt}, \ldots, \widehat{\lambda}_S^{Opt}\}, \tag{29}$$

where $|\Lambda^{Opt}| = S$.

The SMMA estimator is solved as follows:

$$\widehat{\beta}_{SMMA}(w; \Lambda^{Opt}) = \sum_{s=1}^{S} \widehat{w}_s \widehat{\beta}(\widehat{\lambda}_s^{Opt}), \tag{30}$$

where the weight vector is estimated by the MMA criterion,

$$\widehat{w} = \underset{w \in \mathcal{H}_S}{\mathrm{argmin}} \left(y - \widehat{\mu}(w; \Lambda^{Opt})\right)^T \left(y - \widehat{\mu}(w; \Lambda^{Opt})\right) + 2\sigma^2 k(w; \Lambda^{Opt}), \tag{31}$$

and $w = [w_1, w_2, \ldots, w_S]$ is a weight vector in the unit simplex in $\mathbb{R}^S$ with $S \in \mathbb{Z}^+$ such that

$$\mathcal{H}_S = \left\{w \in [0,1]^S : \sum_{s=1}^{S} w_s = 1\right\}. \tag{32}$$

The model averaging estimator $\widehat{\mu}(w)$ is defined as

$$\widehat{\mu}(w; \Lambda^{Opt}) = \sum_{s=1}^{S} w_s P(\widehat{\lambda}_s^{Opt}) y = P(w; \Lambda^{Opt}) y, \tag{33}$$

where the projection matrix for model s is defined as

$$P(\widehat{\lambda}_s^{Opt}) = X^{\widehat{\lambda}_s^{Opt}} (X^{\widehat{\lambda}_s^{Opt} T} X^{\widehat{\lambda}_s^{Opt}})^{-1} X^{\widehat{\lambda}_s^{Opt} T}, \tag{34}$$

and the estimator for model s is given by

$$\widehat{\beta}(\widehat{\lambda}_s^{Opt}) = (X^{\widehat{\lambda}_s^{Opt} T} X^{\widehat{\lambda}_s^{Opt}})^{-1} X^{\widehat{\lambda}_s^{Opt} T} y. \tag{35}$$

Let L index the largest model in dimension from the set of the candidate models, i.e.,

$$L = \underset{s \in \mathcal{S}}{\mathrm{argmax}} |\widehat{\beta}(\widehat{\lambda}_s^{Opt})|, \tag{36}$$

where $|\widehat{\beta}(\widehat{\lambda}_s^{Opt})|$ equals the number of nonzero values in $\widehat{\beta}(\widehat{\lambda}_s^{Opt})$.

Following Hansen (2007), the σ^2 term will be estimated by $\widehat{\sigma}_L^2$, which is given below:

$$\widehat{\sigma}_L^2 = \frac{(y - X_L \widehat{\beta}_L)^T (y - X_L \widehat{\beta}_L)}{n - k_L}. \tag{37}$$

The effective number of parameters $k(w; \Lambda^{Opt})$ is defined as

$$k(w; \Lambda^{Opt}) = \sum_{s=1}^{S} w_s k(\widehat{\lambda}_s^{Opt}), \tag{38}$$

where $k(\widehat{\lambda}_s^{Opt}) = |\widehat{\beta}(\widehat{\lambda}_s^{Opt})|$.

4. Monte Carlo Simulations

This section assesses the performance of the existing model selection and averaging estimators, including the SMMA estimator proposed in this paper, via a small Monte Carlo simulation experiment. Our data generating process (DGP) is

$$y_i = X_i^T \beta + \varepsilon_i, \quad \forall i = 1, 2, \ldots, n, \tag{39}$$

where β is a $p \times 1$ parameter vector with only p_0 number of nonzero parameters.

We further assume that $p_0 < p$ and that the error term $\varepsilon_i \sim i.i.d\,\mathcal{N}(0,1)$. In addition, X_i is randomly drawn from a p-dimensional multivariate normal distribution with zero mean and a co-variance matrix as follows

$$Cov(X_l, X_j) = \begin{cases} 1, & \text{if } l = j \\ 0.5, & \text{otherwise} \end{cases}. \tag{40}$$

To investigate the effect of the number of parameters to sample size ratio (p/n) and the degree of model sparsity (p_0/p) on the performance of different estimation methods, we consider two data examples in this section. The data example 1 from Section 4.1 considers the case where p/n is constant while p_0/p is decreasing. The data example 2 in Section 4.2 simulates the scenario where p_0/p is constant but p/n decreases as n increases.

4.1. Example 1. Constant p/n Ratio

Similar to the example given in Fan and Peng (2004), we set $\beta = \left(\frac{11}{4}, -\frac{23}{6}, \frac{37}{12}, -\frac{13}{9}, \frac{1}{3}, 0, \ldots, 0\right)^T \in \mathbb{R}^p$ with $p = n \times \alpha$ for some constant α. The nonzero parameters, β_0, are defined as

$$\beta_0 = \left(\frac{11}{4}, -\frac{23}{6}, \frac{37}{12}, -\frac{13}{9}, \frac{1}{3}\right)^T. \tag{41}$$

We fix $n = 1000$ and allow α to vary in the interval of $[0.02, 0.98]$. Therefore, we consider a case with an increasing number of redundant regressors while the true model remains fixed with 5 nonzero regressors as α increases from .02 to 0.98, where $\alpha = p/n \in \{0.02, 0.05, 0.1, 0.5, 0.98\}$ and $p \in \{20, 50, 100, 500, 980\}$. If we measure the degree of sparsity by $\delta = 1 - p_0/p$, we see that the model becomes sparser for larger α and $p_0/p \in \{0.25, 0.1, 0.05, 0.01, 0.005\}$. Note that this design allows us to further consider cases where the number of parameters drastically approaches the sample size.

4.2. Example 2. Decreasing p/n Ratio

The second example is similar to Wang et al. (2009), where the dimension of the true model also diverges with the dimension of the full model as n increases. More specifically, $p = [7n^{\frac{1}{4}}]$ where $[a]$ stands for the largest integer no larger than a and the size of the true model $|S_0| = p_0 = [p/3]$ with $\beta_0 \sim U(0.5, 1.5)$. For sample size $n \in \{100, 200, 400, 800, 1600\}$, the respective sizes of the full model are $p \in \{22, 26, 31, 37, 44\}$, and the respective sizes of the true model are $S_0 \in \{7, 8, 10, 12, 14\}$. The number of parameters to sample size ratio is $p/n \in \{0.22, 0.13, 0.07, 0.046, 0.027\}$, and the degree of model sparsity is $\delta = 2/3$. Different from the example given in Section 4.1, this data example maintains a constant degree of model sparsity.

4.3. Monte Carlo Results

For the simulation studies, we investigated the finite sample performances of the estimators introduced in Sections 2 and 3. In addition, we also considered the variants of the aforementioned penalized estimators with the tuning parameters selected by the BIC rather than the conventional GCV. To differentiate, we named the OLS post-SCAD with the the tuning parameters selected by the BIC as the OLS post-SCAD(BIC) estimator. We used the finite sample performance of the OLS estimator as the benchmark for those of the model selection and model averaging estimators. For each data example, a total of 500 simulation replications were conducted.

4.3.1. Model Selection Estimators

The penalized least squares estimators considered in the simulation studies are listed in Table 1 below.

Table 1. Penalized Estimators.

Estimator	
Ridge(GCV)	Ridge(BIC)
OLS post-ridge(GCV)	OLS post-ridge(BIC)
LASSO(GCV)	LASSO(BIC)
OLS post-LASSO(GCV)	OLS post-LASSO(BIC)
Elastic net(GCV)	Elastic net(BIC)
OLS post-elastic net(GCV)	OLS post-elastic net(BIC)
Adaptive LASSO(GCV)	Adaptive LASSO(BIC)
OLS post-adaptive-LASSO(GCV)	OLS post- adaptive LASSO(BIC)
SCAD(GCV)	SCAD(BIC)
OLS post-SCAD(GCV)	OLS post-SCAD(BIC)
MCP(GCV)	MCP(BIC)
OLS post-MCP(GCV)	OLS post-MCP(BIC)

Figures 1 and 2 below present the finite sample performances of the above penalized least squares estimators with the tuning parameters selected by either GCV or BIC. To level the playing field, each estimator was supplied with the same set of candidate tuning parameters $\Lambda = \{\lambda^1, \ldots, \lambda^q\}$ as all the other competing estimators, and $|\Lambda| = q$ with $q \in \mathbb{Z}^+$. Since the conventional LASSO, SCAD, and MCP estimators have already been studied extensively with well-documented finite sample performances, we turn our focus to the finite sample performances of the class of OLS post-selection estimators. For the elastic net estimator, the weights for the l_1 penalty and l_2 penalty were set to 0.5. For a cleaner representation of comparison and to save space, we choose to report only the first six best-performing OLS post-selection estimators among those listed in Table 1.

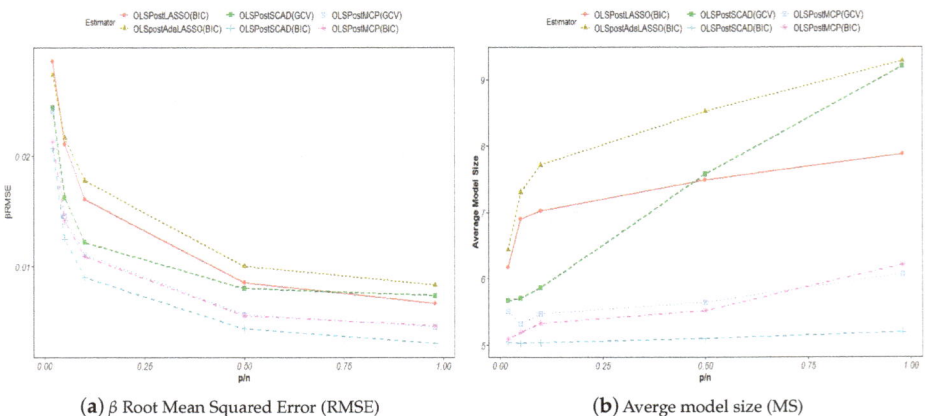

(**a**) β Root Mean Squared Error (RMSE) (**b**) Averge model size (MS)

Figure 1. *Cont.*

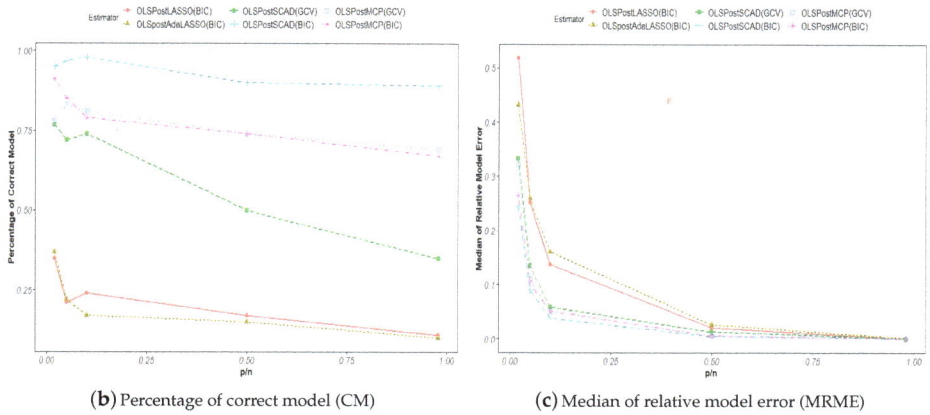

(b) Percentage of correct model (CM)

(c) Median of relative model error (MRME)

Figure 1. Example 1 model selection and estimation accuracy.

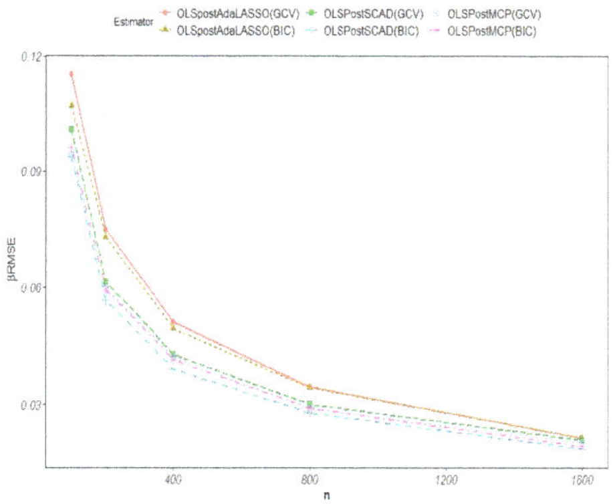

(a) β RMSE

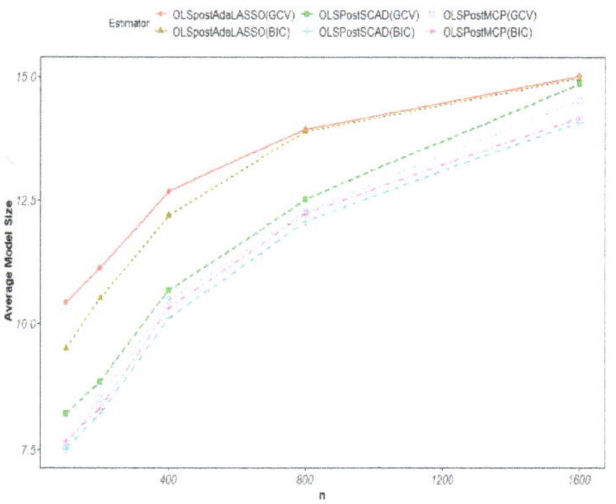

(b) Averge Model Size (MS)

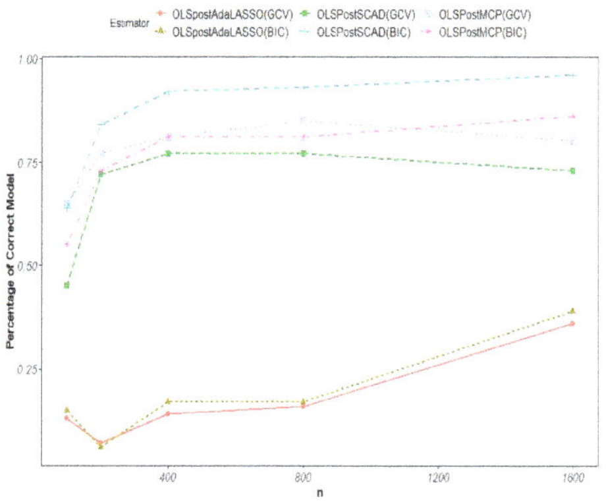

(c) Percentage of Correct Model (CM)

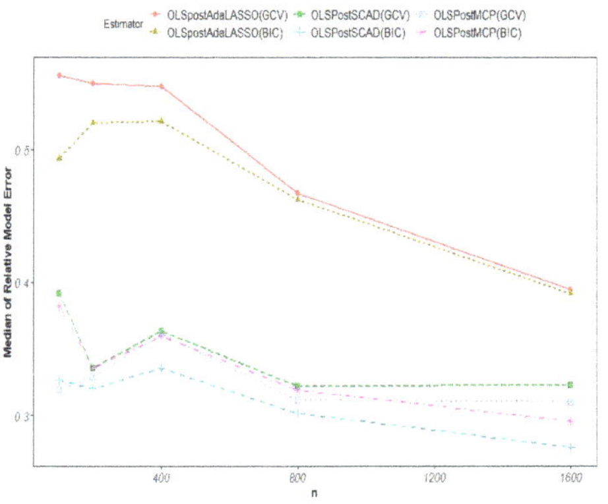

(d) Median of Relative Model Error (MRME)

Figure 2. Example 2 model selection and estimation accuracy.

Table 2 below ranks the first six best-performing OLS post-selection estimators based on the results from data example 1 and data example 2.

Table 2. Performance ranking for the OLS post-selection estimators.

Ranking	Example 1	Example 2
1	OLS post-SCAD(BIC)	OLS post-SCAD(BIC)
2	OLS post-MCP(BIC)	OLS post-MCP(BIC)
3	OLS post-MCP(GCV)	OLS post-MCP(GCV)
4	OLS post-SCAD(GCV)	OLS post-SCAD(GCV)
5	OLS post-LASSO(BIC)	OLS post-adaptive-LASSO(BIC)
6	OLS post-adaptive-LASSO(BIC)	OLS post-adaptive-LASSO(GCV)

For both data examples, it is evident from Figures 1 and 2 above that in finite samples, the OLS post-SCAD(BIC) estimator outperforms the competing estimators consistently by yielding lower root mean squared error (RMSE) for β and higher selection accuracy. The performance of the OLS post-SCAD(BIC) is also insensitive to the changes in the p/n ratio and the p_0/p ratio. Therefore, as long as $p < n$, our findings show that the OLS post-SCAD(BIC) outperforms the competing OLS post-selection estimators regardless of the effective sample size and degree of model sparsity, which are controlled by p/n and p_0/p, respectively. The finite sample performances of the OLS post-LASSO and the OLS post-adaptive-LASSO seem to be affected by changes in the degree of model sparsity and the effective sample size. The simulation results support the conclusion in the literature that the choice of the tuning parameter does play a vital role in the variable selection outcomes. The findings from the two data examples above offer some guidance to empirical researchers who are weighing different approaches for model selection.

4.3.2. Model Averaging Estimators

For the model averaging estimators, we mainly focused on the finite sample performances of the S-BIC, Hansen's MMA, SAE(LASSO) with LASSO as the shrinkage method, and the SMMA estimator proposed in Section 3. The SMMA estimator averages the candidate models produced by the penalized least squares estimators listed in Table 1. The specifications of the candidate models are determined by the set of optimal tuning parameters Λ^{Opt}, which consists of the optimal tuning parameters selected by either the GCV or the BIC approach. For Hansen's MMA, we only considered the pure nested subset models due to the fact that all of the possible combinations of subset models are not computationally feasible given the high-dimensional nature of our data examples. Since in Table 1 there are 24 estimators, which yield 24 candidate models, we also generated 24 candidate models for the MMA, S-BIC, and SAE(LASSO). These candidate models were generated using the program developed by Professor Hansen, and the program is available from Professor Hansen's website. Similar to Hansen (2007), we evaluated the finite sample performances of the model averaging estimators by comparing the β RMSE and the adjusted R^2 for the final averaged model. Due to the high-dimensional sparse nature of the DGP, using the adjusted R^2 helps us avoid the misleadingly high R^2 from including many more predictors that might have been irrelevant in the first place. The adjusted R^2 can also gauge whether the SMMA could better perform the task of identifying the most relevant regressors, which is one of the fundamental goals for statistical learning.

Figure 3 above gives the finite sample performances of the model averaging estimators from both data examples. For data example 1, where the degree of model sparsity increases while the effective sample size decreases with the increase in the p/n, the SMMA outperforms the MMA in terms of yielding a relatively lower β RMSE and slightly higher adjusted R^2 if $p/n < 0.5$. As p/n increases from 0.5 to 0.98, which causes p_0/p to further decrease, resulting in a much sparser model, the SMMA significantly outperforms the competing model averaging estimators in β RMSE and adjusted R^2. The sparser the model and the smaller the effective sample size, the better the SMMA performs. This supports the application of the SMMA estimator when averaging high-dimensional sparse models against modeling uncertainty. Intuitively, a sparser model entails greater modeling uncertainty, which could result from the lack of a unifying theory in guiding the exact specification of the underlying model. Therefore, the SMMA can be a viable option for model averaging, especially for high-dimensional sparse models when it is computationally infeasible to exhaust all possible combinations of subset models.

For data example 2, where the degree of model sparsity is constant and the p/n decreases as the sample size n increases, the SMMA still slightly outperforms other model averaging estimators in β RMSE and adjusted R^2. However, the finite sample performances of the SMMA and MMA estimators tend to be very close as n increases, which indicates rather similar asymptotic properties for both estimators. As a possible direction for future research, one could consider the derivation of the asymptotic properties for the SMMA estimator. But this paper focuses on the numerical comparisons of the SMMA, whose asymptotic properties will be for our future research.

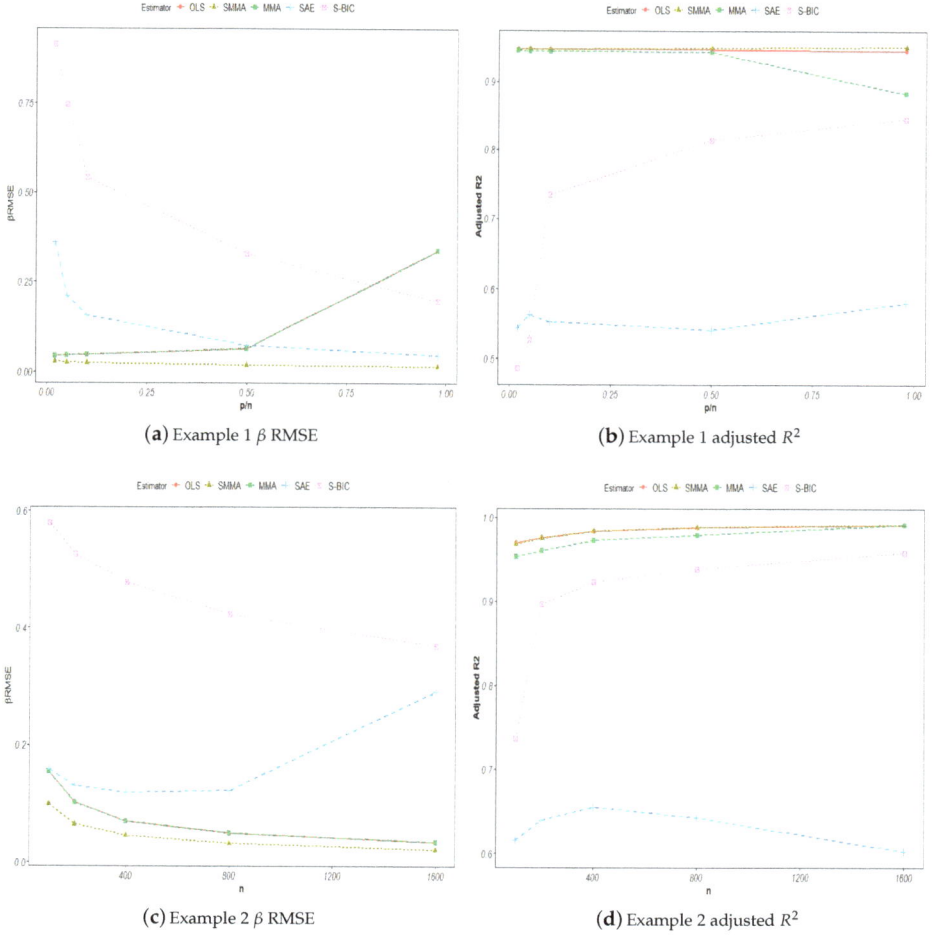

Figure 3. Finite sample performance for model averaging estimators.

5. Conclusions

In this paper, we reviewed some of the conventional model selection and model averaging estimators, and we further proposed a shrinkage Mallows model averaging (SMMA) estimator. Using a Monte Carlo study, we compared the finite sample performances of the reviewed model selection and model averaging estimators. We also investigated the effect of the tuning parameter choice on variable selection outcomes. We aimed to supplement the existing model selection literature by studying the finite sample performances of the class of OLS post-selection estimators via different tuning parameter selection approaches. Our Monte Carlo design further considered the effect of changes in the effective sample size and the degree of model sparsity on the finite sample performances of model selection and model averaging estimators.

The results from our data examples suggest that tuning parameter choice plays a vital role in variable selection and optimal estimation. Given the same tuning parameter selection approach, for the penalized estimators that are already oracle efficient, the corresponding OLS post-selection estimators give a rather similar performance. However, for the same penalized estimators, the performances via different tuning parameter selection approaches are markedly different. The OLS post-SCAD(BIC) estimator gives the best finite sample performance, based on the data examples in our Monte Carlo design. The SMMA performs better given sparser models. The sparser the model and the smaller the effective sample size, the better the SMMA performs. This supports the use of the SMMA estimator when averaging high-dimensional sparse models against modeling uncertainty. This paper is limited by the absence of the derivation of the asymptotic properties for the SMMA estimator. We will leave the derivations of the asymptotic properties for the SMMA estimator to our future studies.

Author Contributions: Both authors contributed to the project formulation and paper preparation.

Funding: This research received no external funding.

Acknowledgments: We thank the anonymous referees for their constructive comments.

Conflicts of Interest: The authors declare no conflict of interest.

References

Belloni, Alexandre, and Victor Chernozhukov. 2013. Least squares after model selection in high-dimensional sparse models. *Bernoulli* 19: 521–47. [CrossRef]

Breheny, Patrick, and Jian Huang. 2011. Coordinate descent algorithms for nonconvex penalized regression, with applications to biological feature selection. *The Annals of Applied Statistics* 5: 232–53. [CrossRef] [PubMed]

Buckland, Steven T., Kenneth P. Burnham, and Nicole H. Augustin. 1997. Model Selection: An Integral Part of Inference. *Biometrics* 53. [CrossRef]

Fan, Jianqing, and Heng Peng. 2004. Nonconcave penalized likelihood with a diverging number of parameters. *The Annals of Statistics* 32: 928–61. [CrossRef]

Fan, Jianqing, and Runze Li. 2001. Variable Selection via Nonconcave Penalized Likelihood and Its Oracle Properties. *Journal of the American Statistical Association* 96: 1348–60. [CrossRef]

Fan, Jianqing, and Runze Li. 2006. Statistical Challenges with High Dimensionality: Feature Selection in Knowledge Discovery. *arXiv*. arXiv:math/0602133.

Fan, Yingying, and Cheng Yong Tang. 2013. Tuning Parameter Selection in High Dimensional Penalized Likelihood. *Journal of the Royal Statistical Society. Series B (Statistical Methodology)* 75: 531–52. [CrossRef]

Gao, Yan, Xinyu Zhang, Shouyang Wang, and Guohua Zou. 2016. Model averaging based on leave-subject-out cross-validation. *Journal of Econometrics* 192: 139–51. [CrossRef]

Hansen, Bruce. 2007. Least Squares Model Averaging. *Econometrica* 75: 1175–89.

Hansen, Bruce. 2014. Model averaging, asymptotic risk, and regressor groups. *Quantitative Economics* 5: 495–530. [CrossRef]

Hansen, Bruce, and Jeffrey Racine. 2012. Jackknife model averaging. *Journal of Econometrics* 167: 38–46. [CrossRef]

Hoerl, Arthur E., and Robert W. Kennard. 1970. Ridge Regression: Biased Estimation for Nonorthogonal Problems. *Technometrics* 12: 55–67. [CrossRef]

Knight, Keith, and Wenjiang Fu. 2000. Asymptotics for lasso-type estimators. *The Annals of Statistics* 5: 1356–78. [CrossRef]

Lehrer, Steven, and Tian Xie. 2017. Box Office Buzz: Does Social Media Data Steal the Show from Model Uncertainty When Forecasting for Hollywood? *Review of Economics and Statistics* 99: 749–55. [CrossRef]

Pötscher, Benedikt M., and Hannes Leeb. 2009. On the Distribution of Penalized Maximum Likelihood Estimators: The LASSO, SCAD, and Thresholding. *Journal of Multivariate Analysis* 100: 2065–82.

Pötscher, Benedikt M., and Ulrike Schneider. 2009. On the Distribution of the Adaptive LASSO Estimator. *Journal of Statistical Planning and Inference* 139: 2775–90. [CrossRef]

Schomaker, Michael. 2012. Shrinkage averaging estimation. *Statistical Papers* 53: 1015–34.

Shi, Peide, and Chih-Ling Tsai. 2002. Regression model selection—A residual likelihood approach. *Journal of the Royal Statistical Society Series B* 64: 237–52. [CrossRef]

Tibshirani, Robert. 1996. Regression Shrinkage and Selection via the Lasso. *Journal of the Royal Statistical Society. Series B (Methodological)* 58: 267–88. [CrossRef]

Tibshirani, Rob, Trevor Hastie, and Jerome Friedman. 2010. Regularization Paths for Generalized Linear Models via Coordinate Descent. *Journal of Statistical Software* 33: 1–22. [CrossRef]

Wang, Hansheng, Bo Li, and Chenlei Leng. 2009. Shrinkage Tuning Parameter Selection with a Diverging Number of Parameters. *Journal of the Royal Statistical Society. Series B (Statistical Methodology)* 71: 671–83. [CrossRef]

Wan, Alan T. K., Xinyu Zhang, and Guohua Zou. 2010. Least squares model averaging by Mallows criterion. *Journal of Econometrics* 156: 277–83. [CrossRef]

Zhang, Cun-Hui. 2010. Nearly unbiased variable selection under minimax concave penalty. *The Annals of Statistics* 38: 894–942. [CrossRef]

Zou, Hui, and Trevor Hastie. 2005. Regularization and Variable Selection via the Elastic Net. *Journal of the Royal Statistical Society. Series B (Statistical Methodology)* 67: 301–20. [CrossRef]

Zou, Hui. 2006. The Adaptive Lasso and Its Oracle Properties. *Journal of the American Statistical Association* 101: 1418–29. [CrossRef]

© 2019 by the authors. Licensee MDPI, Basel, Switzerland. This article is an open access article distributed under the terms and conditions of the Creative Commons Attribution (CC BY) license (http://creativecommons.org/licenses/by/4.0/).

Article

Threshold Stochastic Conditional Duration Model for Financial Transaction Data

Zhongxian Men [1], Adam W. Kolkiewicz [1] and Tony S. Wirjanto [1,2,*]

[1] Department of Statistics and Actuarial Science, University of Waterloo, 200 University Avenue West, Waterloo, ON N2L 3G1, Canada; zhongxianmen@gmail.com (Z.M.); wakolkie@uwaterloo.ca (A.W.K.)
[2] School of Accounting and Finance, University of Waterloo, 200 University Avenue West, Waterloo, ON N2L 3G1, Canada
* Correspondence: twirjant@uwaterloo.ca; Tel.: +1-(519)-888-4567 (ext. 35210)

Received: 15 April 2019; Accepted: 8 May 2019; Published: 14 May 2019

Abstract: This paper proposes a variant of a threshold stochastic conditional duration (TSCD) model for financial data at the transaction level. It assumes that the innovations of the duration process follow a threshold distribution with a positive support. In addition, it also assumes that the latent first-order autoregressive process of the log conditional durations switches between two regimes. The regimes are determined by the levels of the observed durations and the TSCD model is specified to be self-excited. A novel Markov-Chain Monte Carlo method (MCMC) is developed for parameter estimation of the model. For model discrimination, we employ deviance information criteria, which does not depend on the number of model parameters directly. Duration forecasting is constructed by using an auxiliary particle filter based on the fitted models. Simulation studies demonstrate that the proposed TSCD model and MCMC method work well in terms of parameter estimation and duration forecasting. Lastly, the proposed model and method are applied to two classic data sets that have been studied in the literature, namely IBM and Boeing transaction data.

Keywords: stochastic conditional duration; threshold; Bayesian inference; Markov-Chain Monte Carlo; probability integral transform; deviance information criterion

JEL Classification: C10; C41; G10

1. Introduction

In this paper,[1] we propose a threshold Stochastic Conditional Duration (TSCD) model, in which the innovation of a financial duration process is assumed to follow a threshold distribution, where the two component distributions have positive supports, while the log duration process is kept to be the same as that in the classic Stochastic Conditional Duration (SCD) models introduced by Bauwens and Veredas (2004). In addition, we also assume that the state (i.e., the logarithm of the conditional durations) follows a threshold AR(1) process with the threshold level being driven by observed duration processes. The regimes are determined by a threshold parameter, which is estimated from the data. Suitable Markov-Chain Monte Carlo (MCMC) methods are developed within a Bayesian framework in which the parameters of the model and the augmented parameters, being the latent states, are estimated simultaneously by the estimation process. For the in-sample and out-of-sample duration forecasting, we use an auxiliary particle filter (APF) proposed in Pitt and Shephard (1999), from which the filter and predictive distributions of the latent states are approximated by samples of particles from the corresponding distributions. The APF is an efficient method for calculating the

---

[1] This paper is built from materials presented in several earlier working papers by the authors in Men et al. (2013, 2014, 2019).

marginal likelihood of observed data. For model selection and comparison, we employ a deviance information criterion (DIC) proposed by Spiegelhalter et al. (2002).

The remaining parts of this paper are organized as follows. Section 2 introduces the TSCD model. In Section 3, we propose a suitable MCMC method for parameter estimation of the models with a Gamma distribution or a Weibull distribution serving as the component distributions in the model. The latent states are augmented as parameters and estimated as a by-product of the MCMC estimation processes. We simulate the state variables by using a single-move Metropolis-Hastings (MH) algorithm with a univariate normal distribution as the proposal. In Section 4, model diagnostics, model selection, and duration forecasting are presented and discussed. In particular, model assessment is performed by calculating probability integral transforms (PITs) produced from the fitted TSCD models. In Section 5, we conduct simulation studies to assess the performance of the proposed TSCD models and developed estimation methods, while in Section 6 we present empirical results from applications of the proposed TSCD models to two classic/benchmark data sets of IBM and Boeing transactions. In this section, restricted versions of the TSCD models are also estimated and analyzed. Concluding remarks are made in Section 7.

2. Threshold Stochastic Conditional Duration Model

Let y_t denote the observed duration at time t, $t \leq T$, where T is a positive integer representing the sample size. The duration process of y_t is characterized by a product of two independent random variables: a lognormal random variable H_t and a positive random variable ϵ_t. Then, following Bauwens and Veredas (2004), we specify the following set of equations:

$$y_t = H_t \epsilon_t, \quad H_t = \exp(h_t), \qquad t = 1,...,T, \qquad (1)$$
$$h_{t+1} = \mu + \phi(h_t - \mu) + \sigma u_{t+1}, \qquad t = 1,...,T-1, \qquad (2)$$
$$h_1 \sim \mathcal{N}(\mu, \sigma^2/(1-\phi^2)), \qquad (3)$$

where ϵ_t and u_t are assumed to be mutually independent shocks with $u_t \sim \mathcal{N}(0,1)$. For the latent AR(1) process in (2) to be weakly stationary, it is assumed that $|\phi| < 1$. Bauwens and Veredas (2004) assume that ϵ_t follows either a Gamma distribution or a Weibull distribution with scale parameters equal to 1.

In our proposed model, we allow not only the innovation of the duration process to follow a threshold distribution with two component distributions with positive supports, but also the latent states to follow a threshold AR(1) process which switches between two regimes. These two regimes are determined by the previously observed durations according to a threshold level. In particular, the threshold distribution for the innovations of the measurement equation is given by

$$\begin{cases} \epsilon_t \sim \mathcal{D}_1(\delta_1), & \text{if } y_{t-1} \leq r, \\ \epsilon_t \sim \mathcal{D}_2(\delta_2), & \text{if } y_{t-1} > r, \end{cases} \qquad (4)$$

where $\mathcal{D}_1(\delta_1)$ and $\mathcal{D}_2(\delta_2)$ are two generic distributions with positive supports, and δ_1 and δ_2 are the corresponding parameter vectors.

For the log conditional durations, h_t, a threshold AR(1) process is defined as:

$$\begin{cases} h_{t+1} - \mu_1 = \phi_1(h_t - \mu_1) + \sigma_1 u_{1,t+1}, & \text{if } y_t \leq r, \\ h_{t+1} - \mu_2 = \phi_2(h_t - \mu_2) + \sigma_2 u_{2,t+1}, & \text{if } y_t > r, \end{cases} \qquad (5)$$

where $u_{1,t+1}$ and $u_{2,t+1}$ are two independent processes with a standard normal distribution. In the threshold specification in (5), the latent states, h_t, follow separate AR(1) processes in the two different regimes determined by the previously observed duration y_t and the threshold level r. The threshold level r is treated as a free parameter to be estimated by our proposed MCMC method.

For the components of the threshold distribution of ϵ_t, following Bauwens and Veredas (2004), we use either a Gamma distribution or a Weibull distribution. With this assumption, the probability density functions (pdfs) of ϵ_t are given respectively by

$$\begin{cases} f_1(\epsilon_t) = \frac{1}{\Gamma(\gamma_1)} \epsilon_t^{\gamma_1 - 1} \exp\{-\epsilon_t\}, & \text{if } y_{t-1} \leq r, \\ f_2(\epsilon_t) = \frac{1}{\Gamma(\gamma_2)} \epsilon_t^{\gamma_2 - 1} \exp\{-\epsilon_t\}, & \text{if } y_{t-1} > r, \end{cases} \quad (6)$$

with the shape parameters $\gamma_1 > 0$ and $\gamma_2 > 0$, and the scale parameters are all set to 1, and

$$\begin{cases} f_1(\epsilon_t) = v_1 \epsilon_t^{v_1 - 1} \exp\{-\epsilon_t^{v_1}\}, & \text{if } y_{t-1}, \leq r, \\ f_2(\epsilon_t) = v_2 \epsilon_t^{v_2 - 1} \exp\{-\epsilon_t^{v_2}\}, & \text{if } y_{t-1}, > r, \end{cases} \quad (7)$$

with the shape parameters $v_1 > 0$ and $v_2 > 0$ and unit scale parameters. Under these assumptions, the distribution of ϵ_t depends on the shape parameters. At time t, the observation y_t affects not only the distribution of ϵ_{t+1}, but also the distribution of h_{t+1}. In other words, the observation, y_t, contributes to future durations through ϵ_{t+1} and h_{t+1}. The asymmetric property of the marginal distribution of y_{t+1} is influenced by the previously observed duration according to the threshold level r. Importantly, under the threshold distributional assumption, we no longer need to explicitly specify a correlation structure between the observation and the latent process. In addition, as the variance of ϵ_t is not equal to 1, the location parameters in the threshold AR(1) processes are no longer required as well.

Under the TSCD model setup, at each time t, the conditional distribution of y_t is assumed to depend on the previous observation y_{t-1} and the threshold parameter r, i.e., the distributions of the observations will switch between the two regimes with the arrivals of the previously observed durations. Similar to the arguments in De Luca and Gallo (2004, 2009), who work with Autoregressive Conditional Duration (ACD) models, the two regimes can be interpreted as representing two types of behavior of traders in the market, who are respectively informed and uninformed traders. The informed and uninformed traders are assumed to respond differentially to bad news and good news in the market over the sample period. The proposed TSCD models with two regimes are constructed specifically to characterize these time dependent responses, giving rise to a desirably asymmetric pattern in the marginal distributions of the model.

3. Bayesian Inference

In this section, we develop a suitable MCMC method for parameter estimation of the proposed model. Following the literature, all the latent states, h_t, are augmented as parameters and simulated or estimated as a by-product of the derived estimators. For each specified TSCD model, the latent states are simulated one at a time by the slice sampler introduced by Neal (2003).

In the following MCMC algorithm, we assume that the innovation of the mean equation follows a threshold distribution with two, say Gamma, component distributions with $\theta = (\phi_1, \sigma_1, \phi_2, \sigma_2, \gamma_1, \gamma_2, r)$ serving as the parameter vector. Given an observed duration time series of $\mathbf{y} = (y_1, \ldots, y_T)$, the conditional densities of y_t are given by

$$\begin{cases} f(y_t | y_{t-1}, h_t, r) = \frac{1}{\Gamma(\gamma_1)} \exp(-\gamma_1 h_t) y_t^{\gamma_1 - 1} \exp\{-y_t \exp(-h_t)\}, & \text{if } y_{t-1} \leq r, \\ f(y_t | y_{t-1}, h_t, r) = \frac{1}{\Gamma(\gamma_2)} \exp(-\gamma_2 h_t) y_t^{\gamma_2 - 1} \exp\{-y_t \exp(-h_t)\}, & \text{if } y_{t-1} > r. \end{cases} \quad (8)$$

Therefore, the posterior density of $(\theta, \mathbf{h})$ can be conveniently split into two parts according to the threshold parameter r,

$$f(\theta, \mathbf{h}|\mathbf{y}) \propto \prod_{\substack{t=2, \, y_{t-1} \leq r}}^{T} \left[\frac{1}{\Gamma(\gamma_1)} \exp(-\gamma_1 h_t) y_t^{\gamma_1 - 1} \exp\left\{ - y_t \exp(-h_t) \right\} \right]$$
$$\times \prod_{\substack{t=2, \, y_{t-1} > r}}^{T} \left[\frac{1}{\Gamma(\gamma_2)} \exp(-\gamma_2 h_t) y_t^{\gamma_2 - 1} \exp\left\{ - y_t \exp(-h_t) \right\} \right], \qquad (9)$$

where $\mathbf{h} = (h_1, ..., h_T)$. Within the Bayesian inference, the posterior distributions of the parameters in θ, and the latent states, $\mathbf{h}$, can be readily derived from (9).

The TSCD model is completed by specifying prior distributions for all the parameters in θ. For tractability, we assume that the prior distributions of the parameters in θ are mutually independent. The persistence parameters ϕ_1 and ϕ_2 are assumed to have a univariate normal distribution $\phi_i \sim N(0, 5), i = 1, 2$, truncated in the interval $(-1, 1)$. Instead of sampling σ_1 and σ_2, we sample σ_1^2 and σ_2^2. The prior distributions of σ_1^2 and σ_2^2 are $\sigma_i^2 \sim IG(0.25, 5), i = 1, 2$, which are inverse Gamma distributions. For the shape parameters γ_1 and γ_2 we use the half-Cauchy distributions as their prior distributions

$$f(\gamma_i) \propto \frac{1}{1 + \gamma_i^2}, \gamma_i > 0, i = 1, 2. \qquad (10)$$

The half-Cauchy distribution is also used as the prior distribution for the shape parameters of the Weibull components. For the threshold parameter r, we use a uniform distribution between the first and third quartiles of the observations in $\mathbf{y}$. The two quartiles are intended to ensure that there are enough observations in each of the two regimes.

The algorithm of the MCMC estimation procedure for the TSCD model with a threshold Gamma distribution, called TSCD-G model hereafter, is listed in Algorithm 1. The derivation of the full conditionals for the parameters and individual latent state are given explicitly in Step 1 below, where the full conditional of each parameter is defined as the conditional distribution given that other parameters in the model have been sampled.

Algorithm 1: MCMC algorithm for the TSCD-G model.

Step 0. Initialize $\mathbf{h}, \phi_i, \sigma_i, \gamma_i$, i=1, 2, and r
Step 1. Sample $h_t, t = 2, ..., T$
Step 2. Sample γ_1 and γ_2
Step 3. Sample r
Step 4. Sample ϕ_i and $\sigma_i^2, i = 1, 2$
Step 5. Go to **Step 1**.

Step 0. Initialize $\mathbf{h}, \phi_i, \sigma_i, \gamma_i$ and r. To start the MCMC algorithm, the initial values of the parameters of the model are set as $\phi_1 = 0.5, \phi_2 = 0.5, \sigma_1 = 0.12, \sigma_2 = 0.12, \gamma_1 = 0.5, \gamma_2 = 1.5, v_1 = 0.5$ and $v_2 = 1.5$. The initial value of r is set as the mean of the observations, which falls into the interval of the first and third quartiles of the observations. The initial values of $\mathbf{h}$ are generated from the latent AR(1) process with the above initial parameters.

Step 1. Sample $\mathbf{h}$. Here, we only give the full conditionals of $h_t, t = 3, ...T - 1$. The full conditionals of h_2 and h_T are easy to derive and, thus, omitted from this paper. The full conditional of h_t depends on $y_{t+1}, y_t, y_{t-1}, h_{t+1}, h_{t-1}$ and r. Given that r has been sampled previously, the full conditional of h_t can be calculated based on four cases: (i) If $y_t \leq r$ and $y_{t-1} \leq r$, the full conditional of h_t is given by

$$f(h_t|h_{t-1}, h_{t+1}, y_t, \theta_{-r}, y_t \leq r, y_{t-1} \leq r)$$
$$\propto f(y_t|h_t, \theta_{-r}, y_{t-1} \leq r) f(h_t|h_{t-1}, y_{t-1} \leq r, \theta_{-r}) f(h_t|y_t \leq r, h_{t+1}, \theta_{-r})$$
$$\propto \exp(-\gamma_1 h_t) \exp\left\{-y_t \exp(-h_t)\right\}$$
$$\times \exp\left\{-\frac{(h_t - \phi_1 h_{t-1})^2}{2\sigma_1^2}\right\} \times \exp\left\{-\frac{(h_{t+1} - \phi_1 h_t)^2}{2\sigma_1^2}\right\}$$
$$\propto \exp\left\{-y_t \exp(-h_t)\right\} \times \exp\left\{-\frac{(h_t - \mu_t)^2}{2\sigma_t^2}\right\}, \qquad (11)$$

where

$$\mu_t = -\sigma_t^2 \gamma_1 + \frac{\phi_1(h_{t+1} + h_{t-1})}{1 + \phi_1^2}, \qquad \sigma_t^2 = \frac{\sigma_1^2}{1 + \phi_1^2}.$$

Here θ_{-r} defines as a collection of model parameters except for r. Thus, the full conditional of h_t can be sampled by the slice sampler.

Algorithm of the slice sampler for h_t

SS1. Draw u_1 uniformly from the interval $(0,1)$ and set $u_2 = u_1 \exp\left\{-\frac{(h_t - \mu_t)^2}{2\sigma_t^2}\right\}$. Let $u_2 < \exp\left\{-\frac{(h_t - \mu_t)^2}{2\sigma_t^2}\right\}$, then we have

$$\mu_t - \sqrt{-2\sigma_t^2 \log(u_2)} < h_t < \mu_t + \sqrt{-2\sigma_t^2 \log(u_2)}. \qquad (12)$$

SS2. Draw u_3 uniformly from the interval $(0,1)$ and set $u_4 = u_3 \exp\left\{-y_t \exp(-h_t)\right\}$. Let $u_4 < \exp\left\{-y_t \exp(-h_t)\right\}$ then we have

$$h_t > -\log(-\log(u_4)/y_t)$$

SS3. Draw h_t uniformly from the interval determined by the inequalities in (11) and (12) such as

$$h_t \sim U\left(\max\left\{-\log(-\log(u_4)/y_t), \mu_t - \sqrt{-2\sigma_t^2 \log(u_2)}\right\}, \mu_t + \sqrt{-2\sigma_t^2 \log(u_2)}\right).$$

As a brief remark to the above algorithm, we note that in our approach, each h_t is simulated based on its conditional distribution. So conditionally μ_t is known in our situation. Also note that y_{t+1}'s are the only observations available to our model. As we subsequently perform a one-step-ahead prediction for the fitted model, we only need to sample h_{t+1}, and do not need to sample y_{t+1}.

In each MCMC iteration, when we simulate h_t, the sampled value of h_t from the previous MCMC step is set at the initial value. As the full conditionals of h_t in each MCMC step are similar, this initial value should provide a good starting point. As the slice sampler adapts to the form of the density function of the underlying variable, it is more efficient than many other existing samplers. In addition, under certain conditions, Roberts and Rosenthal (1999) also show that the slice algorithm is robust and has geometric periodicity properties. Moreover, Mira and Tierney (2002) prove that the slice sampler has a smaller second-largest eigenvalue, which ensures faster convergence to the underlying distribution. Indeed, in our study, we find that even with only five iterations of our slice algorithm, we can feasibly and efficiently estimate the TSCD models by the MCMC.[2]

The single-move simulation method is popular in the literature and used in Jacquier et al. (2004); Yu et al. (2006); Zhang and King (2008), Men et al. (2015, 2016a, 2016b) among others. The advantage of the slice sampler is that five iterations can give us a point from the underlying distribution unlike the MH algorithm where many generated points must be discarded.

The full conditional of h_t, given (ii) $y_t > r$ and $y_{t-1} \leq r$, is

$$
\begin{aligned}
& f(h_t|h_{t-1}, h_{t+1}, y_t, \theta_{-r}, y_t > r, y_{t-1} \leq r) \\
& \propto f(y_t|h_t, \theta_{-r}, y_{t-1} \leq r) f(h_t|h_{t-1}, y_{t-1} \leq r, \theta_{-r}) f(h_t|y_t > r, h_{t+1}, \theta_{-r}) \\
& \propto \exp(-\gamma_1 h_t) \exp\left\{ - y_t \exp(-h_t)\right\} \\
& \quad \times \exp\left\{ -\frac{(h_t - \phi_1 h_{t-1})^2}{2\sigma_1^2} \right\} \exp\left\{ -\frac{(h_{t+1} - \phi_2 h_t)^2}{2\sigma_2^2} \right\} \\
& \propto \exp\left\{ - y_t \exp(-h_t)\right\} \times \exp\left\{ -\frac{(h_t - \mu_t)^2}{2\sigma_t^2} \right\},
\end{aligned}
\tag{13}
$$

where

$$\mu_t = -\gamma_1 \sigma_t^2 + \frac{a}{b}, \qquad \sigma_t^2 = \frac{1}{b}$$

with $a = \frac{\phi_1 h_{t-1}}{\sigma_1^2} + \frac{\phi_2 h_{t+1}}{\sigma_2^2}$, $\qquad b = \frac{1}{\sigma_1^2} + \frac{\phi_2^2}{\sigma_2^2}.$

The full conditional of h_t is also sampled through the slice sampler. Under the other conditions (iii) $y_t > r$ and $y_{t-1} > r$, and (iv) $y_t \leq r$ and $y_{t-1} > r$, the full condition of h_t can be calculated in the same fashion, and the realized full conditionals of h_t can be sampled through the slice sampler.

Step 2. Sample γ_1 and γ_2. Given that other parameters and the latent states have been sampled from the previous iteration of the MCMC algorithm, the full conditionals of γ_i, $i = 1, 2$, are given respectively by

$$f(\gamma_1|\mathbf{y}, \mathbf{h}, \theta_{-\gamma_1}) \propto \prod_{t=2, y_{t-1} \leq r}^{T} \left(\frac{\exp(-\gamma_1 h_t)}{\Gamma(\gamma_1)} y_t^{\gamma_1 - 1} \right) \frac{1}{1 + \gamma_1^2}, \tag{14}$$

$$f(\gamma_2|\mathbf{y}, \mathbf{h}, \theta_{-\gamma_2}) \propto \prod_{t=2, y_{t-1} > r}^{T} \left(\frac{\exp(-\gamma_2 h_t)}{\Gamma(\gamma_2)} y_t^{\gamma_2 - 1} \right) \frac{1}{1 + \gamma_2^2}. \tag{15}$$

These distributions are not simple distributions that can be simulated directly. Our simple solution to this is to use a random-walk MH method with a univariate normal distribution with mean zero and non-unit variance. The variance can be fined tuned to obtain a reasonable acceptance rate for the MH algorithm. Experience from our study suggests that an acceptance rate between 25% and 55% gives us a more accurate estimate of r in the simulation studies.

---

[2] For further efficiency considerations, Pitt and Shephard (1999) for instance proposes the use of block samplers for h_t for a stochastic volatility (SV) model. We have tried to apply this block sampling scheme to our variant of the TSCD models and found the required computation to be highly intractable.

Step 3. Sample r. The full conditional of r is

$$f(r|\mathbf{y},\mathbf{h},\theta_{-r})$$
$$\propto \prod_{t=2,\,y_{t-1}\leq r}^{T}\left(\frac{\exp(-\gamma_1 h_t)y_t^{\gamma_1-1}}{\Gamma(\gamma_1)}\right)\prod_{t=2,\,y_{t-1}>r}^{T}\left(\frac{\exp(-\gamma_2 h_t)y_t^{\gamma_2-1}}{\Gamma(\gamma_2)}\right). \qquad (16)$$

The full conditional of r is not a simple distribution either. Therefore, again, we use a random-walk MH method to simulate this posterior distribution with a univariate normal distribution $N(0,\sigma_0^2)$, where σ_0 is fined tuned for the random-walk MH method to have a reasonable acceptance rate.

Step 4. Sample ϕ_1, ϕ_2, σ_1^2 and σ^2. The full conditionals of ϕ_i are univariate normal distributions truncated in the interval $(-1,1)$, which can be simulated by a slice sampler. The full conditionals of σ_i^2 are inverse Gamma distributions from which the sampling is relatively easy to carry out. The derivation of these full conditionals are not given in this paper, but they can be found for instance in Men et al. (2016a) or any in prior studies on SV models such as Men et al. (2016b), where MCMC algorithms are used.

To conduct a Bayesian inference in the TSCD model with threshold Weibull component distributions, the estimation algorithm can be derived similarly. As a result, details of these derivations are omitted from the paper.

4. Model Selection, Assessment and Duration Forecasting

4.1. Model Selection

Information criteria such as AIC due to Akaike (1987) and BIC due to Schwarz (1978) are often used for model comparison. For instance, in the study of SV models, Lopes and West (2004) and Zhang and King (2008) use the AIC and the BIC for model selection. It is well-known that the AIC tends to choose a model with a larger number of parameters, while the BIC tends to prefer a model with a smaller number of parameters. It is important to note that in the calculation of the AIC and the BIC, we need to know the exact number of parameters of the model. For hidden Markov models such as the TSCD models proposed in this paper, the number of parameters is difficult to determine since all the latent states are augmented as parameters and highly correlated. For instance, when a TSCD-G model is fitted to a data set with T observations, the number of parameters in the fitted model could be $(T+7)$ or less. However, it is worth reiterating that the AIC and the BIC are functions of both the number of parameters and the sample size. This indicates that the AIC and the BIC are not suitable for discriminating hidden Markov models, including the TSCD models. A new criterion, called the DIC proposed by Spiegelhalter et al. (2002) is used in this paper to discriminate between these models since it does not depend on the number of parameters directly. The DIC is defined as follows:

$$\text{DIC} = \bar{D} + P_D.$$

The first term

$$\bar{D}(\theta,\mathbf{h}) = E_{\theta,\mathbf{h}|\mathbf{y}}[D(\theta,\mathbf{h})], \text{ where } D(\theta,\mathbf{h}) = -2\log f(\mathbf{y}|\theta,\mathbf{h}),$$

represents a Bayesian measure of a model fit. It is called the posterior mean of the deviance. The second term is

$$P_D = \bar{D} - D(\bar{\theta},\bar{\mathbf{h}})$$
$$= E_{\theta,\mathbf{h}|\mathbf{y}}[D(\theta,\mathbf{h})] - 2\log f(\mathbf{y}|\bar{\theta},\bar{\mathbf{h}}),$$

where $D(\bar{\theta},\bar{\mathbf{h}})$ is the deviance of the posterior mean, and P_D is the effective number of parameters, which measures the complexity of the model. Thus, the DIC represents a trade-off between model adequacy and model complexity. When prior information is dominated by the likelihood, we have $p_D = p + o(1)$, where p is the number of parameters in the model. In other words, when likelihood information dominates, we expect that the observed-data DIC is not sensitive to different prior distributions, and p_D is close to p with the difference capturing the amount of prior information.

4.2. Duration Forecasting

To perform duration forecasting via the fitted TSCD models, we use the APF proposed in Pitt and Shephard (1999). In our MCMC method, the conditional of h_t depends on y_t, h_{t-1} and h_{t+1}, while in the APF, the filtered distribution depends on y_t and h_{t-1}, and the predictive distribution of h_t depends on h_{t-1} and y_{t-1}. In addition, the filtered distribution of h_t is also represented by a sample of the conditional distribution of $h_t|y_t$. APF is an efficient recursive algorithm to approximate the filtered and one-step-ahead predictive distributions. The sample likelihood of a specified TSCD model via the successive conditional decomposition is given by

$$f(\mathbf{y}|\theta) = f(y_2|\theta, \mathcal{F}_1) \prod_{t=3}^{T} f(y_t|\mathcal{F}_{t-1}, \theta), \qquad (17)$$

where $\mathcal{F}_t = (y_1, \ldots, y_t)$ is the information known at time t. The conditional density of y_{t+1}, given θ and $\mathcal{F}_t$, has the following expression

$$\begin{aligned} f(y_{t+1}|\mathcal{F}_t, \theta) &= \int f(y_{t+1}|h_{t+1}, \theta, \mathcal{F}_t) dF(h_{t+1}|\mathcal{F}_t, \theta) \\ &= \int f(y_{t+1}|h_{t+1}, \theta, \mathcal{F}_t) f(h_{t+1}|h_t, \theta, \mathcal{F}_t) dF(h_t|\mathcal{F}_t, \theta). \end{aligned} \qquad (18)$$

As it is impossible to obtain an analytical representation of this conditional density function, numerical methods such as the APF method must be employed. The APF algorithm has been used in the context of the SV models such as in Chib et al. (2006); Men et al. (2016b); and in the context of the SCD models such as in Men et al. (2015, 2016a) and among others. It is given in Appendix A. It should point out that the one-step-ahead in-sample and out-of-sample duration forecasting can be constructed with the APF algorithm using the latent AR(1) process. Our experience shows that using 3000 particles is sufficient for our simulation studies and real stock transaction data used to illustrate our estimation approach.

4.3. Model Assessment

There are several statistical tools that can be used to assess the overall model fit of our TSCD model. Our approach in this paper is to analyze the PITs, which was proposed by Diebold et al. (1998). If the fitted TSCD model agrees with the data, the PITs will follow a uniform distribution $U(0,1)$. The Kolmogorov-Smirnov (KS) test, which is designed to examine whether realized observation errors originated from the assumed distribution, is used to assess the distribution of the PITs.

Suppose that $\{f(y_t|\mathcal{F}_{t-1})\}_{t=1}^{T}$ is a sequence of conditional densities of y_t and $\{p(y_t|\mathcal{F}_{t-1})\}_{t=1}^{T}$ is the corresponding sequence of one-step-ahead density forecasts. The PIT of y_t is defined as

$$u(t) = \int_{-\infty}^{y_t} p(z|\mathcal{F}_{t-1}) dz. \qquad (19)$$

Under the null hypothesis that the sequence $\{p(y_t|\mathcal{F}_{t-1})\}_{t=1}^{T}$ coincides with $\{f(y_t|\mathcal{F}_{t-1})\}_{t=1}^{T}$, the sequence $\{u(t)\}_{t=1}^{T}$ corresponds to i.i.d. observations from the distribution $U(0,1)$. In our TSCD model, the PITs can be calculated using the following formulas.

The TSCD-G model: If $y_{t-1} \leq r$ then

$$u(t) \approx \frac{1}{N} \sum_{i=1}^{N} \int_{-\infty}^{y_t} \frac{1}{\Gamma(\gamma_1)} z^{\gamma_1 - 1} \exp(-\gamma_1 h_t^{(i)}) \exp\left\{ -\frac{z}{\exp(h_t^{(i)})} \right\} dz$$

$$= \frac{1}{N} \sum_{i=1}^{N} \frac{1}{\Gamma(\gamma_1)} g(\gamma_1, y_t \exp(-h_t^{(i)})), \tag{20}$$

where $g(\gamma_1, y_t \exp(-h_t))$ is the incomplete Gamma function, and N is the number of particles. Similarly, if $y_{t-1} > r$ then

$$u(t) \approx \frac{1}{N} \sum_{i=1}^{N} \frac{1}{\Gamma(\gamma_2)} g(\gamma_2, y_t \exp(-h_t^{(i)})). \tag{21}$$

The TSCD-W model: If $y_{t-1} \leq r$ then

$$u(t) \approx \frac{1}{N} \sum_{i=1}^{N} \int_{-\infty}^{y_t} v_1 z^{v_1 - 1} \exp(-v_1 h_t^{(i)}) \exp\left\{ -\left(\frac{z}{\exp(h_t^{(i)})}\right)^{v_1} \right\} dz$$

$$= 1 - \frac{1}{N} \sum_{i=1}^{N} \exp\left\{ -\left(\frac{y_t}{\exp(-h_t^{(i)})}\right)^{v_1} \right\}. \tag{22}$$

Similarly, if $y_{t-1} > r$ then

$$u(t) \approx 1 - \frac{1}{N} \sum_{i=1}^{N} \exp\left\{ -\left(\frac{y_t}{\exp(-h_t^{(i)})}\right)^{v_2} \right\}. \tag{23}$$

In the computation of $u(t)$, $h_t^{(i)}$ are particles from the corresponding predictive distribution of h_t with weights $1/N$.

5. Simulation Studies

In this section, we assess the performance of the TSCD models and the MCMC algorithms by simulation studies. Since the component distributions can be either a Gamma or Weibull distribution, we examine two types of the TSCD models. The values of parameters used to generate artificial duration time series are listed in the second column of Table 1 in boldface. We generate 12,000 observations from each TSCD model indexed by these parameters, where the first 10,000 observations are fitted by the corresponding TSCD model and the fitted model is then used for the one-step-ahead in-sample and out-of-sample duration forecasting. The estimated parameters as well as the corresponding standard errors and Bayesian highest probability density (HPD) credible intervals, which can be calculated based on the 2.5% and 97.5% quantiles of the sampled data, are also included in this table. With relatively small standard deviations and narrow credible intervals, we conclude that the estimated parameters are close to their true values.

One way to assess the goodness-of-fit of the TSCD models is to compare the empirical survival function and the hazard function with those calculated from the fitted TSCD models visually. Denote by $f(y)$ and $F(y) = p(Y < y)$ respectively the pdf and cumulative distribution function (cdf) of the observed duration data. Then the survival function and the hazard function of the data are defined as $S(y) = 1 - F(y)$ and $H(y) = f(y)/(1 - F(y))$, respectively. As discussed in Bauwens and Veredas (2004), both the $f(y)$ and $F(y)$ for a given duration data have to be calculated by using a numerical method such as a kernel density fitting method, which can be found in Silverman (1986), pp. 11–13, and Bowman and Azzalini (1997). In addition, numerical integration methods such as the Gaussian quadrature method must be used for the calculation of $F(y)$ as well.

Table 1. True and estimated parameters of the TSCD models based on the simulated duration data.

Parameter	True	Est.	Std.	HPD CI(95%)
Panel A: With Gamma(γ,1) component				
ϕ_1	0.94	0.9368	0.0080	(0.9209, 0.9521)
σ_1	0.12	0.1298	0.0098	(0.1107, 0.1480)
ϕ_2	0.80	0.8014	0.0206	(0.7699, 0.8499)
σ_2	0.19	0.1819	0.0105	(0.1619, 0.2025)
r	3.5	3.5054	0.0035	(3.4978, 3.5106)
γ_1	3.5	3.4677	0.0550	(3.3584, 3.5743)
γ_2	5.0	4.9855	0.0582	(4.8654, 5.0953)
Panel B: With Weibull(v,1) component				
ϕ_1	0.94	0.9346	0.0062	(0.9221, 0.9465)
σ_1	0.12	0.1201	0.0065	(0.1073, 0.1328)
ϕ_2	0.80	0.7940	0.0139	(0.7668, 0.8213)
σ_2	0.19	0.1841	0.0049	(0.1744, 0.1938)
r	0.8	0.7985	0.0014	(0.7956, 0.8005)
v_1	3.5	3.4761	0.0546	(3.3694, 3.5823)
v_2	5.0	4.9703	0.0931	(4.7910, 5.1526)

Given the highly comparable results reported in Table 1 for the Gamma and Weibull component cases, for brevity, we focus only on the Weibull component case in the subsequent discussion. The top panel in Figure 1 compares the empirical survival function of the simulated durations with the conditional survival function based on the TSCD-W model, while the bottom panel plots the corresponding empirical hazard of the simulated data together with the conditional hazard function. It is observed in the presented figures that the empirical survival function and the hazard function implied by the fitted TSCD-W model behave similarly to the empirical counterparts except that there is a very small jump at the threshold value of 0.7983. The reason for this jump is presumably because the threshold level of 0.8 was used in generating the artificial duration time series.

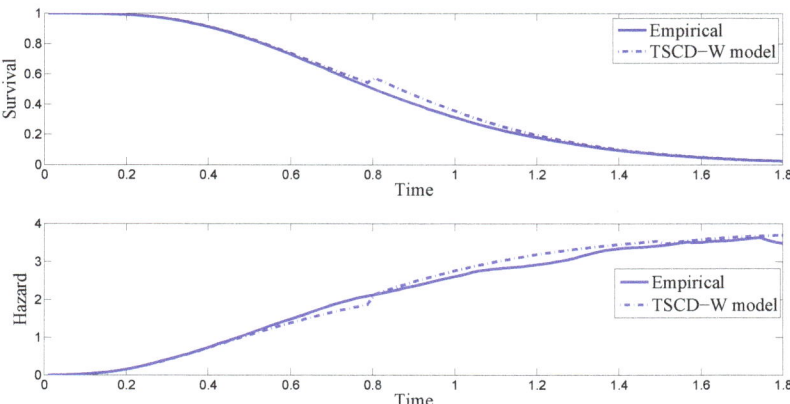

Figure 1. Top Panel: conditional survival function of the TSCD-W model for the simulated durations and its empirical survival function. **Bottom Panel**: the corresponding conditional hazard function for the simulated data and its empirical hazard rate.

To check the convergence of the MCMC algorithms, we plot the histogram and time series of samples simulated from each posterior distribution of the parameters of the TSCD-W model in

Figures 2 and 3, respectively. It can be seen visually that the time series drawn from the full conditionals of parameters are convergent. Subsequent statistical tests also confirm this conclusion.

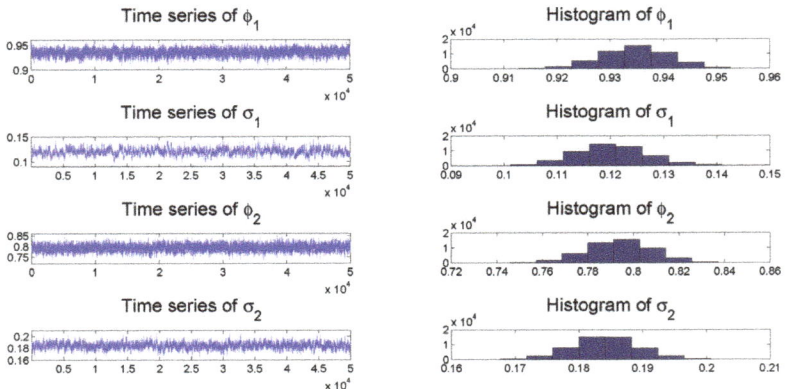

Figure 2. Time series and histograms of the samples drawn from the full conditionals of the parameters in the AR(1) process of the TSCD-W model based on the simulated duration data.

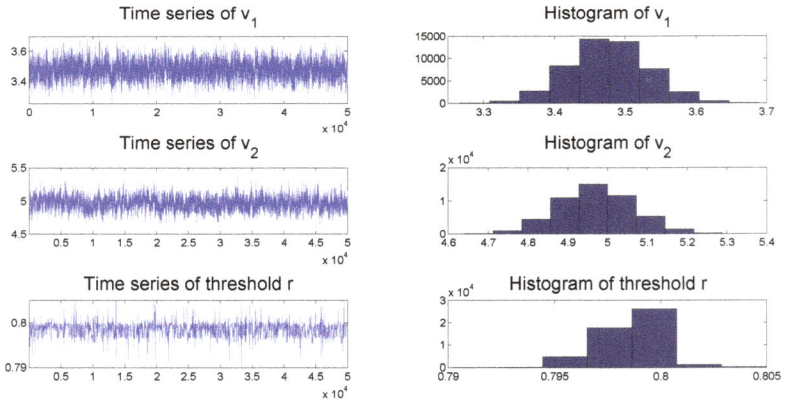

Figure 3. Time series and histograms of the samples drawn from the full conditionals of the parameters in the Weibull component distributions of the TSCD model and the full conditional of threshold based on simulated duration data.

To assess the overall model fit, we consider the PITs calculated from the fitted TSCD-W model. Figure 4 includes the scatter and histogram plots of the PITs. The two horizontal lines in the histogram plot are the 95% confidence intervals of the uniformity, constructed under the normal approximation of a binomial distribution, the calculation of which is detailed in Diebold et al. (1998). It is evident that the PITs originated from the uniform distribution $U(0, 1)$. The KS test statistic for the PITs is calculated as 0.0136 with the corresponding p-value of 0.8916. So, we do not reject the null hypothesis at any reasonable level of significance that the fitted TSCD model with the threshold Weibull innovations agrees with the generated duration data. Figure 5 graphs the cdf of the uniform distribution $U(0, 1)$ together with the empirical cdf of the PITs. The two cdfs appear to be very close with each other, which confirms our earlier conclusion. Figure 6 compares the simulated durations with the filtered and one-step-ahead in-sample and out-of-sample forecasted durations, where the latter is separated by the vertical dotted line. We observe that the forecasted durations resemble the true durations, indicating that our TSCD-W model is again able to give a reasonably accurate forecast of future durations.

In applications to real data, although the true financial durations are not observable, we are reasonably confident that the fitted TSCD-W model can do a good job for duration forecast. While the above analysis is based on the TSCD-W model, we, unsurprisingly, also reach a very similar conclusion for the TSCD-G model.

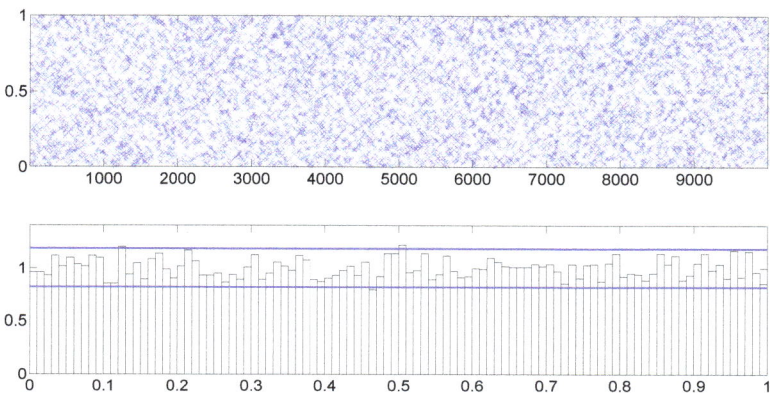

Figure 4. Goodness-of-fit test via the scatter plot (**top**) and the histogram (**bottom**) of the PITs produced by the fitted TSCD-W model based on simulated transaction data. The two horizontal lines in the histogram plot are the 95% confidence intervals of the uniformity, constructed under the normal approximation of a binomial distribution, the calculation of which is detailed in Diebold et al. (1998).

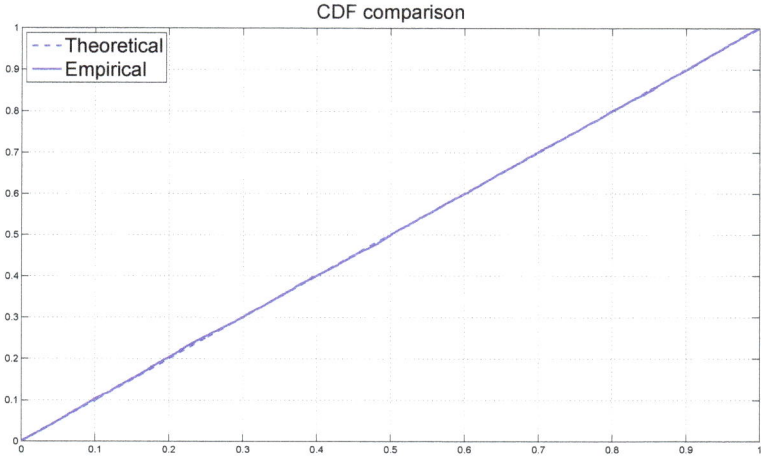

Figure 5. Comparison between the empirical CDF of the PITs and the theoretical CDF of a uniform distribution over the interval [0, 1] based on the TSCD-W model using simulated transaction data.

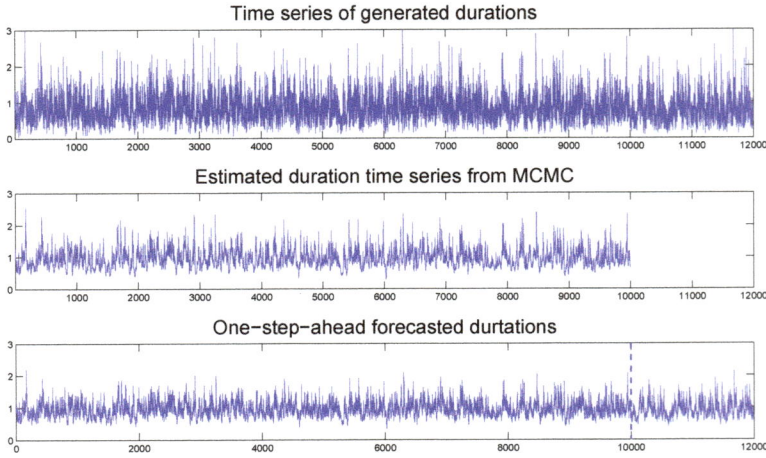

Figure 6. Comparison between observed durations with the estimated and one-step-ahead forecasted conditional durations based on the TSCD-W model using the simulated transaction data.

Overall, the simulation studies carried out above demonstrate that the TSCD models and MCMC methods can recover the true parameters obtained by using the simulated duration data. In addition, duration forecasting can also be adequately performed using the AFP.

6. Empirical Analysis

In this section, we apply the proposed TSCD model to the classic/benchmark IBM and Boeing transaction data. Both data sets have been used previously in Knight and Ning (2008); Xu et al. (2011) and Men et al. (2015, 2016a). The IBM transaction data cover the period from 1 November 1990 to 31 January 1991 with a total of 24,765 transactions, while the Boeing data covers the period from 1 September 2001, to 31 October 2001 with a total of 90,136 observations. These datasets are admittedly from several decades ago. However, the use of these datasets is intended to facilitate a direct comparison between the results obtained from our models and methods with those in the literature (including our own previous studies), which all have conveniently used these same benchmark datasets. The frequency of the data is tick by tick, which records every single transaction that occurs in the market. Its salient feature is irregularly spaced in time and is primarily caused by financial transactions being clustered over time or occurring in a scattered fashion over time. The main implication of the irregular spacing of these data is that the time between any two consecutive market events, which is the financial duration, is a random variable.

Tables 2 and 3 present the estimated parameters of the TSCD models based on the two data sets. The proposed MCMC algorithms were iterated 100,000 times. After the first 50,000 sampled values are discarded as the burn-in to eliminate initial value problems, the parameters and the states were then estimated by sample means. Standard errors and Bayesian HPD intervals are also reported in the two tables. The Bayesian HPD intervals are calculated by the 2.5% and 97.5% quartiles. The relatively small standard errors of these Bayesian HPD intervals indicate that our estimation process is quite efficient.

We note that for the IBM transaction data, the two persistent parameter estimates (e.g., for the TSCD-W model, $\hat{\phi}_1 = 0.9847$ and $\hat{\phi}_2 = 0.8640$) and, to a lesser extent, also the two volatility parameter estimates (e.g., for the TSCD-W model, $\hat{\sigma}_1 = 0.1369$ and $\hat{\sigma}_2 = 0.1397$) of the latent threshold AR(1) processes are quite different from each other. This indicates that at least two latent dynamic market factors that affect the duration innovation in different scales can be captured by the TSCD model.

In other words, the IBM transaction data can be adequately characterized by the two specified threshold processes in the TSCD model. However, for the Boeing transaction data, the parameter estimates between the two regimes are relatively closer to each other (e.g., for the TSCD-W model, $\hat{\phi}_1 = 0.9897$ and $\hat{\phi}_2 = 0.9705$, and $\hat{\sigma}_1 = 0.0703$ and $\hat{\sigma}_2 = 0.0669$).

Table 2. Parameter estimates based on TSCD models based on the IBM transaction data.

Parameter	Est.	Std.	HPD CI(95%)
Panel A: With Gamma(γ,1) components			
ϕ_1	0.9704	0.0061	(0.9588, 0.9818)
σ_1	0.1788	0.0129	(0.1538, 0.2037)
ϕ_2	0.8065	0.0322	(0.7431, 0.8667)
σ_2	0.2096	0.0254	(0.1618, 0.2593)
γ_1	1.0015	0.0135	(0.9768, 1.0278)
γ_2	0.9528	0.0120	(0.9287, 0.9767)
r	1.0337	0.2010	(0.7377, 1.3145)
Panel B: With Weibull(v,1) components			
ϕ_1	0.9847	0.0043	(0.9766, 0.9933)
σ_1	0.1369	0.0090	(0.1180, 0.1535)
ϕ_2	0.8640	0.0290	(0.8223, 0.9018)
σ_2	0.1397	0.0144	(0.1114, 0.1681)
v_1	0.9664	0.0075	(0.9553, 0.9843)
v_2	0.9280	0.0101	(0.9001, 0.9393)
r	0.9622	0.1756	(0.6711, 1.2980)

Table 3. Parameter estimates based on TSCD models based on the Boeing transaction data.

Parameter	Est.	Std.	HPD CI(95%)
Panel A: With Gamma(γ,1) components			
ϕ_1	0.9979	0.0012	(0.9956, 1.0000)
σ_1	0.0573	0.0036	(0.0501, 0.0640)
ϕ_2	0.9923	0.0020	(0.9897, 0.9951)
σ_2	0.0496	0.0040	(0.0430, 0.0599)
γ_1	1.2697	0.0097	(1.2506, 1.2891)
γ_2	1.2959	0.0067	(1.2832, 1.3089)
r	0.3420	0.1363	(0.2778, 0.4682)
Panel B: With Weibull(v,1) components			
ϕ_1	0.9897	0.0014	(0.9869, 0.9923)
σ_1	0.0703	0.0038	(0.0636, 0.0780)
ϕ_2	0.9705	0.0039	(0.9626, 0.9778)
σ_2	0.0669	0.0060	(0.0559, 0.0787)
v_1	1.1415	0.0043	(1.1332, 1.1499)
v_2	1.1081	0.0064	(1.0960, 1.1208)
r	1.1775	0.0974	(0.0965, 1.3085)

Again, given the highly comparable results for the Gamma and Weibull component cases for both datasets reported in Tables 2 and 3, for brevity and without much loss of generality, we focus our ensuing discussion only for the Weibull component case, i.e., the TSCD-W model. However, the fitted TSCD-G model will later be subjected to a formal model discrimination against the fitted TSCD-W model for both datasets.

To check the convergence of the samples drawn from the full conditionals, we again plot the time series and histograms for each parameter of the TSCD-W models based on the Boeing transaction data in Figures 7 and 8. It is visually evident that these time series are convergent. Please note that in our TSCD models, after 50,000 iterations, the generated time series typically converge. Figure 9 compares the duration time series with the filtered (or, Bayesian estimated) durations, and with the one-step-ahead in-sample and out-of-sample forecasted durations. It is observed that the forecasted durations also resemble the true durations closely.

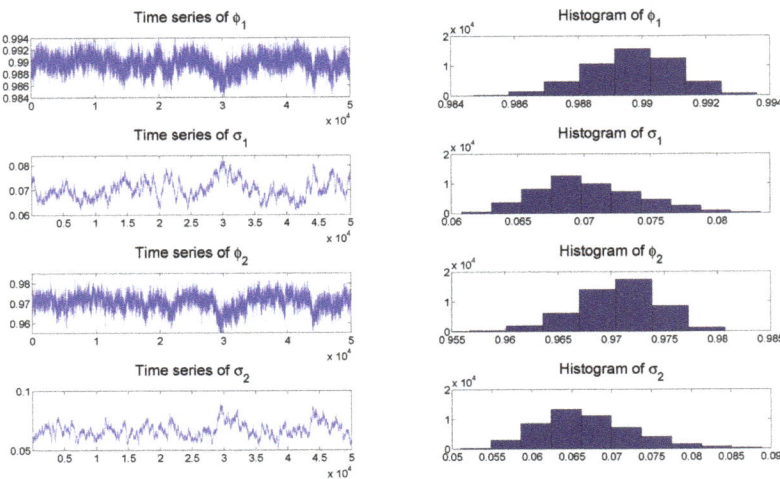

Figure 7. Time series and histograms of the samples drawn from the full conditionals of the parameters in the AR(1) process of the double TSCD-W model based on the Boeing stock duration data.

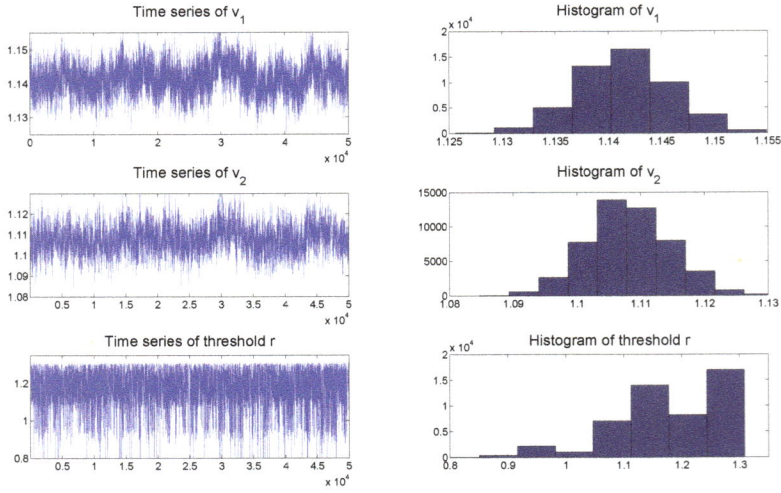

Figure 8. Time series and histograms of the samples drawn from the full conditionals of the parameters of the TSCD-W model based on the Boeing duration data.

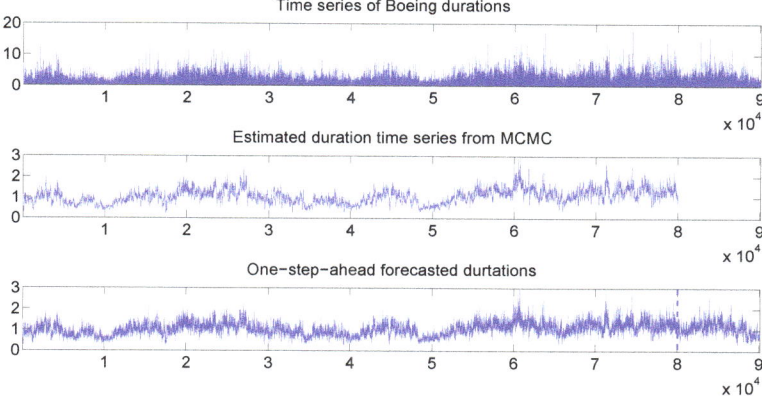

Figure 9. Comparison between observed durations, estimated, and one-step-ahead forecasted conditional durations based on the TSCD-W model using the Boeing stock transaction data.

As we did in the simulation studies, we compare in Figure 10 the empirical survival function of the Boeing durations with the conditional survival function based on the estimated TSCD-W model. The bottom panel plots the corresponding empirical hazard of the Boeing data together with the conditional hazard function. It is observed that the empirical survival function and the hazard function behave similarly to the counterparts implied by the fitted TSCD model except that there is a very small jump at the threshold value of 1.1775 in the hazard function implied by the fitted model.

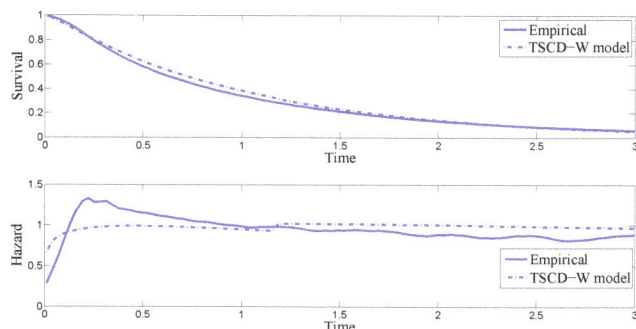

Figure 10. Top Panel: conditional survival function of the TSCD-W model for the Boeing durations and its empirical survival function. Bottom Panel: the corresponding conditional hazard function for the Boeing durations data and its empirical hazard rate.

To check the goodness-of-fit of the model, we plot the scatter and histogram plots of the PITs originated from the fitted TSCD-W model in Figure 11, while Figure 12 plots the empirical cdf of the PITs together with the theoretical cdf of the uniform distribution $U(0,1)$. The plots reveal that the PITs do not appear to follow a uniform distribution over the interval (0,1). The results from the KS test confirm this assertion. The reason for these unfavorable results can be understood by inspecting Figures 11 and 12 where we see that the right tail of the marginal distribution of the data is well fitted, but the left tail of the marginal distribution is less so. The intensity of small durations is around 0.18. Bauwens and Veredas (2004); Feng et al. (2004) and Men et al. (2015, 2016a) also observed a similar lack of fit for their SCD models to duration data. Fractional latent processes have been proposed to improve the fit of the model. Distributional assumptions for the innovations of the duration equation other than the Gamma and Weibull distributions may also prove to be fruitful in this regard.[3]

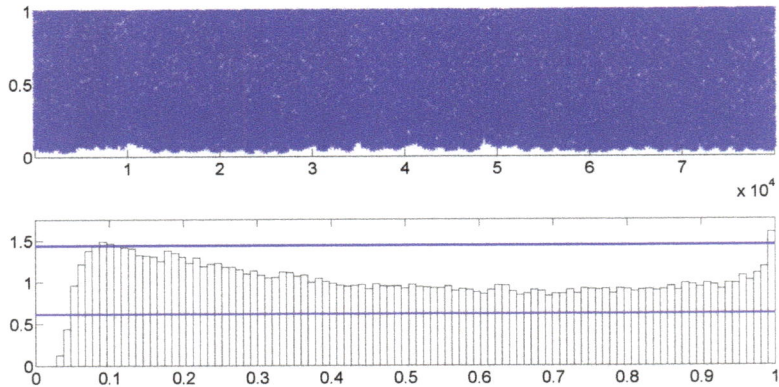

Figure 11. Scatter plot (**top**) and the histogram (**bottom**) of the PITs produced by the fitted TSCD-W model to the Boeing transaction data. The two horizontal lines in the histogram plot are the 95% confidence intervals of the uniformity, constructed under the normal approximation of a binomial distribution, the calculation of which is detailed in Diebold et al. (1998).

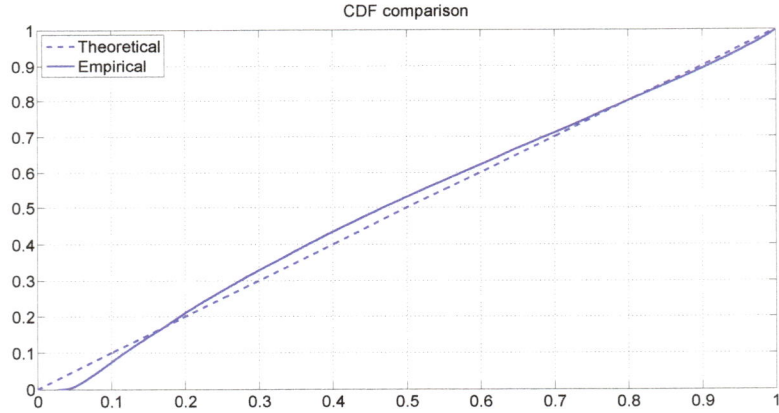

Figure 12. Comparison between the empirical CDF of the PITs and the theoretical CDF of a uniform distribution over the interval (0,1) based on the TSCD-W model to the Boeing transaction data.

Given the above qualification, we next proceed to select a better TSCD model for each of the two data sets of transactions by calculating the DIC values from the four fitted TSCD models. Berg et al. (2004) propose that the DIC be calculated by using the conditional likelihood. It is referred to as the conditional DIC. The conditional DIC is widely used for comparing SV models and is also used in the

---

[3] Another potential source of rejection for the KS statistic may lie in the fact that it is calculated by using estimated parameters in the empirical analysis. This alters the standard limiting distribution of the KS statistics to a non-standard one involving functionals of Brownian bridges.

earlier version of this paper. In this paper, we follow Celeux et al. (2006) in computing the DIC by using an observed-data likelihood. This is referred to as an observed-data DIC. This observed-data DIC is not computed in practice due to the difficulty in evaluating the observed-data likelihood. However, despite its popularity, the Monte Carlo study reported by Chan and Grant (2016) shows that the conditional DIC tends to pick overfitted models (often with negative values of p_D, which is difficult to justify), whereas the observed-data DIC is better able to choose the correct model. The challenge associated with the computation of the observed-data DICs for the proposed TSCD models is overcome by suitably modifying importance sampling algorithms proposed by Chan and Grant (2016) for estimating the observed-data likelihoods for SV models.

The observed-data DIC measures are listed in Table 4. First, note that the computed values of P_D for both models are positive, suggesting a positive penalty for model complexity, which makes sense. Second, for both the IBM and Boeing transaction data, the TSCD-G model is preferred given that the two fitted TSCD-G models have smaller observed-data DIC values compared to the TSCD-W counterparts.[4]

Table 4. Model selection by using the observed-data DIC criterion.

Data	Model	$D(\theta)$	P_D	DIC
IBM	TSCD-G	35,960.8	14.4	35,975.2
	TSCD-W	36,305.7	19.6	36,325.3
Boeing	TSCD-G	146,155.6	15.4	146,171.0
	TSCD-W	147,022.5	20.1	147,042.6

To undertake a further specification analysis, we pre-set $\phi_1 = \phi_2 = \phi$, and $\sigma_1 = \sigma_2 = \sigma$ to arrive at a restricted TSCD (RTSCD) model.[5] Thus, this RTSCD model is obtained by not allowing the latent first-order autoregressive process of the log conditional duration process to switch between the two regimes. However, it still permits the innovations of the duration process to follow a threshold distribution with a positive support. To select a better fitted RTSCD models for the IBM and Boeing transaction data, we compute the observed-data DICs from the models. The values of the observed-data DICs are presented in Table 5. Among the observed-data DIC values, the smallest ones are from the RTSCD-G model, which means that the RTSCD-G model is better suited than the RTSCD-W model for the analysis of the real transaction data of the IBM and Boeing stocks.[6] In addition, the computed DICs for the unrestricted TSCD models are uniformly smaller than those for the RSTCD models, suggesting that the unrestricted TSCD models are the preferred models for both datasets.[7] Thus, for these datasets, the latent first-order autoregressive process of the log conditional duration process switch between the two regimes.

---

[4] The conditional DICs for the TSCD-G model and the TSCD-W model are 35,669.5 and 36,025.1 for the IBM dataset and 145,874.4 and 146,749.1 for the Boeing dataset respectively. These results are comparable with those reported for the unobserved-data DICs.
[5] We thank one of the anonymous reviewers for this suggestion.
[6] The conditional DICs for the RTSCD-G model and the RTSCD-W model are 33,252.8 and 33,557.9 for the IBM dataset and 143,287.3 and 144,758.8 for the Boeing dataset respectively. These results are comparable with those reported for the unobserved-data DICs but in all four cases the effective numbers of parameters, P_D, are negative, implying a negative penalty for model complexity, which is difficult to justify.
[7] The conditional DICs for the RTSCD models are always smaller than those for the unrestricted TSCD models. This is because the effective number of parameters that measures the model complexity is positive in the observed-data DIC, which is expected, and negative in the conditional DIC, which is less plausible. This is consistent with the Monte Carlo study in Chan and Grant (2016). At the same time, the posterior mean deviance, which is used as a Bayesian measure of the model fit, is always negative in both methods.

Table 5. Restricted model selection by using the observed-data DIC criterion.

Data	Model	$D(\theta)$	P_D	DIC
IBM	TSCD-G	35,981.9	10.7	35,992.6
	TSCD-W	36,378.2	12.5	36,390.7
Boeing	TSCD-G	146,182.3	11.9	146,194.2
	TSCD-W	147,064.6	16.3	147,080.9

What is the economic interpretation of the findings in this paper? The findings are consistent with the prediction of the market micro-structure theory (MMT) in finance. The MMT suggests that there are informed and uninformed traders in the financial market. The interaction between the two trader types through information-revealing price formation processes is consistent with the observed financial market behavior. The informed traders will buy if the market price of an asset is below the true value (based on their information set). Conversely, they will sell, if the price is above the value. However, information is not free to the traders, and there are traders who base their trading decisions by observing the asset prices. As this latter trader type is a follower, its actions will be regulated by a distinct innovation process. This difference in behavior is consistent with the introduction of the two regimes for the innovation process in the TSCD model, since the instantaneous rate of transaction can be seen as being different across the two trader types.

7. Concluding Remarks

In this paper, we have proposed a TSCD model to analyze financial duration time series. The innovations of the duration process were assumed to follow a threshold distribution, where component distributions could be either a Gamma distribution or a Weibull distribution. In addition, we also assumed that the logarithm of the conditional durations followed a threshold latent AR(1) process. In the specified TSCD model, we allowed for the informed and uninformed traders in the market. Loosely speaking, these two types of traders have different trading behavior in response to the information arriving in the market. Suitable MCMC methods were developed for Bayesian inference of the parameters of the models in which the latent states were estimated as a by-product. Using the APF, the one-step-ahead in-sample and out-of-sample duration forecasts were carried out in a relatively straightforward way. Simulation studies and applications to two classic/benchmark data set of IBM and Boeing transactions demonstrated that the threshold SCD models work reasonably well in terms of parameter estimation and duration forecasting.

We have also considered a restricted version of the TSCD (RTSCD) model, in which the latent first-order autoregressive process of the log conditional duration process does not switch between the two regimes. We found that the RTSCD-G model performs better than the RTSCD-W model, when they are applied to both the IBM and Boeing transaction data. In addition, the proposed, unrestricted TSCD models uniformly outperform the restricted counterparts for both datasets.

Lastly, one important task remains outstanding at this juncture; i.e., we still need to further improve the empirical fit of the left tail of the marginal distribution of financial duration data. This entails a continued search for an ideal distribution of the financial duration data.

Author Contributions: All three authors contributed almost equally to all aspects of this research. Conceptualization, Z.M., A.W.K. and T.S.W.; methodology, Z.M., A.W.K. and T.S.W.; software, Z.M.; validation, Z.M., A.W.K. and T.S.W.; formal analysis, Z.M., A.W.K. and T.S.W.; investigation, Z.M., A.W.K. and T.S.W.; resources, Z.M.; data curation, Z.M.; writing–original draft preparation, Z.M.; writing–review and editing, T.S.W.; visualization, Z.M.; supervision, A.W.K. and T.S.W.; project administration, T.S.W.; funding acquisition, T.S.W.

Funding: This research was funded by the Social Sciences and Humanities Research Council (SSHRC) of Canada with a grant number Grant Account Number 435-2015-682, and the APC was also funded by the same agency under the same grant account number.

Conflicts of Interest: All three authors declare no conflict of interest.

Appendix A. The APF Algorithm for the TSCD Model

The question is how to sample $(h_{t+1}|\mathcal{F}_{t+1},\theta,)$ given that we have a particle sample from the filter distribution of $(h_t|\mathcal{F}_t,\theta)$. Below we present an algorithm for the TSCD model based on the procedure suggested by Chib et al. (2006):

PF1. Given a sample $\{h_t^{(i)}, i = 1,\ldots,N\}$ from $(h_t|\mathcal{F}_t,\theta)$, calculate the expectation $\hat{h}_{t+1}^{*(i)} = E(h_{t+1}|h_t^{(i)},\mathcal{F}_t)$ and

$$\pi_{it} = f(y_{t+1}|\hat{h}_{t+1}^{*(i)},\theta,\mathcal{F}_{t+1}), i = 1,\ldots,N. \tag{A1}$$

Sample N times with replacement the integers $1,\ldots,N$ with probabilities given by $\hat{\pi}_{it} = \pi_{it}/\sum_{i=1}^N \pi_{it}$. Denote the sampled indexes by $n_1,\ldots,n_N$ and associate these with particles $\{h_t^{(n_1)},\ldots,h_t^{(n_N)}\}$.

PF2. For each value n_i from Step PF1, sample the values $\{h_{t+1}^{*(1)},\ldots,h_{t+1}^{*(N)}\}$ using

$$h_{t+1}^{*(i)} = \phi_1 h_t^{(n_i)} + \sigma_1 u_{t+1}, i = 1,\ldots,N, \text{if } y_t \leq r, \text{or} \tag{A2}$$

$$h_{t+1}^{*(i)} = \phi_2 h_t^{(n_i)} + \sigma_2 u_{t+1}, i = 1,\ldots,N, \text{if } y_t > r, \tag{A3}$$

where $u_{t+1} \sim \mathcal{N}(0,1)$.

PF3. Calculate the weights of the values $\{h_{t+1}^{*(1)},\ldots,h_{t+1}^{*(N)}\}$ as

$$\pi_{it}^* = \frac{f(y_{t+1}|h_{t+1}^{*(i)},\theta,\mathcal{F}_{t+1})}{f(y_{t+1}|\hat{h}_{t+1}^{*(i)},\theta,\mathcal{F}_{t+1})}, \quad i = 1,\ldots,N, \tag{A4}$$

and using these weights resample the values $\{h_{t+1}^{*(1)},\ldots,h_{t+1}^{*(N)}\}$ N times with replacement to obtain a sample $\{h_{t+1}^{(1)},\ldots,h_{t+1}^{(N)}\}$ from the filter distribution of $(h_{t+1}|\mathcal{F}_{t+1},\theta)$. In our implementation we used $N = 3000$.

References

Akaike, Hirotugu. 1987. Factor Analysis and AIC. *Psychometrika* 52: 317–32. [CrossRef]

Bauwens, Luc, and David Veredas. 2004. The Stochastic Conditional Duration Model: A Latent Variable Model for the Analysis of Financial Durations. *Journal of Econometrics* 119: 381–482. [CrossRef]

Berg, Andreas, Renate Meyer, and Jun Yu. 2004. Deviance Information Criterion for Comparing Stochastic Volatility Models. *Journal of Business and Economic Statistics* 22: 107–20. [CrossRef]

Bowman, Adrian W., and Adelchi Azzalini. 1997. *Applied Smoothing Techniques for Data Analysis*. New York: Oxford University Press.

Celeux, Gilles, Florence Forbes, Christian P. Robert, and D. Mike Titterington. 2006. Deviance information criteria for missing data models. *Bayesian Analysis* 1: 651–74. [CrossRef]

Chan, Joshua C. C., and Angelia L. Grant. 2016. On the Observed-Data Deviance Information Criterion for Volatility Modeling. *Journal of Financial Econometrics* 14: 772–802. [CrossRef]

Chib, Siddhartha, Federico Nardari, and Neil Shephard. 2006. Analysis of High Dimensional Multivariate Stochastic Volatility Models. *Journal of Econometrics* 134: 341–71. [CrossRef]

De Luca, Giovanni, and Giampiero M. Gallo. 2004. Mixture Processes for Financial Intradaily Durations. *Studies in Nonlinear Dynamics & Econometrics* 8: 1–12.

De Luca, Giovanni, and Giampiero M. Gallo. 2009. Time-Varying Mixing Weights in Mixture Autoregressive Conditional Duration Models. *Econometric Reviews* 28: 102–20. [CrossRef]

Diebold, Francis X., Todd A. Gunther, and Anthony S. Tay. 1998. Evaluating Density Forecasts with Applications to Financial Risk Management. *International Economic Review* 39: 863–83. [CrossRef]

Feng, Dingan, George J. Jiang, and Peter X. K. Song. 2004. Stochastic Conditional Duration Models with "Leverage Effect" for Financial Transaction Data. *Journal of Financial Econometrics* 2: 390–421. [CrossRef]

Jacquier, E., N. G. Polson, and P. E. Rossi. 2004. Bayesian Analysis of Stochastic Volatility Models with Fat-tails and Correlated Errors. *Journal of Econometrics* 122: 185–212. [CrossRef]

Knight, John L., and Cathy Q. Ning. 2008. Estimation of the Stochastic Conditional Duration Model via Alternative Methods. *Econometrics Journal* 11: 573–92. [CrossRef]

Lopes, Hedibert Freitas, and Mike West. 2004. Bayesian Model Assessment in Factor Analysis. *Statistica Sinica* 14: 41–67.

Men, Zhongxian, Tony S. Wirjanto, and Adam W. Kolkiewicz. 2013. A Threshold Stochastic Conditional Duration Model for Financial Transaction Data. Working Paper. Rimini Centre for Economic Analysis, pp. 30–13. Available online: http://www.rcea.org/RePEc/pdf/wp30_13.pdf./ (accessed on 8 May 2019).

Men, Zhongxian, Tony S. Wirjanto, and Adam W. Kolkiewicz. 2014. A Threshold Stochastic Conditional Duration Model for Financial Transaction Data. Available online: https://ssrn.com/abstract=2241190 (accessed on 8 May 2019).

Men, Zhongxian, Adam W. Kolkiewicz, and Tony S. Wirjanto. 2015. Bayesian Analysis of Asymmetric Stochastic Conditional Duration Models. *Journal of Forecasting* 34: 36–56. [CrossRef]

Men, Zhongxian, Adam W. Kolkiewicz, and Tony S. Wirjanto. 2016a. Bayesian Inference of Asymmetric Stochastic Conditional Duration Models. *Journal of Statistical Computation and Simulation* 86: 1295–1319. [CrossRef]

Men, Zhongxian, Don McLeish, Adam W. Kolkiewicz, and Tony S. Wirjanto. 2016b. Comparison of Asymmetric Stochastic Volatility Models under Different Correlation Structures. *Journal of Applied Statistics* 44: 1350–68. [CrossRef]

Men, Zhongxian, Tony S. Wirjanto, and Adam W. Kolkiewicz. 2019. *Threshold Model for Financial Duration Data*. Unpblished Working Paper. Waterloo: University of Waterloo,

Mira, Antonietta, and Luke Tierney. 2002. Efficiency and Convergence Properties of Slice Samplers. *Scandinavian Journal of Statistics* 29: 1–12. [CrossRef]

Neal, Radford M. 2003. Slice Sampling. *The Annals of Statistics* 31: 705–67. [CrossRef]

Pitt, Michael K., and Neil Shephard. 1999. Filtering via Simulation: Auxiliary Particle Filters. *Journal of the American Statistical Association* 94: 590–99. [CrossRef]

Roberts, G. O., and J. S. Rosenthal. 1999. Convergence of Slice Sampler Markov Chains. *Journal of the Royal Statistical Society Series B (Statistical Methodology)* 61: 643–60. [CrossRef]

Schwarz, Gideon. 1978. Estimating the Dimension of a Model. *Annals of Statistics* 6: 461–64. [CrossRef]

Silverman, Bernard. W. 1986. *Density Estimation for Statistics and Data Analysis*. London: Chapman & Hall.

Spiegelhalter, David J., Nicola G. Best, Bradley P. Carlin, and Angelika van der Linde. 2002. Bayesian Measures of Model Complexity and Fit (with discussion). *Journal of the Royal Statistical Society, Series B* 64: 583–639. [CrossRef]

Xu, Dinghai, John Knight, and Tony S. Wirjanto. 2011. Asymmetric Stochastic Conditional Duration Model—A Mixture-of-Normal Approach. *Journal of Financial Econometrics* 9: 469–88. [CrossRef]

Yu, Jun, Zhenlin Yang, and Xibin Zhang. 2006. A class of nonlinear stochastic volatility models and its implication for pricing currency options. *Computational Statistics and Data Analysis* 51: 2218–31. [CrossRef]

Zhang, Xibin, and Maxwell L. King. 2008. Box-Cox Stochastic Volatility Models with Heavy-tails and Correlated Errors. *Journal of Empirical Finance* 15: 549–66. [CrossRef]

© 2019 by the authors. Licensee MDPI, Basel, Switzerland. This article is an open access article distributed under the terms and conditions of the Creative Commons Attribution (CC BY) license (http://creativecommons.org/licenses/by/4.0/).

Article

Bond Risk Premia and Restrictions on Risk Prices †

Constantino Hevia and Martin Sola *

Department of Economics, Universidad Torcuato Di Tella, Buenos Aires 1428, Argentina; chevia@utdt.edu
* Correspondence: msola@utdt.edu
† We thank Agustín Gutierrez for outstanding research assistance.

Received: 18 August 2018; Accepted: 30 September 2018; Published: 3 October 2018

Abstract: Researchers who estimate affine term structure models often impose overidentifying restrictions (restrictions on parameters beyond those necessary for identification) for a variety of reasons. While some of those restrictions seem to have minor effects on the extracted factors and some measures of risk premia, such as the forward risk premium, they may have a large impact on other measures of risk premia that is often ignored. In this paper, we analyze how apparently innocuous overidentifying restrictions imposed on affine term structure models can lead to large differences in several measures of risk premiums.

Keywords: bond risk premia; affine term structure models; risk prices

JEL Classification: E43; G12

1. Introduction

Understanding bond risk premia remains one of the central issues in empirical finance. Much of this literature uses non-arbitrage affine term structure models (ATSM) to extract risk premium components from bond prices. The purpose of this paper is to analyze how apparently innocuous overidentifying restrictions imposed on ATSMs can lead to large differences in several measures of bond risk premia.

Long-term interest rates can be decomposed into expectations of average future short rates and a risk premium that investors demand for bearing long-term risk (the term premium). Forward interest rates can be split into an expected future interest rate and a risk premium component (the forward premium). Those are the measures of risk premia on which the literature has mostly focused. However, there are other definitions of risk premia that are arguably equally or more relevant from the point of view of market participants. An investor who buys a long-term bond financed by borrowing at a shorter interest rate is exposed to a risk premium (the bond holding risk premium). The return for an investor that writes a forward contract to buy a bond in the future, but closes the contract before the settlement date is also exposed to a risk premium (the holding forward risk premium). The contribution of this paper is to investigate to what extent different restrictions imposed on ATSMs, which often imply modest differences in the term and forward premiums, could lead to large differences in the bond holding and holding forward risk premiums.[1]

Since often the extracted factors, forward premiums and term premiums look similar across restricted ATSM models, researchers tend to choose their preferred models based on the parsimony or forecasting ability of future yields. Yet, overidentifying restrictions unsupported by the data can have

---

[1] Although there is a large literature that has investigated the time variation in expected excess bond returns, it has mostly been done in the context of documenting the failure of the expectations hypothesis. This literature is too large to summarize here, but some widely-cited papers are Fama and Bliss (1987), Campbell and Shiller (1991) and Cochrane and Piazzesi (2005).

a large impact on other measures of risk premia, such as the bond holding risk premium or the holding forward risk premium, particularly at longer horizons. The reason is that small errors compound and get amplified as the holding horizon increases. Therefore, if the objective of the analysis is to understand bond risk premia, researchers should be very careful in not imposing overidentifying restrictions unsupported by the data even though the more parsimonious model may produce similar factors or predict better than the unrestricted model. Those restrictions can be harmful.

The main, and perhaps only, reason to consider affine models of bond prices is to understand risk premia. As noted by Joslin et al. (2011) and Duffee (2011), if the objective of the analysis is to fit a yield curve or to forecast bond yields, little is gained by imposing non-arbitrage restrictions. However, to understand risk premia, non-arbitrage restrictions are of fundamental importance. Unfortunately, there is no clear guidance in the literature on how to impose restrictions on risk prices. This issue has been overlooked in the literature, and this paper is an attempt to fill this gap. To our knowledge, Bauer (2018) is the only paper that studied restrictions on risk prices. He did so from a Bayesian perspective and only focusing on the term premium and excess bond returns. This paper is complementary to Bauer's in that we also analyze restrictions on risk prices, but from a different perspective. In particular, besides the term premium and excess returns, we analyze how restrictions on risk prices affect other measures of risk premia.

We first analyze to what extent usual restrictions imposed on risk prices or factor dynamics imply similar estimated term and forward premiums, but may lead to large differences in excess holding returns and holding forward premiums. The different concepts of risk premia are related among them, and small deviations in estimated forward premiums accumulate and can lead to large differences in expected excess returns of long-term bonds. For example, the bond holding risk premium is proportional to the forward risk premium, where the factor of proportionality increases with the maturity of the bond. Small differences in the estimated one-month forward risk premium, which may seem irrelevant if one focuses only on the forward premium, get amplified by about 120 times when we compute the risk premium associated with holding a 10-year bond financed by borrowing at the one-month interest rate.

Although the argument is general, we base our empirical investigation using the class of arbitrage-free Nelson and Siegel models. The work in Nelson and Siegel (1987) proposed a flexible, yet parsimonious functional form to model the cross-section of bond yields, which is widely used by practitioners and researchers.[2] The work in Christensen et al. (2011) showed that the Nelson and Siegel parametric representation of the yield curve can be made arbitrage-free by including a maturity-specific constant to the traditional Nelson and Siegel model. We use the Nelson and Siegel model because it is easy to estimate, and it is sufficiently general to make our point. We analyze several restrictions on risk prices and factor dynamics that are considered in the literature to analyze risk premia. Although the estimated factors are virtually identical across models, the estimates of risk premia that they produce often vary dramatically because the loadings on those factors change across models.

Using as a baseline the most general arbitrage-free Nelson and Siegel model, we evaluate to what extent the econometric rejections of the restrictions on risk prices are economically relevant (in terms of the estimated risk premia). For example, imposing a diagonal covariance matrix on the evolution of the risk factors is comfortably rejected using standard econometric tests, but the estimated risk premia are similar to those of the unrestricted model. On the other hand, imposing a diagonal matrix on the lagged values of the vector autoregression representation of the risk factors is also rejected, but with a much smaller likelihood ratio statistic. Yet, the estimated risk premiums in the restricted model are very different from those of the unrestricted model.

---

[2] For example, the arbitrage-free Nelson and Siegel model has been used in Christensen et al. (2010), Gürkaynak and Wright (2012), Christensen and Rudebusch (2015), among many others. The reference Diebold and Rudebusch (2012) is a textbook treatment of the dynamic Nelson and Siegel model.

The main practical implication of these results is that, to analyze and forecast risk premia, it is advisable to consider the just identified model. Imposing restrictions that are unsupported by the data may lead to large errors in estimated and forecast measures of risk premia. These observations also have policy implications: to the extent that fluctuations in risk premia have macroeconomic consequences, a policy maker that reacts to spurious changes in risk premia may choose suboptimal policies.

Using an ex-ante empirical analysis, Cochrane and Piazzesi (2005, 2008) argued that excess returns are a function of a single factor and built an affine term structure model imposing this assumption on risk prices. Other papers used likelihood ratios to test whether certain risk prices are zero, e.g., (Joslin et al. 2011). Some restrictions are often motivated on forecasting grounds. For example, Christensen et al. (2011) argued that imposing a diagonal structure on the factor dynamics outperforms a more general model in forecasting the yield curve. Even though this may be the correct procedure when the objective of the exercise is to forecast yields, it may be counterproductive when the objective is to understand risk premia. The reason is well known: even if the "true model" may contain many parameters, it may be outperformed out-of-sample by invalid reductions in the number of free parameters due to parameter uncertainty. When the issue is to understand the evolution and determinants of risk premia, restrictions that are not supported by the data using standard testing procedures may have damaging effects on the evaluation of risk compensation.[3]

The paper is organized as follows. Section 2 describes a general affine term structure model and the four different concepts of risk premia that we consider. Section 3 provides a Nelson–Siegel representation of the affine model that is used in the empirical section of the paper. Section 4 shows the estimation results, and Section 5 analyzes the impact of imposing restrictions on risk prices. Section 6 concludes, and the Appendix contains some proofs.

2. An Affine Model of Bond Prices

Let X_t denote a $k \times 1$ vector of unobserved risk factors that summarizes the information that investors use to price discount bonds. The risk factors evolve as a first order vector autoregression:

$$X_{t+1} = \mu + \Phi X_t + \Gamma u_{t+1}, \tag{1}$$

where Γ is lower triangular and $u_{t+1} \sim$ i.i.d. $N(0, I_k)$.

Investors price nominal cash flows using the one-period stochastic discount factor:

$$\ln M_{t+1} = -\delta_0 - \delta_1' X_t - \frac{1}{2}\Lambda_t'\Lambda_t - \Lambda_t' u_{t+1}. \tag{2}$$

The $k \times 1$ vector Λ_t, referred to as the market price of risk, represents the compensation that investors demand to face shocks to the state vector u_{t+1}. The market price of risk is an affine function of the factors:

$$\Lambda_t = \lambda_0 + \lambda_1 X_t, \tag{3}$$

where λ_0 is a $k \times 1$ vector and λ_1 is a $k \times k$ matrix of coefficients.

The principle of no-arbitrage implies that bond prices satisfy the recursion:

$$P_t^{(n)} = E_t(M_{t+1} P_{t+1}^{(n-1)}). \tag{4}$$

---

[3] One possible concern with the methodology used in this paper is that the 2008–2009 global crisis was characterized by significant asymmetries in the relation between yield spreads and macroeconomic factors (Evgenidis et al. 2017). Clearly, the affine model is unsuitable to study asymmetric responses to the business cycle. Yet, as shown in Hevia et al. (2015), it is possible to extend the affine model of bond yields to allow for discrete changes in the state of the economy using a Markov switching framework, thus capturing asymmetric responses during booms and recessions. The study of restrictions on risk prices in such a context; however, it is beyond the scope of this paper.

As shown by Ang and Piazzesi (2003), log bond prices, $p_t^{(n)} = \ln P_t^{(n)}$, are also an affine function of the risk factors:

$$p_t^{(n)} = A_n + B_n' X_t, \tag{5}$$

where the coefficients A_n and B_n satisfy the recursions:

$$B_{n+1} = \Phi^{*'} B_n - \delta_1, \tag{6}$$

$$A_{n+1} = A_n + \mu^{*'} B_n + \frac{1}{2} B_n' \Gamma \Gamma' B_n - \delta_0, \tag{7}$$

with $A_0 = 0$, $B_0 = 0$ and where μ^* and Φ^* are defined as:

$$\mu^* = \mu - \Gamma \lambda_0$$
$$\Phi^* = \Phi - \Gamma \lambda_1.$$

The continuously-compounded yield on an n-period discount bond is thus:

$$y_t^{(n)} = -p_t^{(n)}/n = a_n + b_n' X_t, \tag{8}$$

with $a_n = -A_n/n$ and $b_n = -B_n/n$.

We are also interested in the expected returns from holding forward contracts on discount bonds. Let $F_t^{(s,n-s)}$ denote the settlement price of a forward contract entered into at time t to buy an $(n-s)$-period discount bond at time $t+s$, with $n > s$. Since two different ways of moving one dollar from t to $t+n$ must cost the same, the law of one price implies:

$$P_t^{(n)} = P_t^{(s)} F_t^{(s,n-s)}. \tag{9}$$

The log forward rate $f_t^{(s,n-s)}$ is the implicit continuously-compounded interest rate of a forward contract with settlement price $F_t^{(s,n-s)}$,

$$F_t^{(s,n-s)} = e^{-(n-s)f_t^{(s,n-s)}}.$$

In terms of bond prices, the log forward rate $f_t^{(s,m-s)}$ is thus:

$$f_t^{(s,n-s)} = \frac{1}{n-s}[p_t^{(s)} - p_t^{(n)}]. \tag{10}$$

Therefore, the bond prices (5) imply that forward rates are affine functions of the factors,

$$f_t^{(s,n-s)} = a_{s,n}^f + b_{s,n}^{f'} X_t,$$

where $a_{s,n}^f = (A_s - A_n)/(n-s)$ and $b_{s,n}^f = (B_s - B_n)/(n-s)$.

In what follows, we use different concepts of returns, all of which are measured on a monthly basis. The h-period log holding return from buying an n-period discount bond at time t and selling it as an $(n-h)$-period bond at time $t+h$ is:

$$r_{b,t \to t+h}^{(n)} = \frac{1}{h}(p_{t+h}^{(n-h)} - p_t^{(n)}).$$

Denote the h-period log return from holding the n-period bond in excess of the yield of an h-period bond by:

$$rx_{b,t \to t+h}^{(n)} = r_{b,t \to t+h}^{(n)} - y_t^{(h)}.$$

Suppose now that, at time t, an investor enters into a forward contract to buy at time $t+s$ an $(n-s)$-period discount bond, but closes the position at time $t+h < t+s$. Closing the position is equivalent to writing a forward contract at time $t+h$ on an $(n-s)$-period bond with settlement date $t+s$. We define the h-period log holding return from holding the proposed forward as the difference between the log-forward rates associated with each of the contracts,

$$r_{f,t\to t+h}^{(s,n-s,h)} = f_t^{(s,n-s)} - f_{t+h}^{(s-h,n-s)}.$$

2.1. Bond Risk Premia

Our goal is to analyze how different restrictions on risk prices affect bond risk premia. However, what risk premium? Risk premia in bond markets are usually defined in terms of deviations from the expectational hypothesis. Four equivalent forms of the expectational hypothesis give rise to different, but related concepts of risk premia,[4]

1. The forward premium: The time t forward rate for loans between times $t+s$ and $t+n$ is the expected $(n-s)$-period yield at time $t+s$ plus a risk premium,

$$f_t^{(s,n-s)} = E_t\left[y_{t+s}^{(n-s)}\right] + \pi_{f,t}^{(s,n-s)}. \qquad (11)$$

2. The bond holding risk premium: The expected h-period log holding return of an n-period bond measured on a monthly rate is the yield of an h-period bond plus a risk premium:

$$E_t[r_{b,t\to t+h}^{(n)}] = y_t^{(h)} + \pi_{hb,t}^{(n,h)}. \qquad (12)$$

3. The term premium: The n-period yield is the average of expected one-period yields plus a risk premium,

$$y_t^{(n)} = \frac{1}{n}\left(\sum_{j=0}^{n-1} E_t y_{t+j}^{(1)}\right) + \pi_{y,t}^{(n)}. \qquad (13)$$

4. The holding forward risk premium: Since buying or writing a forward contract costs zero, any expected return from holding a forward contract is a risk premium,

$$E_t\left[r_{f,t\to t+h}^{(s,n-s,h)}\right] = \pi_{hf,t}^{(s,n-s,h)}, \qquad (14)$$

for all $h, s > h$, and $n > s+h$.

The four definitions of risk premia are equivalent in the sense that if one of them is zero or constant, so are the other three (see the Appendix A). For our purposes, it is useful to express the risk premiums $\pi_{y,t}^{(n)}$, $\pi_{hb,t}^{(n,h)}$ and $\pi_{hf,t}^{(s,n-s,h)}$ as a function of the forward premium $\pi_{f,t}^{(j,1)}$,

$$\pi_{y,t}^{(n)} = \frac{1}{n}\sum_{j=1}^{h} \pi_{f,t}^{(j,1)},$$

$$\pi_{hf,t}^{(s,n-s,h)} = \pi_{f,t}^{(s,n-s)} - E_t\left[\pi_{f,t+h}^{(s-h,n-s)}\right],$$

$$\pi_{hb,t}^{(n,h)} = \frac{n-h}{h}\pi_{f,t}^{(h,n-h)}.$$

---

[4] The work in Cochrane and Piazzesi (2008) considered the definitions of Risk Premia 1 through 3 below. We add the fourth, which states that all expected log holding forward returns are risk premia.

In particular, the bond holding risk premium $\pi_{hb,t}^{(n,h)}$ is proportional to the forward premium $\pi_{f,t}^{(h,n-h)}$, where the factor of proportionality increases with the maturity n of the bond for a given holding period h. Small differences in the estimated forward premium due to invalid parameter restrictions, which may seem irrelevant to the naked eye, accumulate and may drive large and economically meaningful differences in the bond holding risk premium. For example, a 10 basis point difference in the one-month forward premium ($h = 1$) can lead to differences as large as 12 percentage points in the estimated one-month bond holding risk premium associated with holding a 10-year bond ($n = 120$) financed by borrowing at the one-month rate. In this case, the factor of proportionality is $(n-h)/h = 119$.

The closed form expressions of the risk premiums using the structure of the affine model are the following,

$$\pi_{f,t}^{(h,n-h)} = J_f^{(h,n-h)} + \frac{B'_{n-s}}{n-s} \left[\mu^{(s-1)} - \mu^{*(s-1)} + (\Phi^s - \Phi^{*s}) X_t \right], \quad (15)$$

$$\pi_{hb,t}^{(n,h)} = J_{hb}^{(n,h)} + \frac{B'_{n-h}}{h} \left[\mu^{(h-1)} - \mu^{*(h-1)} + \left(\Phi^h - \Phi^{*h} \right) X_t \right], \quad (16)$$

$$\pi_{y,t}^{(n)} = J_y^{(n)} + \frac{B'_1}{n} \sum_{j=0}^{n-1} \left[\mu^{(j-1)} - \mu^{*(j-1)} + \left(\Phi^j - \Phi^{*j} \right) X_t \right], \quad (17)$$

$$\pi_{hf,t}^{(s,n-s,h)} = J_{hf}^{(s,n-s,h)} + \frac{B'_{n-h} - B'_{s-h}}{n-s} \left[\mu^{(h-1)} - \mu^{*(h-1)} + \left(\Phi^h - \Phi^{*h} \right) X_t \right], \quad (18)$$

where we define $\mu^{(j)} = (I + \Phi + \Phi^2 + ... + \Phi^j) \mu$; $\mu^{*(j)} = (I + \Phi^* + \Phi^{*2} + ... + \Phi^{*j}) \mu^*$; and $J_f^{(h,n-h)}$, $J_{hb}^{(n,h)}$, $J_y^{(n)}$ and $J_{hf}^{(s,n-s,h)}$ are time invariant Jensen inequality terms.[5] Note that with risk neutrality (when the physical and risk neutral measure coincide, $\Phi = \Phi^*$), risk premia collapse to the usual Jensen inequality terms.

Even though different restrictions on the parameters of the affine model usually deliver similar estimated risk factors X_t, the evolution of risk premia may vary across these models as long as the matrices Φ and Φ^* are different. Furthermore, for a given holding period h, the bond holding risk premium $\pi_{hb,t}^{(n,h)}$ is more sensitive to differences between Φ and Φ^* than the forward risk premium the longer is the maturity of the bond n. For example, when $h = 1$, the loading of the holding bond risk premia on X_t is $B'_{n-1}(\Phi - \Phi^*)$, while that of the forward premium is $B'_{n-1}(\Phi - \Phi^*)/(n-1)$. Thus, for the bond with the longest maturity in our sample, $n = 120$, the loading of the forward premium on X_t is almost 120 times smaller than that of the bond holding risk premium. Therefore, small differences in the estimated coefficients may lead to very different estimates of bond holding risk premiums for long maturity bonds even though the forward premiums may look similar.[6]

---

[5] The Jensen inequality terms are given by:

$$J_f^{(h,n-h)} = \sum_{j=0}^{s-1} \frac{1}{n-s} \left(B'_j \frac{\Gamma\Gamma'}{2} B_j - B'_{n-s+j} \frac{\Gamma\Gamma'}{2} B_{n-s+j} \right)$$

$$J_{hb}^{(n,h)} = \sum_{j=0}^{h-1} \frac{1}{h} \left(B'_j \frac{\Gamma\Gamma'}{2} B_j - B'_{n-h+j} \frac{\Gamma\Gamma'}{2} B_{n-h+j} \right)$$

$$J_y^{(n)} = -\frac{1}{n} \sum_{j=1}^{n-1} B'_j \frac{\Gamma\Gamma'}{2} B_j$$

$$J_{hf}^{(s,n-s,h)} = \sum_{i=0}^{n-s-1} \frac{1}{n-s} \left(B'_{s-h+i} \frac{\Gamma\Gamma'}{2} B_{s-h+i} - B'_{s+i} \frac{\Gamma\Gamma'}{2} B_{s+i} \right).$$

Proving Expressions (15) through (18) is not particularly difficult, but it is lengthy and tedious. We provide detailed proofs upon request.

[6] The result is reversed if $n/h < h$ (so that $n - h < h$).

3. A Nelson–Siegel Representation of the Affine Model

General unrestricted affine models with unobserved factors are unidentified because the factors can be re-scaled, rotated and translated without affecting the empirical implications of the model. There are several representations of affine models that are identified. We follow Christensen et al. (2011) and use a representation of the arbitrage-free model in which the yield curve adopts an augmented Nelson–Siegel parametrization of the cross-section of bond yields. As noted by Christensen et al. (2011) and Hamilton and Wu (2012), the Nelson–Siegel model is a convenient representation that is econometrically identified (subject to minor identification restrictions) and that is easy to estimate using the method of maximum likelihood. This representation of the ATSM is sufficiently general to make our point that imposing invalid overidentifying restrictions on risk prices, which may look irrelevant from the point of view of some measures of risk premiums, could lead to large differences in other measures of risk premia.

The dynamic Nelson–Siegel model is a three-factor model that fits the cross-section and time series of yield remarkably well (Diebold and Li 2006). Yet, in its traditional representation, the Nelson–Siegel model does not rule out arbitrage opportunities. The work in Christensen et al. (2011) showed that one can augment the Nelson–Siegel model with a maturity-specific constant to render it arbitrage-free. In particular, the yield $y_t^{(n)}$ at any time t as a function of the maturity of the bond n is parametrized as:

$$y_t^{(n)} = a_n + \xi_{1t} + \left(\frac{1-e^{-\theta n}}{\theta n}\right)\xi_{2t} + \left(\frac{1-e^{-\theta n}}{\theta n} - e^{-\theta n}\right)\xi_{3t}, \tag{19}$$

where $(\xi_{1t}, \xi_{2t}, \xi_{3t})'$ are latent variables interpreted as level, slope and curvature factors; and the parameter θ determines the shape of the loadings on the factors.

In the traditional Nelson–Siegel model, $a_n = 0$ for all n. In the arbitrage-free Nelson–Siegel model, the vector of risk factors is $X_t = [\xi_{1t}, \xi_{2t}, \xi_{3t}]'$, and the factor loadings and constant a_n are chosen to satisfy the recursions (6) and (7). As shown by Christensen et al. (2011) in a continuous time setting, rendering the Nelson–Siegel model arbitrage-free requires imposing restrictions on the risk-neutral evolution of the state variables, $X_{t+1} = \mu^* + \Phi^* X_t + \Gamma \eta_{t+1}^*$, where $\mu^* = \mu - \Gamma \lambda_0$, $\Phi^* = \Phi - \Gamma \lambda_1$ and $\eta_{t+1}^* \sim N(0, I)$. The conditions are as follows: consider any 3×1 vector μ^* and a risk-neutral matrix on lagged values Φ^* defined as:

$$\Phi^* = \begin{bmatrix} 1 & 0 & 0 \\ 0 & e^{-\theta} & \theta e^{-\theta} \\ 0 & 0 & e^{-\theta} \end{bmatrix}, \tag{20}$$

where $\theta > 0$. Furthermore, let δ_0 be any number and $\delta_1' = \left[1, \frac{1-e^{-\theta}}{\theta}, \frac{1-e^{-\theta}}{\theta} - e^{-\theta}\right]$. Using these assumptions, the recursions (6) imply:

$$b_n = -B_n/n = \left[1, \frac{1-e^{-\theta n}}{\theta n}, \frac{1-e^{-\theta n}}{\theta n} - e^{-\theta n}\right]', \tag{21}$$

precisely the factor loadings in the Nelson–Siegel representation (19). The maturity-specific constant a_n is set to satisfy (7). Given these values, the parameters of the market price of risk λ_0 and λ_1 are given by $\lambda_0 = \Gamma^{-1}(\mu - \mu^*)$ and $\lambda_1 = \Gamma^{-1}(\Phi - \Phi^*)$.

Identification of the Nelson–Siegel model requires imposing simple restrictions on the parameter δ_0 and the risk-neutral intercept μ^*. As in Dai and Singleton (2000), we set $\delta_0 = 0$. Furthermore, since in the recursion (7), $\mu^{*\prime} B_n$ is a scalar, we can identify a single parameter in μ^*. We set $\mu^{*\prime} = [\mu_1^*, 0, 0]$ and estimate μ_1^* as a free parameter along with the other parameters of the model.

Let $\mathcal{N} > 3$ denote the set of yield maturities observed by the econometrician. Since there are more observed maturities than factors, the model is stochastically singular. One possibility is to assume that three yields, or three linear combinations of yields, are perfectly priced by the model and then to impose classical measurement errors into the remaining yields (see (Hamilton and Wu 2012; Joslin et al. 2011) among others). In contrast, the Nelson–Siegel literature, e.g., (Christensen et al. 2011), assumes that all yields are measured with error, which is an appealing assumption to make since which yields are perfectly priced or measured without error is arbitrary. We follow the latter approach and assume that all yields are observed with uncorrelated measurement errors. Thus, for each yield $y_t^{(n)}$ with $n \in \mathcal{N}$, the arbitrage-free Nelson–Siegel model is represented by the following system of equations:

$$y_t^{(n)} = a_n + \xi_{1t} + \frac{1-e^{-\theta n}}{\theta n}\xi_{2t} + \left(\frac{1-e^{-\theta n}}{\theta n} - e^{-\theta n}\right)\xi_{3t} + v_t^{(n)}, \qquad (22)$$

$$X_{t+1} = \mu + \Phi X_t + \Gamma \eta_{t+1}, \qquad (23)$$

where the state vector $X_t = [\xi_{1t}, \xi_{2t}, \xi_{3t}]'$ is unobserved, the intercept a_n satisfies the recursion (7) and $v_t^{(n)} \sim$ i.i.d. $N(0, \sigma_n^2)$.

Since the risk factors are unobserved, and it is not possible to recover X_t from the observed yields, we use the Kalman filter to evaluate the prediction-error decomposition of the likelihood function. In the unrestricted Nelson–Siegel model, we maximize the log-likelihood function numerically choosing the free parameters μ, Φ, Γ, μ_1^*, θ and σ_n^2 for $n \in \mathcal{N}$. In restricted versions of the Nelson–Siegel model, we impose the appropriate restrictions on the free parameters.

4. Estimation Results

We used data on U.S. Treasury yields of fixed maturities of 3, 6, 12, 24, 36, 48, 60, 72, 84, 96, 108 and 120 months from January 1985 through December 2013. The shortest yield is the three-month treasury constant maturity rate obtained from the Federal Reserve Bank of St. Louis (Series DGS3MO). The remaining yields are from Cochrane (2015), who updated the data in Joslin et al. (2011) until December 2013.

We begin by estimating the unrestricted unobserved factor model imposing the arbitrage-free Nelson–Siegel parametrization discussed above. Using this model as a benchmark, we imposed restrictions commonly used in the literature on the parameters that determined the evolution of the risk factors under the physical measure. Those restrictions were often motivated in terms of forecasting performance or simplicity grounds. In particular, in the baseline case, we did not restrict any of the parameters of the model besides the aforementioned identifying restrictions. Since all the restricted models that we consider are nested, we next tested whether the restrictions were supported by the data using likelihood-ratio tests along with information criteria for in-sample comparisons. More importantly, we assessed the economic relevance of the restrictions by investigating their impact on estimated risk premia.

Table 1 shows the estimation results of the general model along with the log-likelihood value, information criteria and estimated parameter θ of the different restricted models. The general model corresponds to the Nelson–Siegel parametrization without imposing any restriction on the evolution of the state variables. The restricted models impose different constraints on the state equation: we considered a model with a diagonal Φ matrix, as in Christensen et al. (2011); a model with a diagonal Γ matrix, as in Gürkaynak and Wright (2012); and a model in which only shocks that affect the market price of level risk $\Lambda_{1,t}$ (the first element of Λ_t) are priced, in the spirit of Cochrane and Piazzesi (2005, 2008). Under this last parametrization, the matrix λ_1 had non-zeros only in the first row, and only the first element of the vector λ_0 was non-zero.[7]

---

[7] Since Cochrane and Piazzesi (2005, 2008) developed a four-factor model (level, slope, curvature factors plus a return forecasting) factor, their results and ours are not exactly comparable. Yet, after some pre-estimation analysis, they argued that only shocks to their forecasting factor affected the market price of level risk $\Lambda_{1,t}$. Since the forecasting factor captures information of the level, slope and curvature of the yield curve (and possibly some other information), we captured their restrictions on risk prices by allowing shocks to the three factors to affect only the market price of level risk and set all the other elements of the matrix λ_1 (the second and third rows) to zero.

Table 1. Estimates of arbitrage-free Nelson and Siegel models.

Unrestricted Arbitrage-Free Nelson and Siegel Model

Parameters of the VAR(1) process for the yield curve factors $(\xi_{1t}, \xi_{2t}, \xi_{3t})$

μ ($\times 1000$) Φ Γ ($\times 1000$)

$$\begin{bmatrix} 0.1654 \\ (0.0630) \\ 0.0079 \\ (0.0716) \\ -0.4064 \\ (0.1633) \end{bmatrix} \quad \begin{bmatrix} 0.967 & -0.006 & 0.023 \\ (0.014) & (0.015) & (0.011) \\ -0.016 & 0.960 & 0.027 \\ (0.016) & (0.016) & (0.013) \\ 0.096 & 0.055 & 0.901 \\ (0.033) & (0.034) & (0.028) \end{bmatrix} \quad \begin{bmatrix} 0.274 & 0 & 0 \\ (0.013) & & \\ -0.247 & 0.200 & 0 \\ (0.016) & (0.008) & \\ -0.120 & 0.035 & 0.678 \\ (0.045) & (0.038) & (0.029) \end{bmatrix}$$

Other parameters

$\theta = 0.0403\,(0.001)$ $\mu_1^Q\,(\times 1000) = 0.0094\,(0.0009)$

Log-likelihood = 33,225.3   Akaike = $-66,386.5$ Schwarz = $-66,263.2$

Model with diagonal Φ matrix
Log-likelihood = 33,200.7   Akaike = $-66,349.4$ Schwarz = $-66,249.2$ $\theta = 0.0402$
LR statistic = 49.14   p-value = 0.000

Model with diagonal Γ matrix
Log-likelihood = 3,084.4   Akaike = $-66,110.9$ Schwarz = $-65,999.2$ $\theta = 0.0407$
LR statistic = 281.61   p-value = 0.000

Model with only market price of level risk
Log-likelihood = 33,185.0   Akaike = $-66,322.0$ Schwarz = $-66,229.6$ $\theta = 0.0401$
LR statistic = 80.47   p-value = 0.000

The likelihood ratio tests and the information criteria suggested that none of the models were valid restrictions of the general model. Yet, the estimated risk factors X_t and the parameter θ, which governed the evolution of the risk factors under the risk-neutral measure, were virtually the same in all models (Figure 1 and Table 1). Since bond prices depend only on the parameters of the risk neutral measure (determined only by θ and μ_1^* in the Nelson–Siegel parametrization), the four models provided a virtually identical characterization of the cross-section of bond yields. Risk premiums, however, depend on the evolution of the risk factors under the physical measure, which did vary in the different models. Alternatively, the estimated values of the parameters λ_0 and λ_1, displayed in Table 2, differed substantially across models, often even with different signs.

Table 2. Estimated market prices of risk parameters.

Unrestricted model				Diagonal Φ model			
$\Gamma\lambda_0(\times 1000)$	$\Gamma\lambda_1$			$\Gamma\lambda_0(\times 1000)$	$\Gamma\lambda_1$		
$\begin{bmatrix} 0.156 \\ 0.008 \\ -0.406 \end{bmatrix}$	$\begin{bmatrix} -0.0333 \\ -0.0159 \\ 0.0958 \end{bmatrix}$	$\begin{matrix} -0.0063 \\ -0.0004 \\ 0.0553 \end{matrix}$	$\begin{matrix} 0.0233 \\ -0.0119 \\ -0.0592 \end{matrix}$	$\begin{bmatrix} 0.010 \\ -0.034 \\ -0.033 \end{bmatrix}$	$\begin{bmatrix} -0.0030 \\ 0 \\ 0 \end{bmatrix}$	$\begin{matrix} 0 \\ 0.0285 \\ 0 \end{matrix}$	$\begin{matrix} 0 \\ -0.0386 \\ -0.0064 \end{matrix}$
Diagonal Γ model				Only market price of level risk			
$\Gamma\lambda_0(\times 1000)$	$\Gamma\lambda_1$			$\Gamma\lambda_0(\times 1000)$	$\Gamma\lambda_1$		
$\begin{bmatrix} 0.091 \\ 0.068 \\ -0.359 \end{bmatrix}$	$\begin{bmatrix} -0.0184 \\ -0.0266 \\ 0.0841 \end{bmatrix}$	$\begin{matrix} 0.0009 \\ -0.0066 \\ 0.0628 \end{matrix}$	$\begin{matrix} 0.0116 \\ -0.0001 \\ -0.0617 \end{matrix}$	$\begin{bmatrix} 0.135 \\ -0.115 \\ -0.062 \end{bmatrix}$	$\begin{bmatrix} -0.0273 \\ 0.0233 \\ 0.0125 \end{bmatrix}$	$\begin{matrix} 0.0009 \\ -0.0008 \\ -0.0004 \end{matrix}$	$\begin{matrix} 0.0150 \\ -0.0128 \\ -0.0068 \end{matrix}$

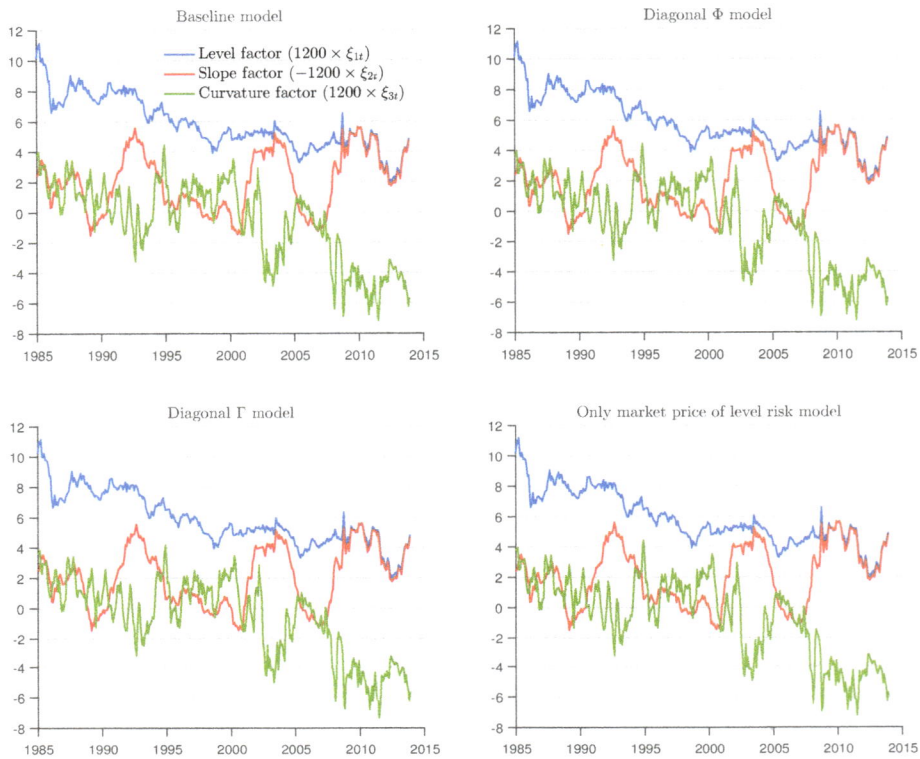

Figure 1. Estimated unobserved factors and empirical level, slope and curvature.

5. Risk Premia and Restrictions on Risk Prices

In this section, we analyze how imposing different restrictions on the general model affects the four measures of risk premium discussed above.

5.1. The Forward Risk Premium

The forward risk premium can be computed from forecasts of the future yield curve (Equation (11)). To the extent that these forecasts are similar to those obtained from reduced form vector autoregression, the forward risk premium would be almost model independent (see Joslin et al. 2011, Hamilton and Wu 2012 and Duffee (2011)).

In Figure 2, we show the estimated forward premiums in the four versions of the model. The upper left panel displays the premium associated with opening a forward contract with a settlement date one year ahead ($s = 1$ using our notation) on a bond that matures in one year ($n - s = 1$). In general, the notation s-for-$(n - s)$ forward represents the premium associated with opening a forward contract with settlement date s years ahead on a bond that matures in $n - s$ years. Except for the factor model in which only the market price of level risk matters, the forward premium is roughly similar across models, particularly for longer term bonds. Although not shown in the figure, all forward premiums move almost one-to-one with the slope factor ξ_{2t} of the yield curve. In the following subsections, we show how these small differences in the forward premium across models get amplified when considering other definitions of risk premium.

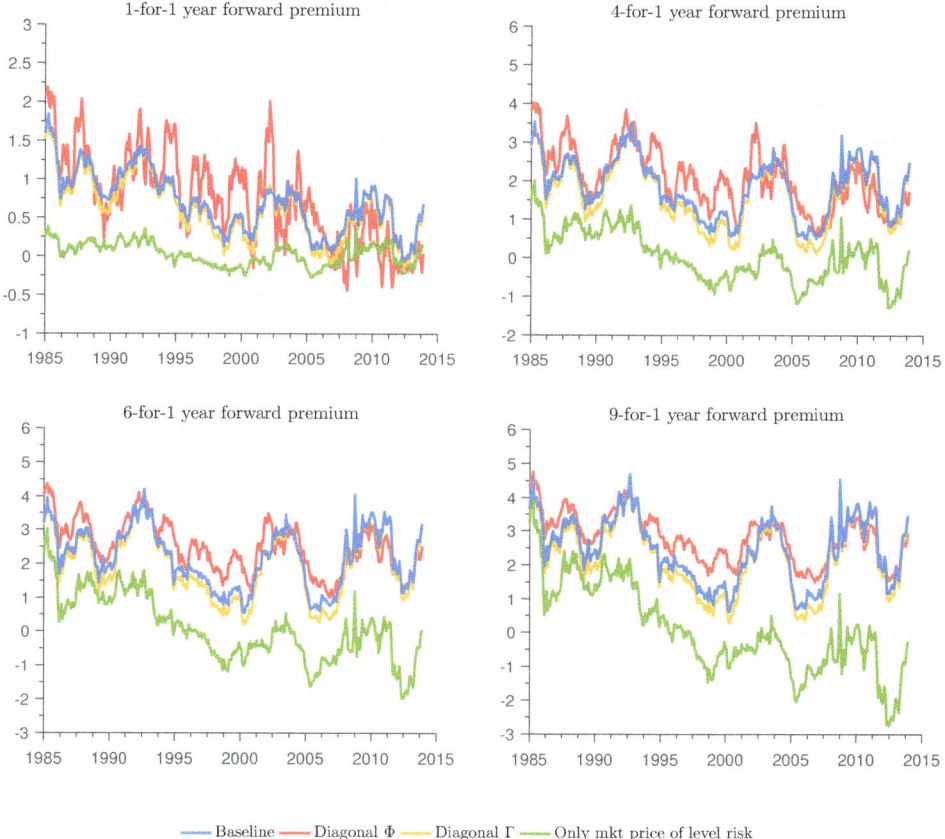

Figure 2. Forward premium: different models and bonds.

5.2. The Bond Holding Risk Premium

Given that the risk factors are virtually identical in the four models, differences in the estimated risk premiums come from differences in the factor loadings. Therefore, looking at factor loadings is a natural way to evaluate how sound the overidentifying restrictions are, we use Equation (16) to analyze those factor loadings in the case of the bond holding risk premium for different bond maturities and holding periods. Results are expressed in annualized percentage terms.

The three plots on the left panel of Figure 3 show the loadings on the factors ($\xi_{1t}, \xi_{2t}, \xi_{3t}$), respectively, of the one-month bond holding risk premium as a function the maturity of the bond (buy and hold for one month an n period bond), for the four different models. The right panel displays the same loadings, but holding the position for one year.

The restrictions imposed on the models are economically relevant. In the baseline (unrestricted) model, and for both holding periods, the importance of the level factor ξ_{1t} increases with the maturity of the bond, while that of the slope factor ξ_{2t} is maximized (in absolute value) at about 84 months (seven years) when holding the bond for one month and is always decreasing in maturity when holding the bond for one year. The loading on the curvature factor ξ_{3t} is almost zero for bonds with maturities up to 40 months and then becomes negative and decreasing for bonds of longer maturities. In contrast, the model with a diagonal Φ matrix works quite differently: the contribution of the level factor ξ_{1t} also increases (almost linearly) with the maturity of the bond, but by a much smaller rate than in the baseline model. On the other hand, the contribution of the curvature factor ξ_{3t} is now positive and increasing with the maturity of the bond for both holding periods. Those differences are economically relevant: a unit increase in the level factor leads to an increase in the one-month bond premium of over two percentage points for a 10-year bond in the baseline model, but of less than 0.5 percentage points in the diagonal Φ model.

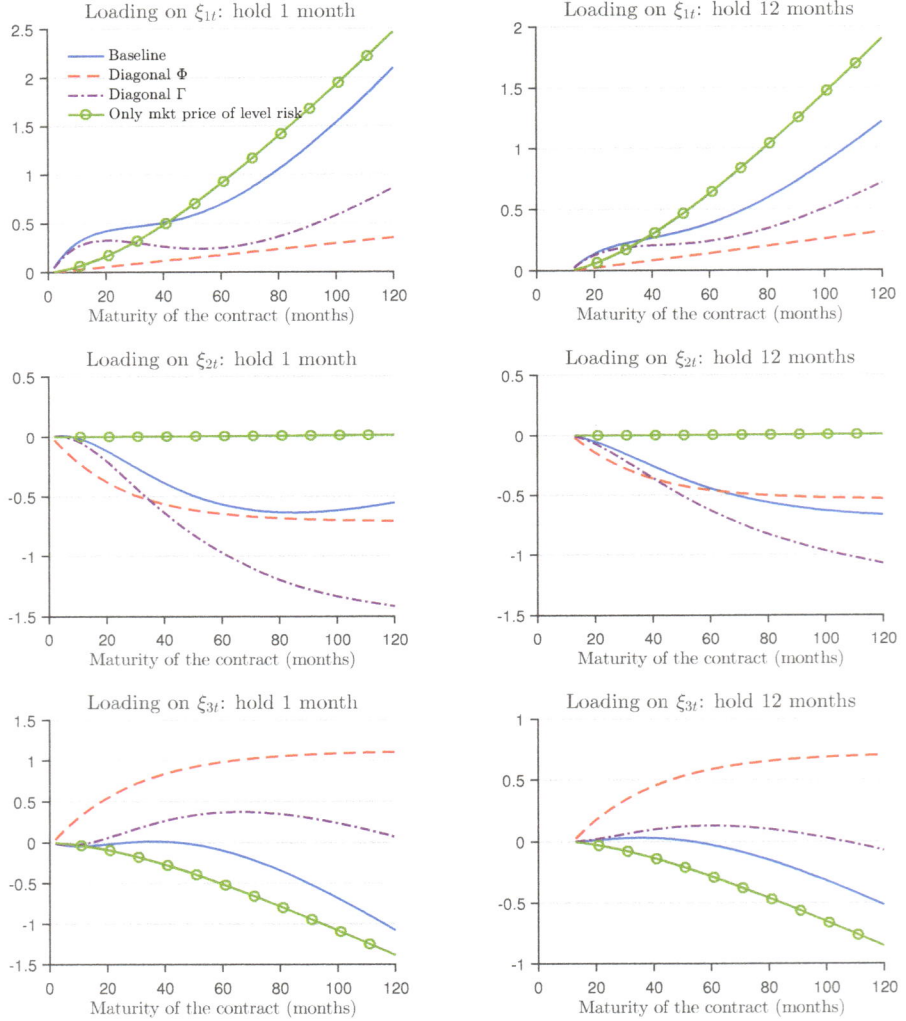

Figure 3. Loadings on factors: one-month and one-year excess holding returns.

Perhaps surprisingly, the factor loadings of the model with a diagonal Γ matrix are quite different from those of the baseline model. In the diagonal Γ model, the loading on the level factor is half of that in the baseline model, the loading on the slope factor is twice as large and the loading on the curvature factor is mostly positive, while that in the baseline model is mostly negative. Yet, as we show below, those differences in the loadings tend to cancel out, and the evolution of the bond holding risk premium in the restricted model is similar to that in the baseline model.

The factor loadings of the model with only the market price of level risk (only the first row of λ_1 is non-zero) are very different from those of the baseline model. The influence of the slope factor is virtually zero for all bond maturities and holding periods. This prediction is at odds with those of the other models, in which the slope factor has a significant impact on all measures of risk premia. Interestingly, for this restricted model, the importance of the level factor when holding long-term bonds is not only very similar to that in the baseline model, but also dominates quantitatively the influence of the other factors. This observation suggests that the evolution of the bond holding risk premium will be very different from that of the baseline model when considering short maturity bonds, but similar when considering longer term bonds.

We next evaluate the evolution over time of the bond holding risk premium derived from the four models. If a restricted model is statistically rejected, but it generates an estimated risk premium that is similar to that in the baseline model, one could claim that the statistical rejection is not economically relevant.[8] On the other hand, when a restricted model produces a risk premium that is substantially different from that in the baseline model, we say that the statistical rejection also has economic relevance.

Figure 4 shows one-month bond holding excess returns for 1-year, 5-year, 7-year and 10-year bonds for the different models. Consistent with the information in Figure 3, which shows that the loadings on the level and slope factors increase in absolute value with the maturity of the bond, we observe that the risk premia of long maturity bonds are substantially more volatile than those of shorter maturity bonds. The excess return from holding one-year bonds reaches a peak of around two percentage points, while those of the 5-, 7- and 10-year bonds are around six and 12 percentage points, respectively. Comparing this results with those presented in Figure 1, it is apparent that excess holding returns move closely with the slope factor, especially for longer maturity bonds.

The model with a diagonal Γ matrix is the one that displays the smaller differences in the bond holding risk premium relative to the baseline model: the differences are centered on zero, and their magnitudes are smaller than those of the other restricted models. Which model differs the most relative to the baseline, however, depends on the maturity of the bond. For the one-year bond, the model with only the market price of level risk is, by far, the most different from the baseline, with differences reaching 100 percentage points of excess holding returns. This model, however, delivers risk premiums similar to those of the baseline model for long-term bonds. As Figure 3 shows, in this model, the level factor dominates the contribution of the other two factors, and in that sense, it is similar to the baseline model. The second most different model is that with a diagonal Φ matrix. This model often produces differences of about 200 percentage points larger or smaller relative to the baseline (for example, in mid-2002).

---

[8] Of course, those differences may be relevant in other dimensions such as forecasts of future yields. Nevertheless, models with good forecasting performance, such as the diagonal Φ model (Christensen et al. 2011), may produce poor estimates of risk premia in sample.

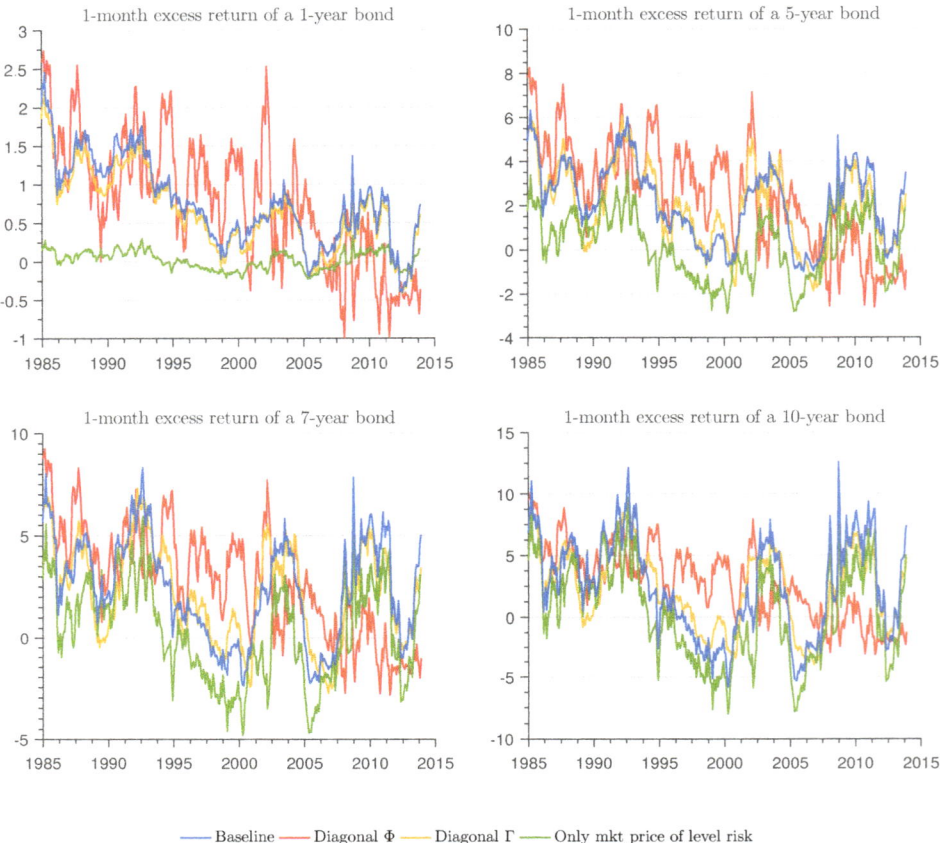

Figure 4. One-month expected excess returns: different models and bonds.

Figure 5 displays the 6-month, 1-year, 5-year and 7-year excess returns from holding a 10-year bond. A pattern that emerges from the figure is that the risk premiums associated with longer maturity bonds are highly contemporaneously correlated with the slope factor ξ_{2t} (see Figure 1). As with the one-month excess holding returns, the model that is closest to the baseline is that with a diagonal Γ matrix.

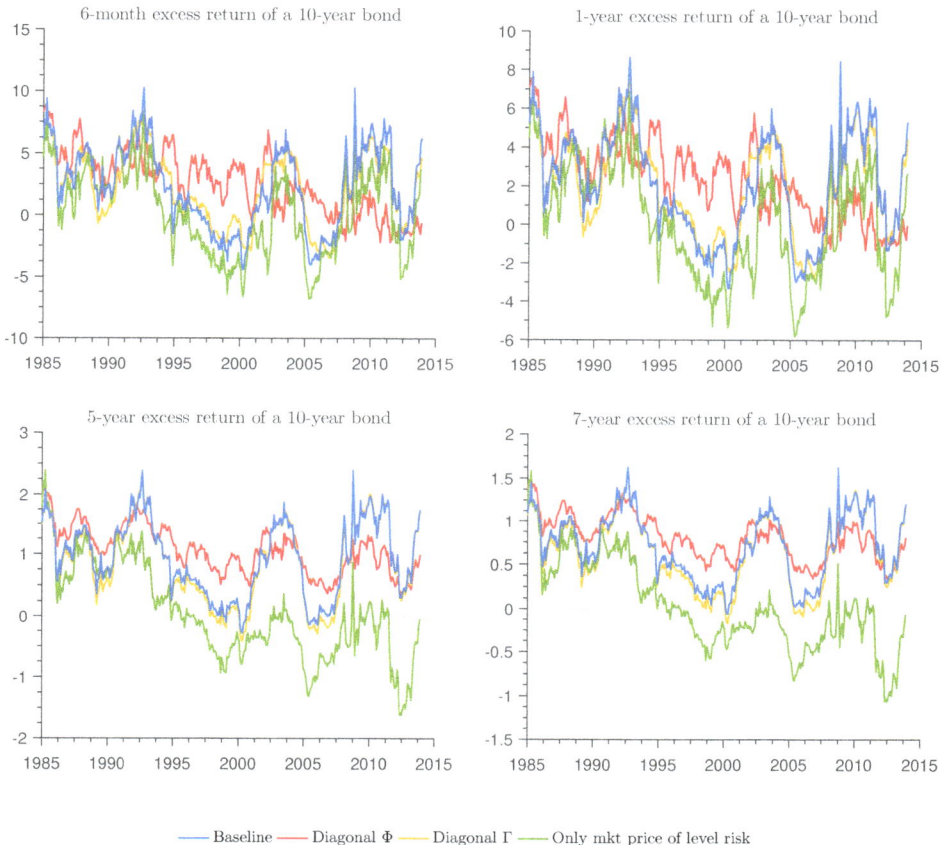

Figure 5. Expected returns on a 10-year bond: different models and holding periods.

5.3. The Term Premium

The n-period term premium is difference between the yield on an n-period zero coupon bond and the average of expected future short rates, where the average is taken between today and $n-1$ periods ahead. Figure 6 shows, in the different panels, the evolution of the term premium using 1-year, 4-year, 6-year and 10-year bonds for the baseline and the restricted models. Two messages follow from this plot. First, the term premium moves closely with the slope factor (ξ_{2t}) especially for long maturity bonds. Second, the violations of the expectational hypothesis, as represented by the volatility of the term premium, become more apparent the longer the bond is under consideration. In particular, while the 10-year term premium can be as high as four percentage points and very volatile, the one-year term premium is smaller and less volatile, although it is far from constant and displays a decreasing trend over time. As for restrictions on risk prices, we still find that the model with a diagonal Γ matrix produces the term premium that is closest to the baseline.

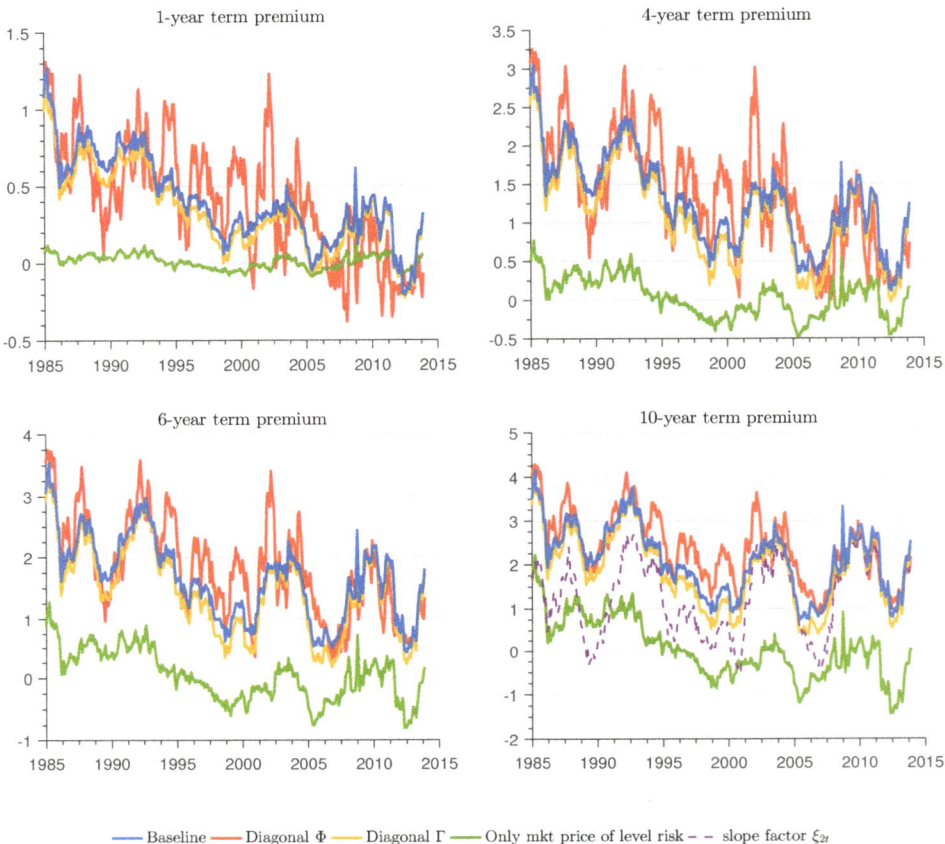

Figure 6. Term premium: different models and bonds.

5.4. The Holding Futures Risk Premium

Here, we consider the premium from holding a forward contract for a number of periods and selling it before the settlement date. Figure 7 displays the factor loadings of the one-month (left panels) and one-year (right panels) holding forward risk premium as a function of the settlement date, for the different models. As in the case of the bond holding return, the shape of the loadings differ substantially depending on the restrictions that we impose on the models. While the loadings on the level and slope factors (ξ_{1t} and ξ_{2t}) have a U-shape in the baseline model, the loading on the level factor in the model with a diagonal Γ matrix is flat and close to zero, and the loading on the slope factor is negative and increases towards zero in the model with a diagonal Φ matrix. Likewise, in the model with only market price of level risk, the loading on the level factor increases with the settlement date, and that on the slope factor is virtually zero.

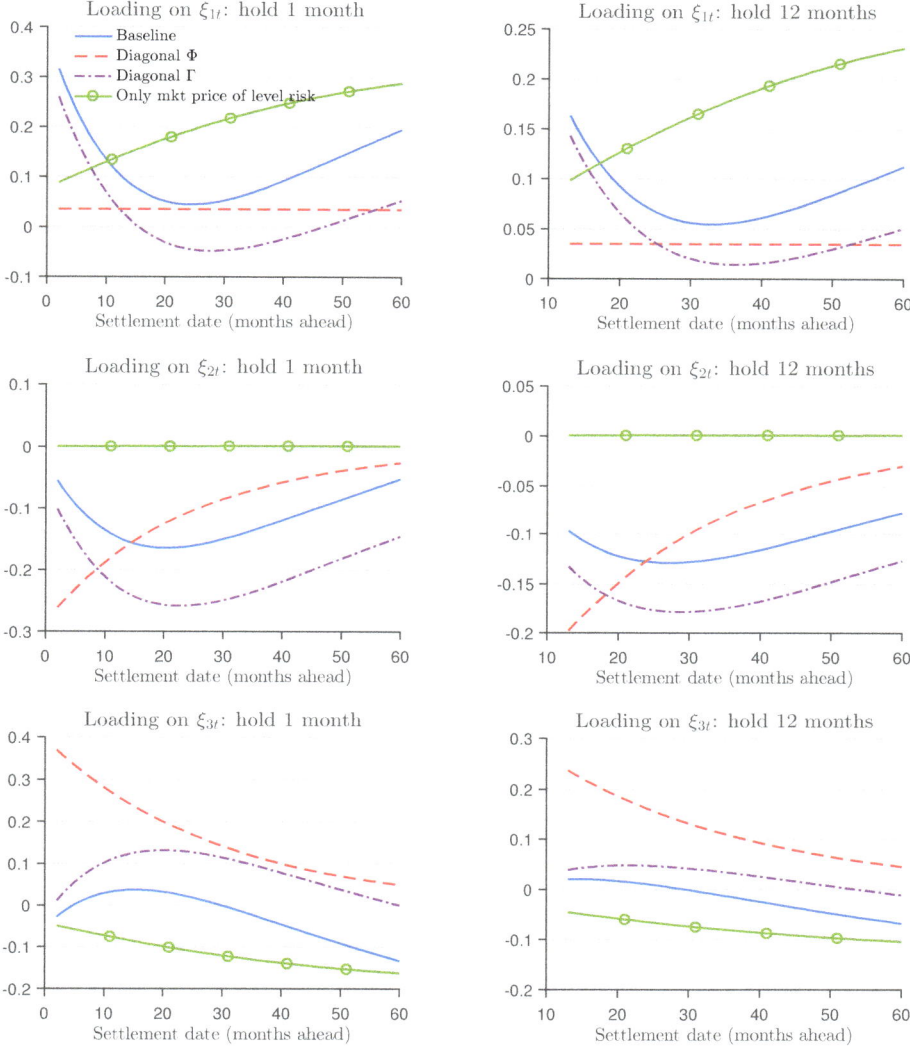

Figure 7. Loadings on factors: one-month and one-year holding forward returns.

Figures 8 and 9 show the evolution of the one-month and one-year holding forward risk premiums. Three patterns emerge from the figures. First, the holding forward risk premiums are much smaller than the bond holding risk premiums (excess bond returns). Second, the holding forward premium is also highly contemporaneously correlated with the slope factor ξ_{2t}. Third, the difference between the restricted models and the baseline tend to follow a pattern similar to the bond holding risk premium.

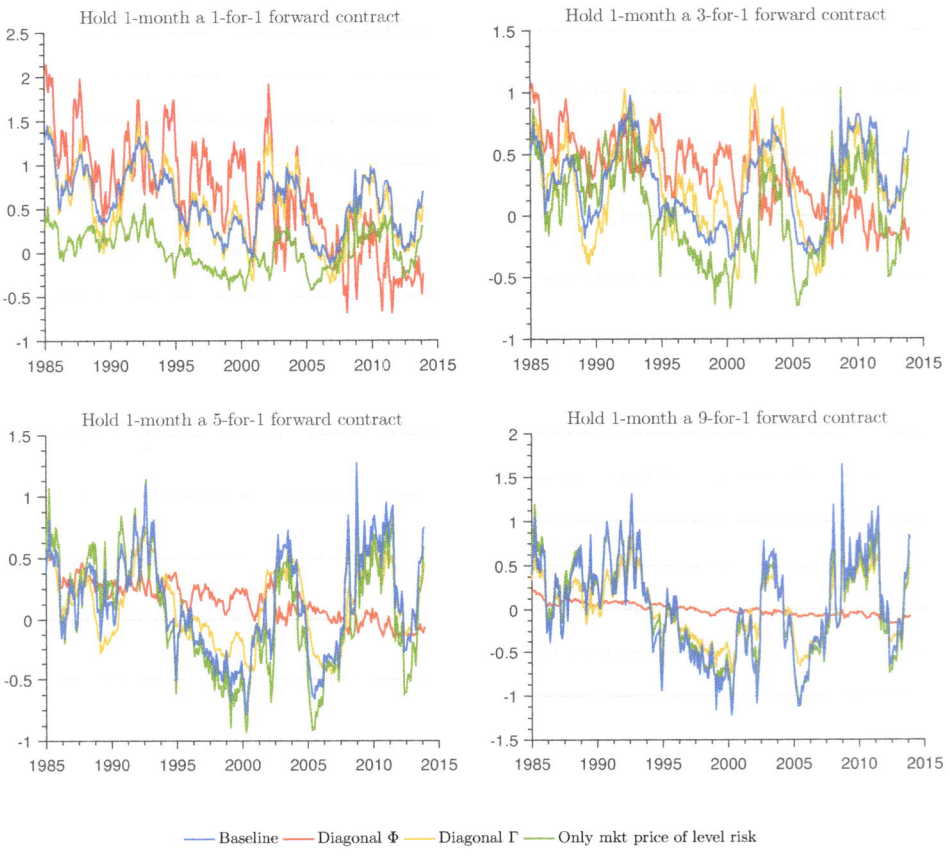

Figure 8. One-month holding forward risk premium.

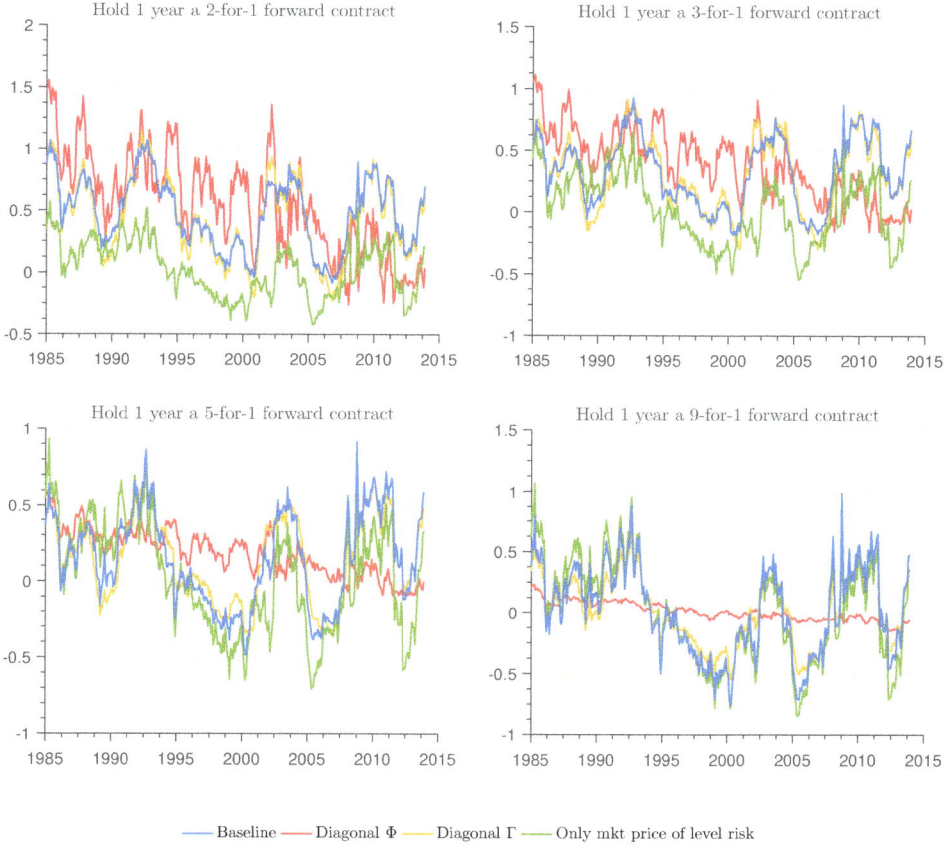

Figure 9. One-year holding forward risk premium.

6. Final Remarks

In this paper, we analyzed how different restrictions on risk prices affect bond risk premia. The model that imposes a diagonal Φ matrix and that with "only market price of level risk" are not only statistically rejected, but also produce measures of risk premia that are very different from those of the unrestricted model. Yet, there are models, such as that with a diagonal Γ matrix, that are also rejected on statistical grounds, but that produce measures of risk premia very similar to those from the baseline model. This result follows because restrictions on Γ have a minor impact on the market price of risk parameters. Any difference with the baseline model is of second order and comes from the indirect effect of the restrictions on the constants A_n, and because the estimates of the remaining, common, parameters may be somewhat different.

In the baseline model, the forward premium is always positive, while the excess holding risk premium is often negative. We found that the slope factor moves almost one-to-one with several measures of risk premia, which suggests that looking at the empirical slope of the yield curve (which is highly correlated with the slope factor that we extract from the model) gives an accurate description of risk premia in bond markets. Furthermore, as has been documented many times, we find that the expectational hypothesis of the term of the structure of interest rates is at odds with the data.

In terms of how restrictions on risk prices affect risk premia, we found that the differences across models in the estimated forward premium are modest, but they get amplified when considering excess holding risk premiums. There are, however, cases in which the restricted models seem to work well. For example, the one-month excess return of a 10-year bond for the model with "only market price of level risk" is quite similar to that from the baseline model. This happens because the loading of the risk premium on the level factor increases with the maturity of the bond and dominates movements in risk premia relative to the contribution of the other factors, but only for long maturity bonds.

In sum, imposing overidentifying restrictions affect the evolution of risk premia dramatically in some cases (such as when Φ is diagonal), but not so much in others (such as when Γ is diagonal). Often, researchers impose overidentifying restrictions to reduce the number of parameters to estimate or for other reasons, such as forecasting performance, even though they are statistically rejected. Our exercises suggest that this practice is inappropriate, since it is difficult to know a priori when the restrictions will have a significant impact on estimated risk premia. Of course, there is no harm in imposing the restrictions if they are not statistically rejected. However, since there is no theoretical guidance on how to impose them and one gains at best a few degrees of freedom by finding the appropriate restrictions, we believe that it is advisable to focus on the just-identified case whenever the objective of the study is to understand risk premia.

Author Contributions: C.H. and M.S. contributed equally to the paper.

Funding: This research received no external funding.

Conflicts of Interest: The authors declare no conflicts of interest.

Appendix A

In the text, we claim that the four concepts of risk premia $\pi_{f,t}^{(s,n-s)}$, $\pi_{hb,t}^{(n,h)}$, $\pi_{y,t}^{(n)}$ and $\pi_{hf,t}^{(s,n-s,h)}$ are equivalent, in the sense that if one of them is zero or constant, so are the other three. That the risk premiums $\pi_{f,t}^{(s,n-s)}$, $\pi_{hb,t}^{(n,h)}$, and $\pi_{y,t}^{(n)}$ are equivalent is a well-known result. Here, we prove that the holding forward risk premium $\pi_{hf,t}^{(s,n-s,h)}$ is also equivalent to the other three.

Consider the equations that define the forward risk premium at times t and $t+h$,

$$f_t^{(s,n-s)} = E_t\left[y_{t+s}^{(n-s)}\right] + \pi_{f,t}^{(s,n-s)},$$

$$f_{t+h}^{(s-h,n-s)} = E_{t+h}\left[y_{t+s}^{(n-s)}\right] + \pi_{f,t+h}^{(s-h,n-s)}.$$

Taking expectations as of time t in the second equation gives:

$$E_t\left[f_{t+h}^{(s-h,n-s)}\right] = E_t\left[y_{t+s}^{(n-s)}\right] + E_t\left[\pi_{f,t+h}^{(s-h,n-s)}\right]$$

Subtracting this expression from the first equation, one obtains:

$$f_t^{(s,n-s)} - E_t\left[f_{t+h}^{(s-h,n-s)}\right] = \pi_{f,t}^{(s,n-s)} - E_t\left[\pi_{f,t+h}^{(s-h,n-s)}\right].$$

However, since the holding forward risk premium is given by:

$$\pi_{hf,t}^{(s,n-s,h)} = E_t\left[f_t^{(s,n-s)} - f_{t+h}^{(s-h,n-s)}\right],$$

it follows that:

$$\pi_{hf,t}^{(s,n-s,h)} = \pi_{f,t}^{(s,n-s)} - E_t\left[\pi_{f,t+h}^{(s-h,n-s)}\right].$$

Therefore, if the forward risk premium $\pi_{f,t}^{(s,n-s)}$ is zero (or constant), so is the holding forward risk premium $\pi_{hf,t}^{(s,n-s,h)}$ for any $(s, n-s, h)$.

Conversely, suppose that $\pi_{\mathsf{hf},t}^{(s,n-s,h)}$ is zero or constant for all $(s, n-s, h)$. In particular, setting $s = h$ and $n - s = 1$ for any h, it follows that:

$$f_t^{(s,n-s)} = E_t\left[f_{t+h}^{(s-h,n-s)}\right] + \pi_{\mathsf{hf}}^{(s,n-s,h)},$$
$$f_t^{(h,1)} = E_t\left[f_{t+h}^{(0,1)}\right] + \pi_{\mathsf{hf}}^{(h,1,h)}.$$

However, $f_{t+h}^{(0,1)} = y_{t+h}^{(1)}$, so that:

$$f_t^{(h,1)} = E_t\left[y_{t+h}^{(1)}\right] + \pi_{\mathsf{hf}}^{(h,1,h)}.$$

Rearranging and using the definition of $\pi_{\mathsf{f},t}^{(h,1)}$ gives $\pi_{\mathsf{f},t}^{(h,1)} = \pi_{\mathsf{hf}}^{(h,1,h)}$. Since $\pi_{\mathsf{hf}}^{(h,1,h)}$ is zero or constant, so is $\pi_{\mathsf{f},t}^{(h,1)}$ for all h. However, using $\pi_{\mathsf{y},t}^{(n)} = \frac{1}{n}\sum_{j=1}^{h}\pi_{\mathsf{f},t}^{(j,1)}$, it then follows that if $\pi_{\mathsf{hf}}^{(h,1,h)}$ is zero or constant, so is $\pi_{\mathsf{y},t}^{(n)}$ for all n. Therefore, the holding forward risk premium is equivalent to the term premium and, therefore, to the other two definitions of risk premium. This completes the proof that the four definitions of risk premiums are equivalent.

References

Ang, Andrew, and Monika Piazzesi. 2003. A no-arbitrage vector autoregression of term structure dynamics with macroeconomic and latent variables. *Journal of Monetary Economics* 50: 745–87. [CrossRef]

Bauer, Michael D. 2018. Restrictions on risk prices in dynamic term structure models. *Journal of Business & Economic Statistics* 36: 196–211.

Campbell, John, and Robert Shiller. 1991. Yield spreads and interest rate movements: A bird's eye view. *Review of Economic Studies* 58: 495–514. [CrossRef]

Christensen, Jens H. E., and Glenn D. Rudebusch. 2015. Estimating shadow-rate term structure models with near-zero yields. *Journal of Financial Econometrics* 13: 226–59. [CrossRef]

Christensen, Jens, Jose Lopez, and Glenn Rudebusch. 2010. Inflation expectations and risk premiums in an arbitrage-free model of nominal and real bond yields. *Journal of Money, Credit and Banking* 42: 143–78. [CrossRef]

Christensen, Jens H. E., Francis X. Diebold, and Glenn D. Rudebusch. 2011. The affine arbitrage-free class of Nelson–Siegel term structure models. *Journal of Econometrics* 164: 4–20. [CrossRef]

Cochrane, John H. 2015. *Comments on "Robust Bond Risk Premia" by Michael Bauer and Jim Hamilton*. Working paper. Chicago: University of Chicago, unpublished.

Cochrane, John H., and Monika Piazzesi. 2005. Bond risk premia. *American Economic Review* 95: 138–60. [CrossRef]

Cochrane, John H., and Monika Piazzesi. 2008. *Decomposing the Yield Curve*. Technical Report 18. Society for Economic Dynamics.

Dai, Qiang, and Kenneth J. Singleton. 2000. Specification analysis of affine term structure models. *Journal of Finance* 55: 1943–78. [CrossRef]

Diebold, Francis X., and Canlin Li. 2006. Forecasting the term structure of government bond yields. *Journal of Econometrics* 130: 337–64. [CrossRef]

Diebold, Francis X., and Glenn D. Rudebusch. 2012. *Yield Curve Modeling and Forecasting: The Dynamic Nelson–Siegel Approach*. Number 9895 in Economics Books. Princeton: Princeton University Press.

Duffee, Gregory R. 2011. *Forecasting with the Term Structure: The Role of No-Arbitrage Restrictions*. Economics Working Paper Archive 576. Baltimore: The Johns Hopkins University, Department of Economics.

Evgenidis, Anastasios, Athanasios Tsagkanos, and Costas Siriopoulos. 2017. Towards an asymmetric long run equilibrium between stock market uncertainty and the yield spread. A threshold vector error correction approach. *Research in International Business and Finance* 39: 267–79. [CrossRef]

Fama, Eugene, and Robert R. Bliss. 1987. The information in long-maturity forward rates. *American Economic Review* 77: 680–92.

Gürkaynak, Refet S., and Jonathan H. Wright. 2012. Macroeconomics and the Term Structure. *Journal of Economic Literature* 50: 331–67. [CrossRef]

Hamilton, James D., and Jing Cynthia Wu. 2012. Identification and estimation of gaussian affine term structure models. *Journal of Econometrics* 168: 315–31. [CrossRef]

Hevia, Constantino, Martin Gonzalez Rozada, Martin Sola, and Fabio Spagnolo. 2015. Estimating and Forecasting the Yield Curve Using A Markov Switching Dynamic Nelson and Siegel Model. *Journal of Applied Econometrics* 30: 987–1009. [CrossRef]

Joslin, Scott, Kenneth Singleton, and Haoxiang Zhu. 2011. A new perspective on gaussian dynamic term structure models. *Review of Financial Studies* 24: 926–70. [CrossRef]

Nelson, Charles R., and Andrew F. Siegel. 1987. Parsimonious Modeling of Yield Curves. *The Journal of Business* 60: 473–89.

© 2018 by the authors. Licensee MDPI, Basel, Switzerland. This article is an open access article distributed under the terms and conditions of the Creative Commons Attribution (CC BY) license (http://creativecommons.org/licenses/by/4.0/).

Article

Stationary Threshold Vector Autoregressive Models

Galyna Grynkiv [1] and Lars Stentoft [1,2,*]

1. Department of Economics, University of Western Ontario, Social Science Centre, London, ON N6A 5C2, Canada; ggrynkiv@uwo.ca
2. Department of Statistical and Actuarial Sciences, University of Western Ontario, Western Science Centre, London, ON N6A 5B7, Canada
* Correspondence: lars.stentoft@uwo.ca; Tel.: +1-519-661-2111 (ext. 85311)

Received: 15 June 2018; Accepted: 3 August 2018; Published: 5 August 2018

Abstract: This paper examines the steady state properties of the Threshold Vector Autoregressive model. Assuming that the trigger variable is exogenous and the regime process follows a Bernoulli distribution, necessary and sufficient conditions for the existence of stationary distribution are derived. A situation related to so-called "locally explosive models", where the stationary distribution exists though the model is explosive in one regime, is analysed. Simulations show that locally explosive models can generate some of the key properties of financial and economic data. They also show that assessing the stationarity of threshold models based on simulations might well lead to wrong conclusions.

Keywords: asset price bubbles; explosive regimes; multivariate nonlinear time series; steady state distributions; TVAR models

JEL Classification: C1; C3; C5; G1

---

1. Introduction

Correct theoretical and empirical modelling of financial time series remains challenging. First of all, the usual linear framework often falls short of properly describing the data, which, instead, exhibit important nonlinear features. Secondly, economic theory regularly results in models with multiple equilibria and asymmetries which the time series model should be able to accommodate. Finally, data is often interconnected and hence simple univariate models generally fall short of appropriately describing the complex nature of the data. The Global Financial Crisis in 2007–2008 demonstrated this very clearly and reinforced the need to use a multivariate nonlinear framework in economic models, in general, and in empirical finance, in particular.

Among the many possible candidate nonlinear models, threshold models are particularly interesting and they have been extensively used in the existing empirical literature. These models are straightforward generalizations of linear models. For example, the simple two regime Threshold Autoregressive (TAR) model specifies a different autoregressive structure for each of the regimes and a threshold variable that determines which regime is active. These models are therefore relatively simple to estimate, and, since at time *t* the regime state is known, they are more suitable for forecasting than other nonlinear models, in particular hidden Markov models. Finally, TAR models allow for reasonably simple tests of the linear structure against nonlinear alternatives and to test the number of regimes. The multivariate generalization of the TAR model instead uses vector autoregressive structures in the regimes and is therefore naturally referred to as the Threshold Vector AutoRegressive (TVAR) model (Hubrich and Teräsvirta 2013; Tsay 1998).

Empirical studies have used threshold models to explore the asymmetry of shocks and nonlinear relationship between variables in financial markets and data from the real and monetary economy.

For instance, TVAR models are widely used to study the asymmetric effect of fiscal and monetary policies in different credit, interest rate and inflationary regimes (Balke 2000; Fazzari et al. 2015; Shen and Chiang 1999). Balke (2000), for example, studies the propagation of shocks to output growth, the Federal Funds rate, inflation and measures of credit conditions during "tight" and "normal" credit market conditions using a TVAR framework with two regimes. The results suggest that shocks have a larger effect on output in "tight" credit regimes and that contractionary monetary shocks are more effective than expansionary ones. A similar approach is followed by Calza and Souza (2006) to study the transmission of monetary shocks across two credit regimes in the EU area and by Li and St-Amant (2010) to evaluate the effect of financial stress conditions on monetary policy effectiveness in Canada.

Another important application of threshold models has been to study the business cycle. For example, Altissimo and Violante (2001) study the joint dynamics of US output and unemployment using a bivariate TVAR model for recessions and expansions. Here, the lagged feedback variable, which measures the depth of the recession, defines the regime. The resulting model is a VAR with a fixed number of lags when the economy is in expansion and a time varying lag order when the economy is in recession. The authors find that nonlinearities are statistically significant only for unemployment, but it transmits to output through cross-correlation. Further evidence on the usefulness of threshold models for analysing the business cycle can be found in Koop and Potter (1999), Peel and Speight (1998), Koop et al. (1996), and Potter (1995), amongst others.

Threshold models are also popular in financial markets studies to explore the asymmetric relation between variables. In particular, a common application of TAR models includes determining the threshold effect in price movements related to transaction cost (Yadav et al. 1994). The threshold autoregressive conditional heteroskedastic class of models has been applied to study the nonlinear effect in volatility processes (Rabemananjara and Zakoian 1993). Finally, multivariate threshold models have been extensively used in studying the dynamics in stock prices, returns, volatilities, inflation and economic activity (Barnes 1999; Griffin et al. 2007; Huang et al. 2005; Li et al. 2015). Griffin et al. (2007), for example, study the joint dynamics of stock market turnover, returns and volatility in 46 countries using a TVAR model with two regimes that are separated by the sign of the past return. The authors conclude that small negative return shocks, rather than large ones, are the drivers for the decrease in turnover after a decrease in returns. Li et al. (2015) study the interaction between Shanghai and Shenzhen stock markets in a bivariate three regime TVAR model where the threshold variable is the average difference of the log returns between the two markets. Their results suggest that the strength of interaction between markets is regime dependent. In particular, the Shanghai market leads most of the time, except for the third regime, where both markets interact simultaneously. A detailed review of the application of threshold models in empirical economics can be found in Hansen (2011).

One challenge with nonlinear time series models, in general, and by extension therefore also with threshold models, in particular, is to assess model stationarity. Establishing stationarity is important as it is a fundamental assumption in most theoretical research. Indeed, the asymptotic properties of estimators in threshold models are generally established under a set of standard regularity conditions, which include the existence of finite higher order moments and the strict stationarity of the data generating process (Tsay 1998). Moreover, existing inference approaches assume stationarity of the data generating process (Hansen 1996, 2000; Tsay 1998) and violation of this assumption might lead to spurious nonlinearity (Calza and Souza 2006) and could invalidate the use of, e.g., Hansen (1996) simulated p-values for inference.

While significant progress has been made to establish conditions which ensure stationarity for the univariate threshold case under realistic assumptions (Brockwell et al. 1992; Chan and Tong 1985; Chen et al. 2011; Knight and Satchell 2011; Petruccelli and Woolford 1984), to the best of our knowledge, very little is known about the multivariate extension. See Chen et al. (2011) for an extensive review about recent findings regarding the stationarity of TAR models. If one was to use the general approach from this literature to establish the stationarity of TVAR models, it would require proving the convergence of an infinite sum of products of random matrices. This is clearly difficult and likely explains the absence of theoretical results for the TVAR model.

In this paper, we fill this gap in the existing literature and analyse the properties of the TVAR model in detail. To achieve this, we assume that the trigger variable is exogenous and that the regime process follows a Bernoulli distribution. We first derive necessary and sufficient conditions for second order stationarity, which are not present in the previous literature, when the variance–covariance matrices of the random vector and the error process are assumed to have full rank. Next, we characterize the joint conditional distribution of the data generating process when the error vector follows a multivariate normal distribution. Finally, we derive the unconditional distribution for a special case of the TVAR model, and we demonstrate that, in this case, the distribution of the threshold model is an infinite mixture of normals. This shows that TVAR models are very general and can accommodate many of the stylized features of financial data.

As a first interesting application of our results, we consider the special case where the elements of the random vector are positively correlated and we describe a model that is explosive in one regime, but still allows for the existence of steady state distribution. A similar idea was introduced in Knight et al. (2014) in the univariate case as a so-called "locally explosive model". In particular, they study the univariate threshold autoregressive model with exogenous trigger and its application to bubble formation. We expand the notion of locally explosive models to the bivariate TVAR model. The derived conditions for the existence of the stationary distribution have simple economic intuition and are easy to interpret. In particular, our results show that, in the stationary model, there is a trade-off between autoregressive dependence in the regime and the probability of the regime.

Next, we conduct an empirical analysis of the locally explosive models. In the absence of explicit theoretical conditions that guarantee stationarity of the model, the previous literature suggested to establish stationarity indirectly by demonstrating, using a simulation study, that the estimated model does not appear to contradict the stability assumption. To assess this procedure, we simulate the bivariate locally explosive TVAR model for different distributions of the regimes. Our results show that a simulation study aimed at verifying stability of a particular model might give inconclusive or even wrong results. Specifically, we show that the simulation exercise may very well fail to reject stability of non-stationary TVAR models when the probability of the explosive regime is low.

Finally, we empirically document that the locally explosive TVAR model can be associated with bubble formation processes. In fact, our simulated locally explosive models appear to possess explosive and unit root behaviour while overall remaining stationary. These properties are implied by the definition of bubbles prevailing in the current literature and formally described by Evans (1991) and Phillips and Yu (2011). Our results, therefore, should encourage further research into multivariate threshold models and their use to study the formation of and existence of bubbles in financial data.

The structure of the paper is as follows: In Section 2, we derive the necessary and sufficient conditions for second order stationarity and for the existence of a stationary distribution for the TVAR model. This section also derives closed form solutions for the stationary distribution. In Section 3, we consider the so-called locally explosive models, in which the TVAR model is explosive in one regime, while overall remaining stationary. This section also presents some interesting special cases and reports the results from a simulation study. Finally, Section 4 concludes the paper. All proofs can be found in Appendix A and Appendix B contains additional figures.

2. The Threshold Vector Autoregressive Model

Throughout this paper, we consider the threshold vector autoregressive model given by

$$Y_t = \Phi^1 I(X_{t-1} \in R_1) Y_{t-1} + \Phi^2 I(X_{t-1} \in R_2) Y_{t-1} + \epsilon_t, \qquad (1)$$

where Y_t is a $(n \times 1)$ random vector, Φ^1 and Φ^2 are $(n \times n)$ parameter matrices, where n is the number of time series, $I()$ is the indicator function, X_t is an *iid* random variable, which determines the regime, and ϵ_t is a sequence of independent multivariate random vectors, such that $E(\epsilon_t) = 0$ and $Var(\epsilon_t) = \Sigma$, $\forall t$, where Σ is positive definite with full rank. We assume that $E(\epsilon_t|X_s) = 0$ for all $s \leq t$ and that the sequence $(\epsilon_t, X_t), t \geq 1$, is *iid*.

The regime process is defined as $S_t = I(X_t \in R_2)$, $\forall t$, where $Prob(X_t \in R_2) = \pi$ and $Prob(X_t \in R_1) = 1 - \pi$, with $R_1 \cup R_2 = R$ and $R_1 \cap R_2 = \emptyset$. From this, it follows that S_t is an *iid* Bernoulli variable with $S_t = 0$ with probability $1 - \pi$ and $S_t = 1$ with probability π. Using S_t, Equation (1) can be rewritten as $Y_t = (\Phi^1 + S_{t-1}\Phi^0)Y_{t-1} + \epsilon_t$, where $\Phi^0 = \Phi^2 - \Phi^1$. If we further denote by $B_t = S_t\Phi^0 - \pi\Phi^0$, where $E(B_t) = 0$, $\forall t$, the model in Equation (1) can be rewritten as a Random Coefficient Model (RCM) (see Nicholls and Quinn (1982)) given by

$$Y_t = (\Phi + B_{t-1})Y_{t-1} + \epsilon_t, \qquad (2)$$

where $\Phi = \Phi^1 + \pi\Phi^0 = (1 - \pi)\Phi^1 + \pi\Phi^2$.

In the following sections, we examine the TVAR model specified above in detail. First, we provide the necessary and sufficient conditions under which the TVAR model is second order stationary. We also derive expressions for the moments and the stationary solution to the model given in Equation (1). Secondly, we derive the distribution associated with this data generating process. For simplicity, we assume only two regimes in Equation (1). However, the theoretical results obtained here can easily be generalized to multiple regimes.

2.1. Stationarity of the TVAR Model

Theorem 1 provides conditions under which the TVAR model above is second order stationary, i.e., that $E(Y_t)$ is constant and $Cov(Y_t, Y_{t+h})$ depends only on the lag h.

Theorem 1. *The process Y_t, $t = 0, 1, 2, ...$ defined in Equation (1) is second order stationary with positive definite covariance matrix $V = Var(Y_0)$ if and only if:*

1. *$\mu = 0$, where μ is a mean of the initial vector, $\mu = E(Y_0)$,*
2. *the covariance matrix V solves $V - \Phi V \Phi' - E(B_{t-1} V B'_{t-1}) = \Sigma$, and*
3. *$|\lambda| < 1$, where λ is the maximum eigenvalue of the matrix $(1 - \pi)\Phi^1 \otimes \Phi^1 + \pi \Phi^2 \otimes \Phi^2$.*

Proof. See Appendix A. □

Condition 3 of Theorem 1 provides a simple and intuitive eigenvalue condition for establishing second order stationarity of the TVAR model in Equation (1). We note that conditions similar to what we present here have been derived previously, though this has been done using alternative and, we believe, less realistic and empirically interesting assumptions (see, e.g., Nicholls and Quinn (1981), Feigin and Tweedie (1985) and Saikkonen (2007)). In particular, Nicholls and Quinn (1981), Feigin and Tweedie (1985) as well as Saikkonen (2007) assume independence of the error term, ϵ_t, and the threshold variable, X_t. We do not have this assumption and instead make a, we believe, far less restrictive assumption of the exogeneity of the threshold variable, X_t, i.e., $E(\epsilon_t|X_t)$, which does not rule out, for example, the possibility that the threshold variable X_t could be a part of the ϵ_t process.

Condition 2 of Theorem 1 provides an expression for calculating the covariance matrix of the second order stationary process Y_t. Notice that, after vectorization of this expression, we can obtain a closed form formula for this. Remark 1 provides this formula.

Remark 1. *From vectorization of the expression $V - \Phi V \Phi' - E(B_{t-1} V B'_{t-1}) = \Sigma$, the equation for the variance of Y_t can be obtained from*

$$vecV = (I - \Phi \otimes \Phi - \pi(1 - \pi)\Phi^0 \otimes \Phi^0)^{-1} vec\Sigma. \qquad (3)$$

Theorem 2 provides an expression for the stationary solution to the model in Equation (1) and the corresponding conditions for the existence of this solution. Theorem 2 also shows that this solution is unique and strictly stationary.

Theorem 2. *Assume that V is positive definite with full rank. Then, the TVAR model in Equation (1) has a unique stationary solution given by*

$$Y_t = \epsilon_t + \sum_{n=1}^{\infty} \left(\prod_{k=1}^{n} \Phi + B_{t-k} \right) \epsilon_{t-n}, \tag{4}$$

if and only if $|\lambda| < 1$, where λ is the maximum eigenvalue of the matrix $(1-\pi)\Phi^1 \otimes \Phi^1 + \pi \Phi^2 \otimes \Phi^2$.

Proof. See Appendix A. □

In Remark 2, we provide the restriction on the eigenvalues of the matrix Φ, which is necessary for the stationary model in Equation (1) and follows from Theorems 1 and 2. This condition is more tractable, and it is used in Section 3 to simplify the analysis of the stationary TVAR model with one explosive regime.

Remark 2. *Let the process Y_t, $t = 0, 1, 2, ...$ defined in Equation (1) be stationary with positive definite covariance matrix V. Then, the maximum eigenvalue of the matrix Φ is less than 1.*

Proof. See Appendix A. □

The results of Theorems 1 and 2 can be extended to TVAR models with more than one lag. Corollary 1 presents the conditions for the stationarity of the TVAR model, which contains more than one lag.

Corollary 1. *Consider the following two-regime TVAR model with p lags in each regime*

$$Y_t = I(X_{t-1} \in R_1) \sum_{j=1}^{p} \Phi^{1j} Y_{t-j} + I(X_{t-1} \in R_2) \sum_{j=1}^{p} \Phi^{2j} Y_{t-j} + \epsilon_t, \tag{5}$$

where the properties of X_t and ϵ_t are those following Equation (1). This model has a unique stationary solution given by

$$Z_t = \eta_t + \sum_{n=1}^{\infty} \left(\prod_{k=1}^{n} A + D_{t-k} \right) \eta_{t-n}, \tag{6}$$

where Z_t and η_t are $np \times 1$ vectors given by $Z_t' = [Y_t', Y_{t-1}', Y_{t-2}', ... Y_{t-(p-1)}']$ and $\eta_t = [\epsilon_t', 0, 0, .., 0]$, respectively, and $D_t = (S_t - \pi)A^2 + (\pi - S_t)A^1$, with A^i, $i = 1, 2$, defined as

$$A^i = \begin{pmatrix} \Phi^{i1} & \Phi^{i2} & \Phi^{i3} & ... & \Phi^{i(p-1)} & \Phi^{ip} \\ I_n & 0 & 0 & ... & 0 & 0 \\ 0 & I_n & 0 & ... & 0 & 0 \\ 0 & 0 & I_n & ... & 0 & 0 \\ ... & ... & ... & ... & ... & ... \\ 0 & 0 & 0 & ... & I_n & 0 \end{pmatrix},$$

if $|\lambda| < 1$, where λ is the maximum eigenvalue of the matrix $(1-\pi)A^1 \otimes A^1 + \pi A^2 \otimes A^2$, and only if $|\lambda_1| < 1$, where λ_1 is the maximum eigenvalue of the matrix $A = (1-\pi)A^1 + \pi A^2$.

Proof. See Appendix A. □

The distinctive feature of the TVAR model is that it is a linear Vector Autoregresive Model (VAR) in each of the regimes and an interesting question therefore is how the stability of each regime contributes to the stationarity of the whole TVAR model. Knight and Satchell (2011) investigate this question in detail for the univariate TAR model and Niglio et al. (2012) provide evidence that, when the univariate TAR model is stationary in both regimes, the whole TAR model cannot explode. The more interesting situation, however, occurs when the model in Equation (1) is explosive in one of the regimes.

The results of Theorems 1 and 2 can be used to analyse this particular situation, one in which the TVAR model in Equation (1) is explosive in one of the regimes. For example, the following example shows that the TVAR model can still be stationary in that case provided the probability to be in the explosive regime is not too large. See also Section 3 for further analysis.

Example. Consider the model in Equation (1), where $\Phi^1 = \begin{pmatrix} 0.70 & 0.21 \\ 0.31 & 0.80 \end{pmatrix}, \Phi^2 = \begin{pmatrix} 0.20 & 0.32 \\ 0.10 & 0.25 \end{pmatrix}$ and $\pi = Prob(X_t \in R_2) = 0.3$. Since one of the eigenvalues of Φ^1 is equal to 1.01, the model is not stationary in regime one. On the other hand, $(1-\pi)\Phi^1 \otimes \Phi^1 + \pi\Phi^2 \otimes \Phi^2 = \begin{pmatrix} 0.36 & 0.12 & 0.12 & 0.0 \\ 0.16 & 0.41 & 0.06 & 0.14 \\ 0.16 & 0.06 & 0.41 & 0.14 \\ 0.07 & 0.18 & 0.18 & 0.47 \end{pmatrix}$, and its maximum eigenvalue $\lambda = 0.78$. Thus, overall the model is stationary.

2.2. The Stationary Distribution

In this section, we describe the stationary distribution associated with the model in Equation (1). Throughout this section, we assume that $\epsilon_t \sim N(0, \Sigma)$ are independent random vectors. Let Y_t be defined by Equation (4) and let $S_n(t) = \prod_{k=1}^{n}(\Phi + B_{t-k})$, $n \geq 1$, with $S_0(t) = 1$. It then follows that

$$Y_t = \epsilon_t + \sum_{n=1}^{\infty} S_n(t)\epsilon_{t-n}. \tag{7}$$

From this, we have that

$$Y_t | S_n(t) \sim N(0, \Sigma + \sum_{n=1}^{\infty} S_n(t)\Sigma S'_n(t)), \tag{8}$$

and from the definition of $S_n(t)$ we notice that the stationary distribution of Y_t is a complicated mixture of Normal distribution. Since it is difficult to establish the distribution of Y_t in general, we will derive it under the assumption that $\Phi^1 = 0$. In this case, if Y_t denotes returns, then prices follow a random walk in regime 1.

From Equation (8), we see that the characteristic function of Y_t conditioned on $S_n(t)$ is given by

$$\phi(t, Y_t | S_n(t)) = exp\left(-\frac{1}{2}t\Sigma t' - \frac{1}{2}t\sum_{n=1}^{\infty} S_n(t)\Sigma S'_n(t)t'\right). \tag{9}$$

Notice that, when $\Phi^1 = 0$ and $\Phi^2 = \Psi$, then $B_t = (S_t - \pi)\Psi$ and $\Phi = \pi\Psi$, and hence $S_n(t) = \prod_{k=1}^{n} S_{t-k}\Psi$. Note also that $\prod_{k=1}^{n} S_{t-k}\Psi\Sigma\prod_{k=1}^{n} S_{t-k}\Psi = \prod_{k=1}^{n} S_{t-k}\Psi\Sigma\prod_{k=1}^{n} \Psi'$. The conditional characteristic function in Equation (9) therefore becomes

$$\phi(t, Y_t | S_n(t)) = exp\left(-\frac{1}{2}t\Sigma t' - \frac{1}{2}t\sum_{n=1}^{\infty}\prod_{k=1}^{n} S_{t-k}\Phi^2\Sigma\prod_{k=1}^{n}\Phi^{2'}t'\right). \tag{10}$$

Given the conditional characteristic function and the distribution of $S_n(t)$, we can obtain the unconditional characteristic function and the marginal stationary distribution of Y_t. The results are presented in Theorem 3.

Theorem 3. *The stationary distribution of the TVAR process with $\Phi^1 = 0$ and $\Phi^2 = \Psi$ has the following characteristic function*

$$\phi(t, Y_t) = (1-\pi) \sum_{K=0}^{\infty} \pi^K exp\left(-\frac{1}{2} t \sum_{n=0}^{K} \Psi^n \Sigma \Psi'^n t\right). \tag{11}$$

Moreover, the probability distribution function is given by

$$f(Y_t) = (1-\pi) \sum_{K=0}^{\infty} \pi^K N\left(0, \sum_{n=0}^{K} \Psi^n \Sigma \Psi'^n\right), \tag{12}$$

where $N(A, B)$ is the multivariate normal distribution function with mean A and covariance matrix B.

Proof. See Appendix A. □

Theorem 3 is a generalization of a result for the univariate threshold autoregressive process developed in Knight and Satchell (2011) and shows that when $\Phi^1 = 0$ the distribution function of Y_t given in Equation (12) is an infinite mixture of multivariate Normals. This type of distribution can generate excess kurtosis. Such distributional characteristics are interesting when it comes to analysing financial markets and economic problems, since it can accommodate the special features of this type of data. For instance, the distributions of equity returns and typical measures of the realized volatility are characterized by large kurtosis. Thus, the theorem shows that TVAR models can be used to study these processes.

3. Locally Explosive TVAR Models

Threshold autoregressive models where one regime is non-stationary are related to the so-called locally explosive models. Knight et al. (2014) defines the locally explosive model as a model in which some regimes may be explosive, but the whole model has a stationary distribution. They study univariate threshold models and apply the idea of locally explosive models to investigate the formation of bubbles. In this section, we generalize the notion of locally explosive models to the bivariate setting. In order to do so, we need to link the stationarity of the whole model in Equation (1) provided in Theorems 1 and 2 to the stability of the model in each particular regime. Notice that the locally explosive models considered in this paper are models, which are state explosive. When $X_t = t$ instead the TVAR model is related to the models derived in Phillips and Yu (2009) and Phillips et al. (2011) where the explosive behaviour is defined in the time series context.

The derived conditions for the existence of a stationary solution are conditions on the matrix $(1-\pi)\Phi^1 \otimes \Phi^1 + \pi \Phi^2 \otimes \Phi^2$, and it is not in general possible to relate the eigenvalues of this matrix to the eigenvalues of the parameter matrices Φ^1 and Φ^2 without adding extra structure. In the following section, we therefore consider a bivariate TVAR model, where the parameter matrices Φ^1 and Φ^2 have either positive entries only or are upper triangular. We first obtain the conditions on the parameter matrices under which the locally explosive TVAR model remains stationary. We next provide a simulation study to examine the characteristics of this model and show that graphically it is very difficult to assess model stationarity using simulated data.

3.1. Special Cases of the TVAR Model

We consider the special case where Y_t in Equation (1) is bivariate and the parameter matrices have positive entries. We introduce the following additional notation for $\Phi^1 = \begin{pmatrix} \phi^1_{11} & \phi^1_{12} \\ \phi^1_{21} & \phi^1_{22} \end{pmatrix}$ and $\Phi^2 = \begin{pmatrix} \phi^2_{11} & \phi^2_{12} \\ \phi^2_{21} & \phi^2_{22} \end{pmatrix}$. The following corollary to Theorems 1 and 2 provides conditions in terms of the individual ϕ's, under which the TVAR model is second order stationary. These conditions do not rule out the possibility of an explosive regime, and, if we assume that one regime is explosive, we derive the conditions on the coefficient matrix of the stationary regime.

Corollary 2. *Let the matrices Φ^1 and Φ^2 have positive entries. If $(1-\pi)(\phi_{j1}^1 + \phi_{j2}^1)^2 + \pi(\phi_{i1}^2 + \phi_{i2}^2)^2 < 1$, $\forall i, j = 1, 2$, then the model in Equation (1) is stationary. Moreover, if the model in Equation (1) is explosive in one of the regimes $x \in \{1, 2\}$, then $(\phi_{i1}^{-x} + \phi_{i2}^{-x}) < 1$, $\forall i = 1, 2$, where $-x \in \{1, 2\} \setminus \{x\}$.*

Proof. See Appendix A. □

Corollary 2 shows that if the model in Equation (1) is explosive in one regime, the persistence of the variables in this regime is restricted by the probability of the regime and the persistence, defined as the column sum of the coefficients of Φ^1 or Φ^2 respectively, of the variables in the other regime. In other words, Corollary 2 states that there is a trade-off between how persistent a given regime can be and the probability of this particular regime. In addition, when the conditions of Corollary 2 hold and one of the regimes is explosive, the sum of the coefficients of the other regime's matrix is naturally bounded by one.

Corollary 2 provides sufficient conditions for stationarity of the model, even when the underlying relationship is explosive in one of the regimes. We believe that the above finding might be useful for a number of financial and macroeconomic models. In fact, the assumption of positive entries only in Φ^1 and Φ^2 is not very restrictive for economic research and there are a variety of well documented cases with positive relationships between variables and their lags. For example, it is documented to be the case for asset returns and asset market illiquidity, consumption and GDP, volatility and trading volume and inflation and stock volatility, among many other pairs (Amihud and Mendelson 1986; Engle and Rangel 2008; Jagannathan et al. 2000; Wang and Yau 2000).

When we add slightly more structure and assume that Φ^1 and Φ^2 are triangular matrices with nonnegative diagonal entries, we can derive the necessary conditions directly in terms of the eigenvalues of Φ^1 and Φ^2. Corollary 3 summarizes these findings.

Corollary 3. *Let the process Y_t, $t = 0, 1, 2, ...$ defined in Equation (1) be stationary. Then, the following conditions hold:*

1. $\lambda_1^2 \lambda_2^2 \leq \frac{1}{\pi}$,
2. $\lambda_1^1 \lambda_2^1 \leq \frac{1}{(1-\pi)}$,
3. $\lambda_1^1 \lambda_2^2 \leq \sqrt{\frac{1}{(1-\pi)\pi}}$, *and*
4. $\lambda_1^2 \lambda_2^1 \leq \sqrt{\frac{1}{(1-\pi)\pi}}$,

where λ_1^i and λ_2^i are the eigenvalues of the matrix Φ^i, $i = 1, 2$.

Proof. See Appendix A. □

Since the eigenvalues of a triangular matrix are its diagonal entries, Corollary 3 could equivalently be stated as follows.

Corollary 4. *Let the process Y_t, $t = 0, 1, 2, ...$ defined in Equation (1) be stationary. Then, the following conditions hold:*

1. $\phi_{11}^2 \phi_{22}^2 \leq \frac{1}{\pi}$,
2. $\phi_{11}^1 \phi_{22}^1 \leq \frac{1}{(1-\pi)}$,
3. $\phi_{11}^1 \phi_{22}^2 \leq \sqrt{\frac{1}{(1-\pi)\pi}}$, *and*
4. $\phi_{11}^2 \phi_{22}^1 \leq \sqrt{\frac{1}{(1-\pi)\pi}}$.

Corollaries 3 and 4 illustrate explicitly that there is a trade-off between how persistent a regime in the TVAR model can be and the probability of that regime while ensuring the overall stationarity of the process. Again, it is noteworthy that the stationarity of the TVAR model does not rule out the possibility of an explosive regime, but it restricts the value of the own autoregressive coefficients.

3.2. Simulation

Second order stationarity implies that means, variances and covariances are time-invariant and finite. If stationarity is not satisfied, however, it could be that shocks to the data generating process could lead to a time series that have unbounded moments. Previously, and in the absence of explicit stationarity conditions such as the ones derived in this paper, the literature instead suggested to verify that the estimated model does not contradict stability assumptions by use of simulation studies (Hubrich and Teräsvirta 2013). Specifically, the literature proposed to switch off the noise and simulate the estimated model for different histories. If the generated series converge to the same point, the natural conclusion would be that the simulated model is stationary. In contrast, finding at least one starting point that leads to an explosive time series would be sufficient to invalidate the stationarity assumption.

In this section, we perform a graphical analysis to "test" the stationarity of the TVAR model as suggested in the existing literature for different locally explosive TVAR models. Our results show that this "test" does not always allow us to draw the correct conclusion and the outcome of it is affected by the distribution of the explosive regime and the persistence of this regime. To be specific, we simulate the bivariate TVAR model in Equation (1) with different parameter values. We generate time series from the model of length equal to $n = 250$, which is equivalent to one year of daily observations. The number of simulations is equal to $m = 200$. The initial values of the time series, Y_0, are equally distributed over the interval given by $[-0.15, 0.24]$ for the first series and equally distributed over the interval given by $[-0.17, 0.23]$ for the second series. In Appendix B, we report additional results when $n = 2000$ to check the robustness of our result.

The parameter values used in the simulation study are shown in Table 1. As the table shows, regime 2 is by construction always (locally) explosive and we vary the value of π, the probability of regime 2, such that the overall TVAR model can be stationary or non-stationary. This is indicated by the maximum eigenvalue of the matrix $(1-\pi)\Phi^1 \otimes \Phi^1 + \pi \Phi^2 \otimes \Phi^2$, which is reported in column six labelled λ_{max}. In particular, we define three groups of models, such that models within each group have the same coefficient matrices, but the probability to be in the explosive regime 2, π, varies.

Models 1–6 are more strongly related to lags in the explosive regime 2 than in regime 1. We contrast our models such that the persistence of the models in the second regime is stronger in group 2 than group 1. When the second regime is mildly explosive, like the models from group 1, this regime has to occur very frequently, in order to make the whole TVAR model non-stationary. In contrast, model 6 is unstable even when the probability to be in the explosive regime is as low as 30%. This confirms numerically that, when one regime is not stable, the distribution of the regimes is crucial for the stationarity of the whole TVAR model.

Figure 1 shows the simulated paths from models 1–3. When π is fairly low (Panel a), the time series appear stationary. When π gets larger and λ is closer to 1, the simulated model looks like a unit root (Panel b). While models 1 and 2 generate spikes, the simulated series return to the initial level all the time, a characteristic of stationary processes. When $\pi = 0.7$ (Panel c), the series is no longer stable and this is also evident from the figure. This conclusion is also valid when $n = 2000$ (see Figure A1 in Appendix B).

Figure 2 shows the simulated paths from models 4–6. These models are very persistent in regime 2 and they can generate huge spikes even when the probability of this regime is low (Panels a and b). Both models 4 and 5 look like unit root models, which explode, though they return to the initial level afterwards. Thus, the simulation exercise cannot reject stability of model 5, even though it is non-stationary by construction. The simulation study though does reject stability of model 6, when the probability to be in the explosive regime increases to 50% (Panel c). Thus, the results of the simulation might be misleading about non-stationary TVAR model with low probability of the explosive regime. The result of the simulation of models 4–6 prevails when $n = 2000$ (see Figure A2 in Appendix B). It is of course impossible to check all starting points in a simulation study and we might simply not be lucky enough to have a starting point that allows rejecting stability of the model.

Table 1. Parameter values used in simulating the bivariate TVAR model.

Group	Model	Regime 1, Φ^1		Regime 2, Φ^2		Probability of Regime 2, π	λ_{max}
1	1	0.2 0.3	0.3 0.4	0.3 0.5	0.8 0.8	0.3	0.72
	2	0.2 0.3	0.3 0.4	0.3 0.5	0.8 0.8	0.5	0.95
	3	0.2 0.3	0.3 0.4	0.3 0.5	0.8 0.8	0.7	1.18
2	4	0.2 0.3	0.3 0.4	1.1 1.2	1.2 1.05	0.1	0.84
	5	0.2 0.3	0.3 0.4	1.1 1.2	1.2 1.05	0.3	1.8
	6	0.2 0.3	0.3 0.4	1.1 1.2	1.2 1.05	0.5	2.8
3	7	0.9 0.7	0.05 0.3	0.3 0.2	0.8 0.8	0.1	0.95
	8	0.9 0.7	0.05 0.3	0.3 0.2	0.8 0.8	0.3	0.99
	9	0.9 0.7	0.05 0.3	0.3 0.2	0.8 0.8	0.5	1.03

Notes: This table shows the parameter values used in the simulated TVAR models. The distribution of the regimes is Bernoulli with probability to be in regime 2 equal to π. Notice that regime 2 is not stable in any of the models. In the right-hand column, we report the maximum eigenvalue of the matrix $(1-\pi)\Phi^1 \otimes \Phi^1 + \pi\Phi^2 \otimes \Phi^2$, λ_{max}.

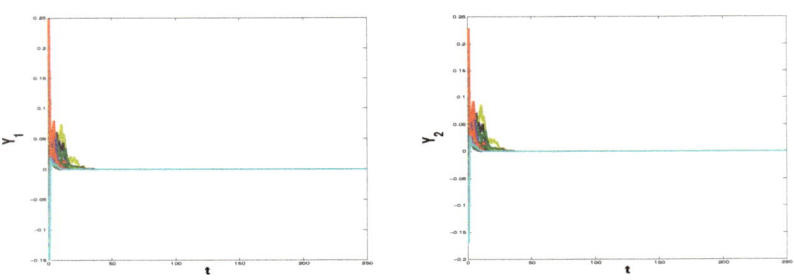

(a) Model 1, $\pi = 0.3$

Figure 1. Cont.

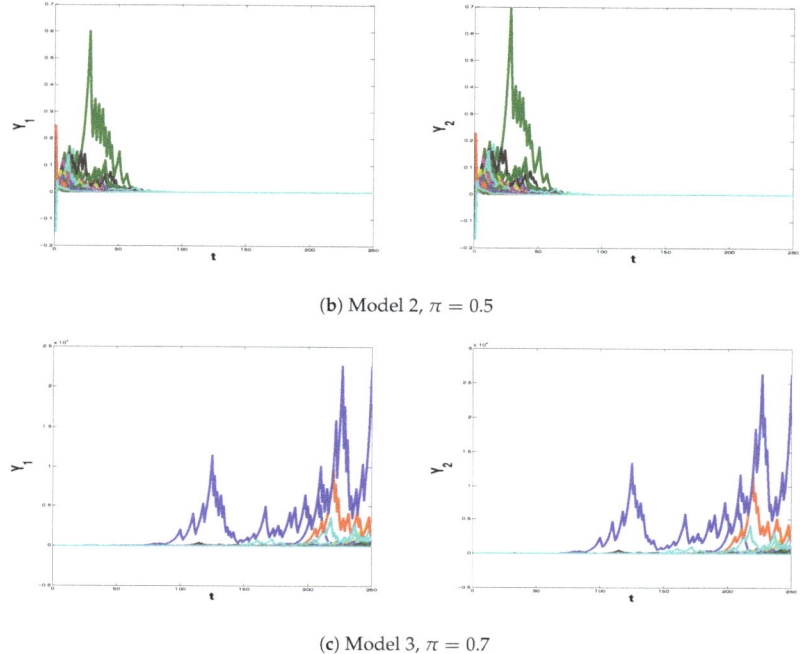

(b) Model 2, $\pi = 0.5$

(c) Model 3, $\pi = 0.7$

Figure 1. Simulated paths represented by different colors from models 1–3 for different set of histories over a $n = 250$ period using $m = 200$ simulated paths. The parameters are those from Table 1 and the probability to be in the explosive regime 2 is equal to π.

Models 7–9 describe a type of relationship, where a particular time series is more strongly related with its own lag in regime 1 and with the other time series in regime 2. These models are quite persistent in regime 1, but still remain stationary in this regime. Figure 3 shows the simulated paths from these models. The explosive performance of model 9 is evident from Panel c. The conclusion, however, is not clear about model 8. This model is quite persistent in both regimes, thus it can generate growing series, like those shown in Panel b, and simulation of model 8 may in fact lead to rejecting the stability of a stationary model. However, we cannot reject stability of the model when $n = 2000$ (Panel b of Figure A3 in Appendix B). In fact, when the length of the simulated time series is increased to $n = 2000$, the series from model 8 grows first but then returns to the initial level later on. Thus, the results from simulating model 8 show that the conclusion from this type of simulation study may also be sensitive to the sample size used in the simulation.

Figure 4 shows the simulated Y_{1t} from TVAR models 4 and 5 specified in Table 1. We end this section by noting that the simulated series of Y_t shown could be associated with data generating processes of financial or economic bubbles. Evans (1991) defines periodically collapsing explosive processes of bubbles such that the explosive behaviour of this process prevails through the whole sample, with non zero probability to collapse when it faces some threshold level. Phillips and Yu (2011) suggest a locally explosive process of bubbles, where asset prices transit from a unit root regime to an explosive regime and claim that this approach is consistent with other propagation mechanisms in financial markets like rational bubbles, exuberant responses to economic fundamentals and herd behaviour. Our simulation exercise shows that a simple bivariate locally explosive yet globally stationary TVAR model can generate unit root or explosive behaviour, which is consistent with these existing definitions of bubbles. An open question in the literature relates to how one can test for bubbles. In a recent paper, Ahmed and Satchell (2018) examine the performance of the Generalized Sup Augmented Dickey Fuller test proposed by Phillips et al. (2015) for the detection of explosive roots in univariate TAR models. They show that the power of the test drops considerably even though locally explosive regimes continue to be present when the process has a stationary distribution. We conjecture that this conclusion generalizes to the multivariate setting used in our paper.

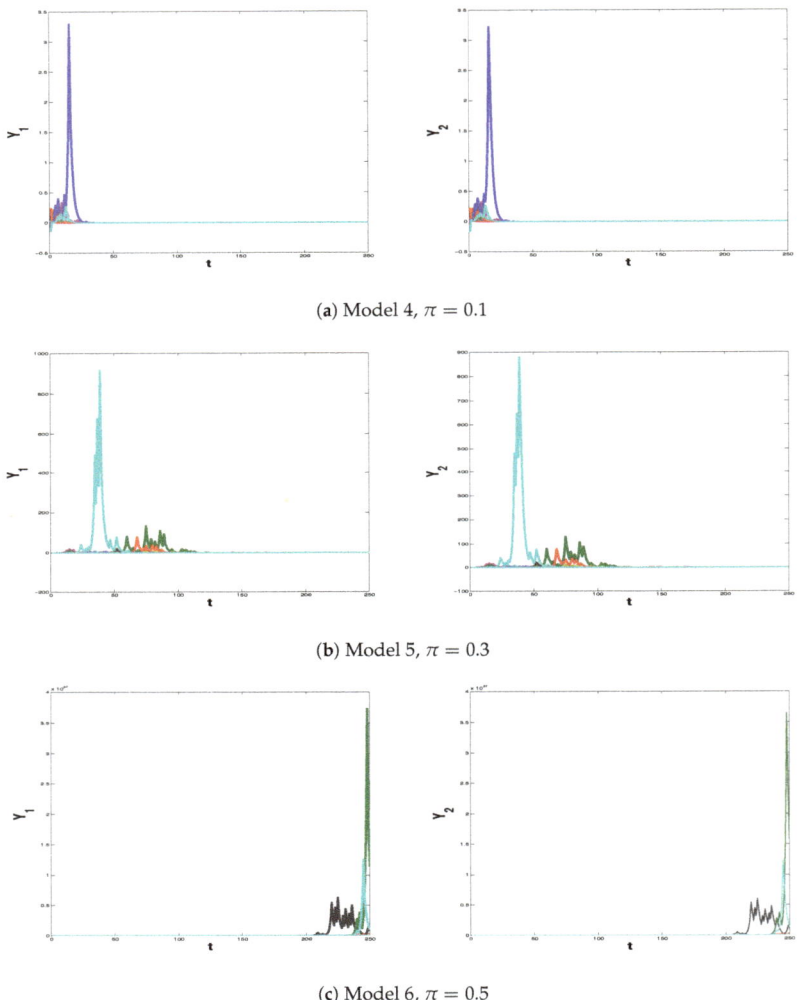

(a) Model 4, $\pi = 0.1$

(b) Model 5, $\pi = 0.3$

(c) Model 6, $\pi = 0.5$

Figure 2. Simulated paths represented by different colors from models 4–6 for different set of histories over a $n = 250$ period using $m = 200$ simulated paths. The parameters are those from Table 1 and the probability to be in the explosive regime 2 is equal to π.

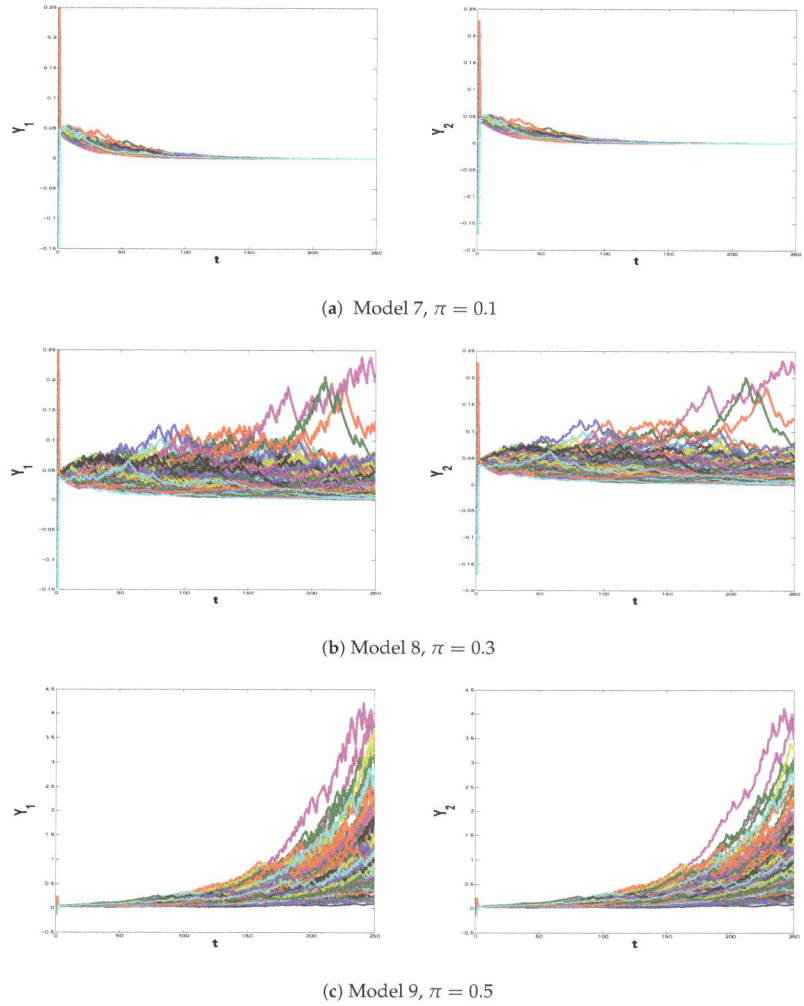

Figure 3. Simulated paths represented by different colors from models 7–9 for different set of histories over a $n = 250$ period using $m = 200$ simulated paths. The parameters are those from Table 1 and the probability to be in the explosive regime 2 is equal to π.

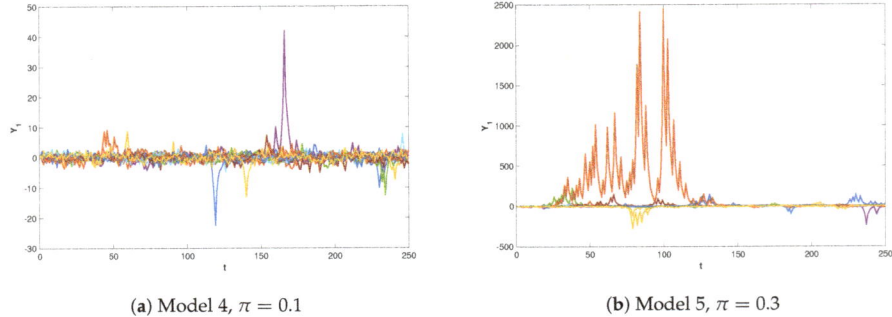

(a) Model 4, $\pi = 0.1$ (b) Model 5, $\pi = 0.3$

Figure 4. Simulated paths of Y_{1t} of model in Equation (1) represented by different colors with parameters from models 4 and 5 for over $n = 250$ period, where $\epsilon_t \in N\{0,1\}$ The parameters are those from Table 1 and the probability to be in the explosive regime 2 is equal to π.

4. Conclusions

This paper derives the necessary and sufficient conditions for the existence of a stationary distribution of the TVAR model with two regimes, when the regime process follows a Bernoulli distribution. These results are, to the best of our knowledge, unavailable in the existing literature. We further derive a closed form solution for the stationary distribution in the special case when there is no autoregressive structure in one of the regimes.

When the variables of interest are positively related, we describe a bivariate TVAR model, which is explosive in one regime, but allows for a stationary distribution along with finite moments. These results are related to so-called locally explosive models and our results extend the notion of locally explosive univariate processes to the bivariate case. We show that such models may remain stationary and, to ensure this, there is a trade-off between the persistence in a given regime and the probability of this regime.

In an empirical application, we simulate from various bivariate TVAR models, which are explosive in one of the regimes. We show how these models can capture the unit root and explosive behaviour, usually implied by the literature on bubble formation. We also demonstrate that a simulation study may fail to reject the stability of non-stationary TVAR models, when the probability of the explosive regime is low.

Author Contributions: The authors contributed equally to all aspects of this paper.

Funding: This research was funded by the Danish National Research Foundation grant number [DNRF78].

Acknowledgments: The authors would like to thank John Knight (deceased), Sergii Pypko, Charles Saunders, Tim Conley, Adlai Fisher, participants at the 2016 NFA Meeting, the 4th Annual Doctoral Workshop in Applied Econometrics at the University of Toronto and the University of Western Ontario Econometric Workshop and three anonymous referees for valuable comments and suggestions.

Conflicts of Interest: The authors declare no conflict of interest.

Appendix A. Proofs

Proof of Theorem 1. We first prove necessity. Let Y_t be second order stationary such that $E(Y_t) = \mu$. Taking expectation of Equation (2), we have that $\mu = (1 - \Phi)^{-1} * 0 = 0$. From Equation (2), we have that

$$(Y_t - \mu)(Y_t - \mu)' = (B_{t-1}\mu + (\Phi + B_{t-1})(Y_{t-1} - \mu) + \epsilon_t)(B_{t-1}\mu + (\Phi + B_{t-1})(Y_{t-1} - \mu) + \epsilon_t)'. \quad (A1)$$

Taking expectations on both sides of Equation (A1) and noticing that the expectation of cross products are zero, we have

$$Var(Y_t) = Var(B_{t-1}\mu) + Var((\Phi + B_{t-1})(Y_{t-1} - \mu)) + Var(\epsilon_t), \tag{A2}$$

which can be rewritten as

$$Var(Y_t) = V = Var(B_{t-1}\mu) + \Phi Var(Y_{t-1})\Phi' + E(B_{t-1}Var(Y_{t-1})B'_{t-1}) + Var(\epsilon_t), \tag{A3}$$

or

$$V = \Phi V \Phi' + E(B_{t-1}VB'_{t-1}) + \Sigma. \tag{A4}$$

It then follows that,

$$V - \Phi V \Phi' - E(B_{t-1}VB'_{t-1}) = \Sigma. \tag{A5}$$

By definition, Σ is a positive definite matrix of full rank. Conlisk (1974) and Conlisk (1976) show there is a unique positive definite V if and only if the maximum of the moduli of $\Phi \otimes \Phi + E(B_{t-1} \otimes B_{t-1})$ is less than 1. Notice that $E(B_{t-1} \otimes B_{t-1}) = \pi(1-\pi)\Phi^0 \otimes \Phi^0$ and $\Phi \otimes \Phi + \pi(1-\pi)\Phi^0 \otimes \Phi^0 = \pi\Phi^2 \otimes \Phi^2 + (1-\pi)\Phi^1 \otimes \Phi^1$. Thus, the conditions used in Conlisk (1974) and Conlisk (1976) transform to $|\lambda| < 1$, where λ is the maximum eigenvalues of the matrix $\pi\Phi^2 \otimes \Phi^2 + (1-\pi)\Phi^1 \otimes \Phi^1$.

We now show sufficiency. Let conditions 1–3 hold. Taking expectation of Equation (2) at $t = 1$ shows that $E(Y_1) = E(Y_0) = \mu$. Iterating further, it is possible to show that $E(Y_t) = \mu$, $\forall t$. Similarly, calculating the variance of Equation (2) at $t = 1$ shows that $Var(Y_1) = \Phi V \Phi' + E(B_{t-1}VB'_{t-1}) + \Sigma = V = Var(Y_0)$. Iterating further, it is possible to show that $Var(Y_t) = V$, $\forall t$. Since $\lambda < 1$, it follows from Conlisk (1974) and Conlisk (1976) that V is positive definite. Premultiplying Equation (2) by Y_{t+h} and taking expectations, we have

$$cov(Y_t, Y_{t+h}) = (\pi\Phi^2 \otimes \Phi^2 + (1-\pi)\Phi^1 \otimes \Phi^1)cov(Y_t, Y_{t+h-1}). \tag{A6}$$

Iterating further, we have

$$cov(Y_t, Y_{t+h}) = (\pi\Phi^2 \otimes \Phi^2 + (1-\pi)\Phi^1 \otimes \Phi^1)^h cov(Y_t, Y_t) = (\pi\Phi^2 \otimes \Phi^2 + (1-\pi)\Phi^1 \otimes \Phi^1)^h V. \tag{A7}$$

Thus, the process Y_t, $t = 0, 1, 2, ...$ is second-order stationary. □

Proof of Theorem 2. Let Y_t be stationary and defined by Equation (4), i.e., the moments of Y_t exist and they are finite. Then, from Equation (7), it follows that

$$E(Y_tY'_t) = E\left(\sum_{n=0}^{\infty} S_n(t)\epsilon_{t-n}\epsilon'_{t-n}S'_n(t)\right).$$

We may rewrite this in *vec* form as

$$\begin{aligned}
vecE(Y_tY'_t) &= vecE\left(\sum_{n=0}^{\infty} S_n(t)\epsilon_{t-n}\epsilon'_{t-n}S'_n(t)\right) \\
&= E\left(\sum_{n=0}^{\infty} S_n(t) \otimes S_n vec(\epsilon_{t-n}\epsilon'_{t-n})\right) \\
&= E\left(vec(\epsilon_t\epsilon'_t) + \sum_{n=1}^{\infty} \prod_{k=1}^{n}(\Phi + B_{t-n}) \otimes (\Phi + B_{t-n})vec(\epsilon_{t-n}\epsilon'_{t-n})\right).
\end{aligned}$$

Since $\prod_{k=0}^{n} A_k \otimes \prod_{k=0}^{n} B_k = \prod_{k=0}^{n} A_k \otimes B_k$ for any matrices A_k and B_k whenever the matrix product exists, the later can be rewritten as

$$vecE(Y_t Y_t') = \sum_{n=0}^{\infty} (\Phi \otimes \Phi + E(B_{t-n} \otimes B_{t-n}))^n vec\Sigma.$$

Then,

$$vecV = \sum_{n=0}^{\infty} (\pi \Phi^2 \otimes \Phi^2 + (1-\pi)\Phi^1 \otimes \Phi^1)^n vec\Sigma. \tag{A8}$$

Furthermore, since $(\pi \Phi^2 \otimes \Phi^2 + (1-\pi)\Phi^1 \otimes \Phi^1) vecV = \sum_{n=1}^{\infty} (\pi \Phi^2 \otimes \Phi^2 + (1-\pi)\Phi^1 \otimes \Phi^1)^n vec\Sigma = vecV - vec\Sigma$, we have that

$$vecV - (\pi \Phi^2 \otimes \Phi^2 + (1-\pi)\Phi^1 \otimes \Phi^1) vecV = vec\Sigma,$$

or

$$vecV - (\Phi \otimes \Phi + E(B_{t-n} \otimes B_{t-n})) vecV = vec\Sigma,$$

which is equivalent to

$$V - \Phi V \Phi - E(B_{t-n} V B_{t-n}) = \Sigma. \tag{A9}$$

Since V and Σ are both positive definite, the maximum eigenvalue of $\Phi \otimes \Phi + E(B_{t-n} \otimes B_{t-n})$ is less than 1 (Conlisk 1974, 1976). Thus, the the maximum eigenvalue of $(1-\pi)\Phi^1 \otimes \Phi^1 + \pi \Phi^2 \otimes \Phi^2$, λ, is less than 1.

We now prove sufficiency. Let all the eigenvalues of the matrix $(1-\pi)\Phi^1 \otimes \Phi^1 + \pi \Phi^2 \otimes \Phi^2$ be less than 1. Following Nicholls and Quinn (1982), we consider

$$W_r(t) = \epsilon_t + \sum_{n=1}^{r} \prod_{k=1}^{n} (\Phi + B_{t-k}) \epsilon_{t-n} = \sum_{n=0}^{r} S_{n-1}(t) \epsilon_{t-n}. \tag{A10}$$

Given that the eigenvalues of the matrix $(1-\pi)\Phi^1 \otimes \Phi^1 + \pi \Phi^2 \otimes \Phi^2$ are less than 1, the limit $W(t)$ of $W_r(t)$ exists in mean square and thus in probability. Moreover, $W(t) = \epsilon_t + \sum_{n=1}^{\infty} (\prod_{k=1}^{n} \Phi + B_{t-k}) \epsilon_{t-n}$ satisfies Equation (2) and $W(t)$ is stationary. Now, suppose $U(t)$ is another stationary solution of Equation (2) and define

$$X(t) = W(t) - U(t). \tag{A11}$$

By definition, $X(t) = (\Phi + B_{t-1}) X(t-1)$, $E(X(t)) = 0$ and $X(t)$ is stationary. Then $E(X(t)X'(t)) = \Phi E(X(t-1)X'(t-1)\Phi') + E(B_{t-1} E(X(t-1)X'(t-1)) B_{t-1})$. Since $X(t)$ is stationary, and $\Phi \otimes \Phi + E(B_{t-1} \otimes B_{t-1}) = (1-\pi)\Phi^1 \otimes \Phi^1 + \pi \Phi^2 \otimes \Phi^2$, we have $(I - ((1-\pi)\Phi^1 \otimes \Phi^1 + \pi \Phi^2 \otimes \Phi^2)') vec E(X(t)X'(t)) = 0$. However, since the eigenvalues of $(1-\pi)\Phi^1 \otimes \Phi^1 + \pi \Phi^2 \otimes \Phi^2$ are less then 1, $E(X(t)X'(t))=0$. Thus, $W(t) = U(t)$, and $W(t)$ is the unique solution of Equation (2). Since $W(t)$ is the same for all t, it is also the strictly stationary solution of Equation (2). □

Proof of Remark 2. Following Theorems 1 and 2, the maximum eigenvalue of $\Phi \otimes \Phi + E(B_{t-n} \otimes B_{t-n})$ is less than 1. Consider $S = \Sigma + E(B_{t-n} V B_{t-n})$ and $K = V$. S and K are positive definite, since Σ and V are positive definite. From Equation (20), we have that

$$K - \Phi K \Phi = S.$$

From Barnett and Storey (1970), it follows that the maximum eigenvalue of Φ is less than 1. □

Proof of Corollary 1. Given the definitions of Z_t, η_t, and $A^i, i = 1, 2$, we can rewrite the model in Equation (5) in its companion form

$$Z_t = A^1 I(X_{t-1} \in R_1) Z_{t-1} + A^2 I(X_{t-1} \in R_2) Z_{t-1} + \eta_t. \tag{A12}$$

Now, define $A = (1 - \pi)A^1 + \pi A^2$. Then, the model in Equation (A12) can be rewritten as a Random Coefficient Model (Nicholls and Quinn 1982) given by

$$Z_t = (A + D_t)Z_{t-1} + \eta_t, \qquad (A13)$$

where $D_t = (S_t - \pi)A^2 + (\pi - S_t)A^1$, such that $ED_t = 0$.

The proof of sufficient conditions are similar to the proof of Theorem 2 and it suffices to show necessity. Define $\Omega = varZ_t$ and assume it exists and that it is finite. Notice that $\eta(t) = (1, 0, 0, .., 0) \otimes \epsilon(t) = l \otimes \epsilon(t)$. Define $H = ll'$. Then, following the first part of the proof of Theorem 2, we have

$$vec\Omega = \sum_{n=0}^{\infty}(A \otimes A + ED_{t-n} \otimes D_{t-n})^n vec(H \otimes \Sigma). \qquad (A14)$$

Following the same strategy as in the proof of Theorem 2, it is straightforward to show that

$$\Omega = A\Omega A + ED'_{t-n}\Omega D_{t-n} + H \otimes \Sigma. \qquad (A15)$$

Let $z' = [z'_1, ...z'_p]$ be the left eigenvector of the matrix A with corresponding eigenvalue λ and z_i are $n \times 1$ vectors. Then,

$$(1 - \lambda^2)z'\Omega z = z'_1 \Sigma z_1 + z'ED'_{t-n}\Omega D_{t-n}z.$$

Since Ω is positive semidefinite, $ED'_{t-n}\Omega D_{t-n}$ is positive semidefinite. Since Σ is positive definite, $|\lambda| < 1$ when $z_1 \neq 0$. Now let $z_1 = 0$. Since z' is the left eigenvector of A with eigenvalue λ, we have the following system of equations:

$$z'_1 \Phi^i + z'_{i+1} = \lambda z'_i, \qquad \forall i = 1, .., p - 1,$$

and

$$z'_1 \Phi^p = \lambda z'_p.$$

Since $\lambda \neq 0$, $z_p = 0$. Thus, $z_i = 0$, $\forall i = 1, .., p - 1$. However, since $z \neq 0$, this contradicts that $z_1 = 0$. □

Proof of Theorem 3. The characteristic function of Y_t is

$$\phi(t, Y_t) = E_{S_n(t)}\left(exp\left(-\frac{1}{2}t\Sigma t' - \frac{1}{2}t\sum_{n=1}^{\infty}S_n(t)\Sigma S'_n(t)t'\right)\right). \qquad (A16)$$

Thus, it is defined by the distribution of $S_n(t)$. Since $\sum_{n=1}^{\infty}S_n(t) = \sum_{n=1}^{\infty}\prod_{k=1}^{n}S_{t-k}\Psi$, the probability space of $\sum_{n=1}^{\infty}S_n(t)$ is $\{0, \sum_{n=1}^{K}\Psi^n, K \geq 1\}$, and $\sum_{n=1}^{\infty}S_n(t)$ has a Geometric distribution with $P(\sum_{n=1}^{\infty}S_n(t) = 0) = (1 - \pi)$ and $P(\sum_{n=1}^{\infty}S_n(t) = \sum_{n=1}^{K}\Psi^n) = (1 - \pi)\pi^K$. It follows that

$$\begin{aligned}
\phi(t, Y_t) &= E_{S_n(t)}\left(exp\left(-\frac{1}{2}t\Sigma t' - \frac{1}{2}t\sum_{n=1}^{\infty}\prod_{k=1}^{n}S_{t-k}\Psi\Sigma(\prod_{k=1}^{n}S_{t-k}\Psi)'t'\right)\right) \\
&= (1 - \pi)exp\left(-\frac{1}{2}t\Sigma t'\right) + (1 - \pi)\sum_{K=1}^{\infty}\pi^K exp\left(-\frac{1}{2}t\sum_{n=1}^{K}\Psi^n\Sigma\Psi'^n t'\right) \\
&= (1 - \pi)\sum_{K=0}^{\infty}\pi^K exp\left(-\frac{1}{2}t\sum_{n=0}^{K}\Psi^n\Sigma\Psi'^n t'\right).
\end{aligned}$$

Integrating the above expression, we have that the probability distribution function of Y_t is a weighted average of normal distributions

$$f(t, Y_t) = (1 - \pi) \sum_{K=0}^{\infty} \pi^K N\left(0, \sum_{n=0}^{K} \Psi^n \Sigma \Psi'^n\right),$$

where $N(A, B)$ is the multivariate normal distribution with mean A and covariance matrix B. □

Proof of Corollary 2. The Perron–Frobenius theorem states that, for a matrix X with positive entries, there is a unique maximum eigenvalue λ such that $\min_i \sum_j x_{ij} \leq \lambda \leq \max_i \sum_j x_{ij}$. Let λ^2 be the maximum eigenvalue of matrix Φ^2. Then, $1 \leq \lambda^2 \leq \max_{i \in \{1,2\}} (\phi_{i1}^2 + \phi_{i2}^2)$. Let λ be the maximum eigenvalue of $(1 - \pi)\Phi^1 \otimes \Phi^1 + \pi \Phi^2 \otimes \Phi^2$. Then,

$$\lambda \leq \max_{i \in \{1,2\}} F_i((1 - \pi)\Phi^1 \otimes \Phi^1 + \pi \Phi^2 \otimes \Phi^2), \tag{A17}$$

where $F_i()$ denotes the column sum for each row i. From the last equation, we have that $\lambda \leq \max_{i \in \{1,2\}} F_i((1 - \pi)\Phi^1 \otimes \Phi^1 + \pi \Phi^2 \otimes \Phi^2) \leq (1 - \pi) \max_{i \in \{1,2\}} (\phi_{i1}^1 + \phi_{i2}^1)^2 + \pi \max_{i \in \{1,2\}} (\phi_{i1}^2 + \phi_{i2}^2)$. Since the condition of the corollary holds for any $i, j = 1, 2$, we have that

$$(1 - \pi) \max_{i \in \{1,2\}} (\phi_{i1}^1 + \phi_{i2}^1)^2 + \pi \max_{i \in \{1,2\}} (\phi_{i1}^2 + \phi_{i2}^2) < 1. \tag{A18}$$

Thus, $\lambda < 1$ and, from Theorems 1 and 2, the model in Equation (1) is stationary. Now, suppose the model is explosive in regime 2 and let λ^2 be the maximum eigenvalue of matrix Φ^2. Then, from the Perron–Frobenius theorem,

$$1 \leq \lambda^2 \leq \max_{i \in \{1,2\}} (\phi_{i1}^2 + \phi_{i2}^2). \tag{A19}$$

Equations (A18) and (A19) show that $1 \leq (\max_{i \in \{1,2\}} (\phi_{i1}^2 + \phi_{i2}^2))^2 < \frac{1}{\pi} - \frac{(1-\pi)}{\pi} \max_{i \in \{1,2\}} (\phi_{i1}^1 + \phi_{i2}^1)^2$ and thus $(\phi_{i1}^1 + \phi_{i2}^1) < 1$ for any $i = 1, 2$. □

Proof of Corollary 3. From Remark 2, we know that, if the model is stationary, then the eigenvalues of the matrix Φ are less than 1. Let λ_1 and λ_2 be the eigenvalues of matrix $\Phi = (1 - \pi)\Phi^1 + \pi \Phi^2$ where $\Phi^1 = \begin{pmatrix} \phi_{11}^1 & \phi_{12}^1 \\ 0 & \phi_{22}^1 \end{pmatrix}, \Phi^2 = \begin{pmatrix} \phi_{11}^2 & \phi_{12}^2 \\ 0 & \phi_{22}^2 \end{pmatrix}$. Then it follows that,

$$\lambda_1 \lambda_2 = \det \Phi = (1 - \pi)^2 \lambda_1^1 \lambda_2^1 + \pi^2 \lambda_1^2 \lambda_2^2 + \pi(1 - \pi)\phi_{11}^1 \phi_{22}^2 + \pi(1 - \pi)\phi_{22}^1 \phi_{11}^2. \tag{A20}$$

Since ϕ_{11}^i and $\phi_{22}^i, i = 1, 2$ are nonnegative,

$$\lambda_1 \lambda_2 \geq (1 - \pi)^2 \lambda_1^1 \lambda_2^1 + \pi^2 \lambda_1^2 \lambda_2^2. \tag{A21}$$

Now suppose $\lambda_1^2 \lambda_2^2 \geq 1$ and $\pi \geq \sqrt{\frac{1}{\lambda_1^2 \lambda_2^2}}$. Since Φ^1 and Φ^2 are upper triangular matrices with nonnegative diagonal entries, we have that

$$\lambda_1 \lambda_2 \geq \pi^2 \lambda_1^2 \lambda_2^2 \geq 1. \tag{A22}$$

Thus, there is an eigenvalue of Φ, which is greater than 1. From Theorem 2, it follows that the process $Y_t, t = 0, 1, 2, ...$ is not stationary. Similarly, it can be shown that the process Y_t is not stationary when condition 2 of Corollary 3 does not hold. □

Appendix B. Additional Figures

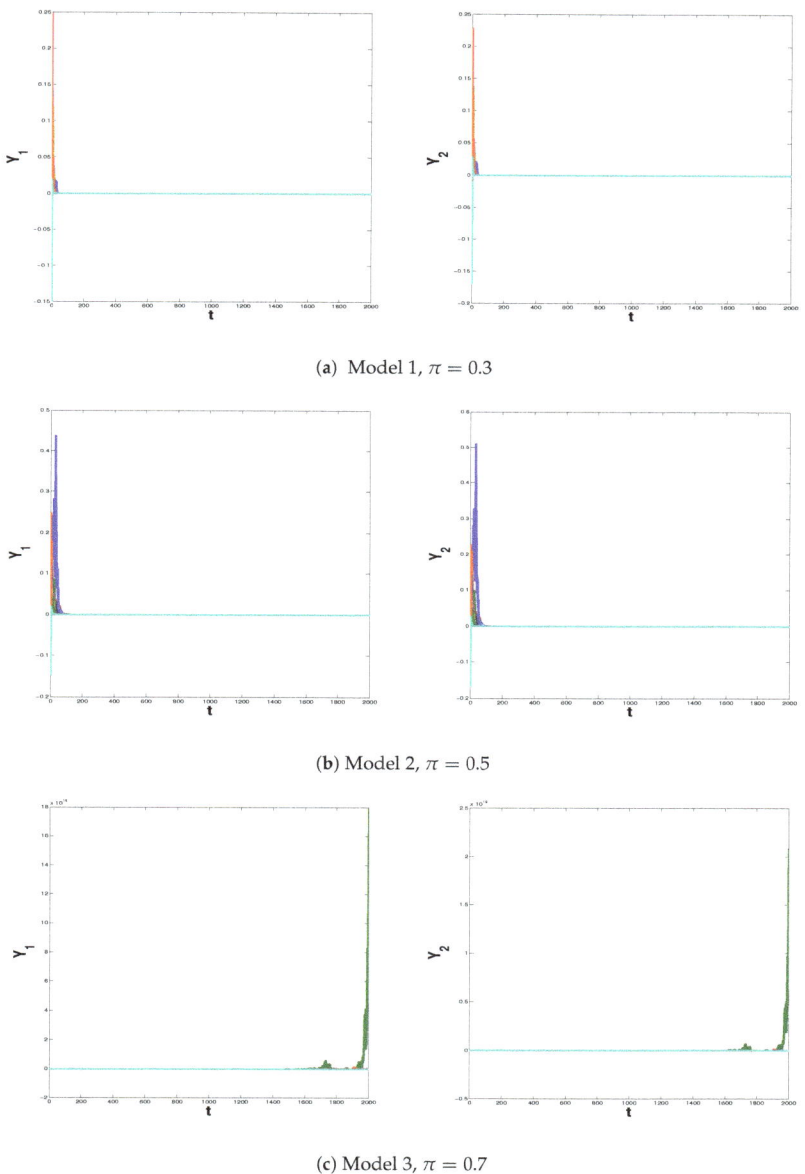

Figure A1. Simulated paths represented by different colors from models 1–3 for a different set of histories over an $n = 2000$ period using $m = 200$ simulated paths. The parameters are those from Table 1 and the probability to be in the explosive regime 2 is equal to π.

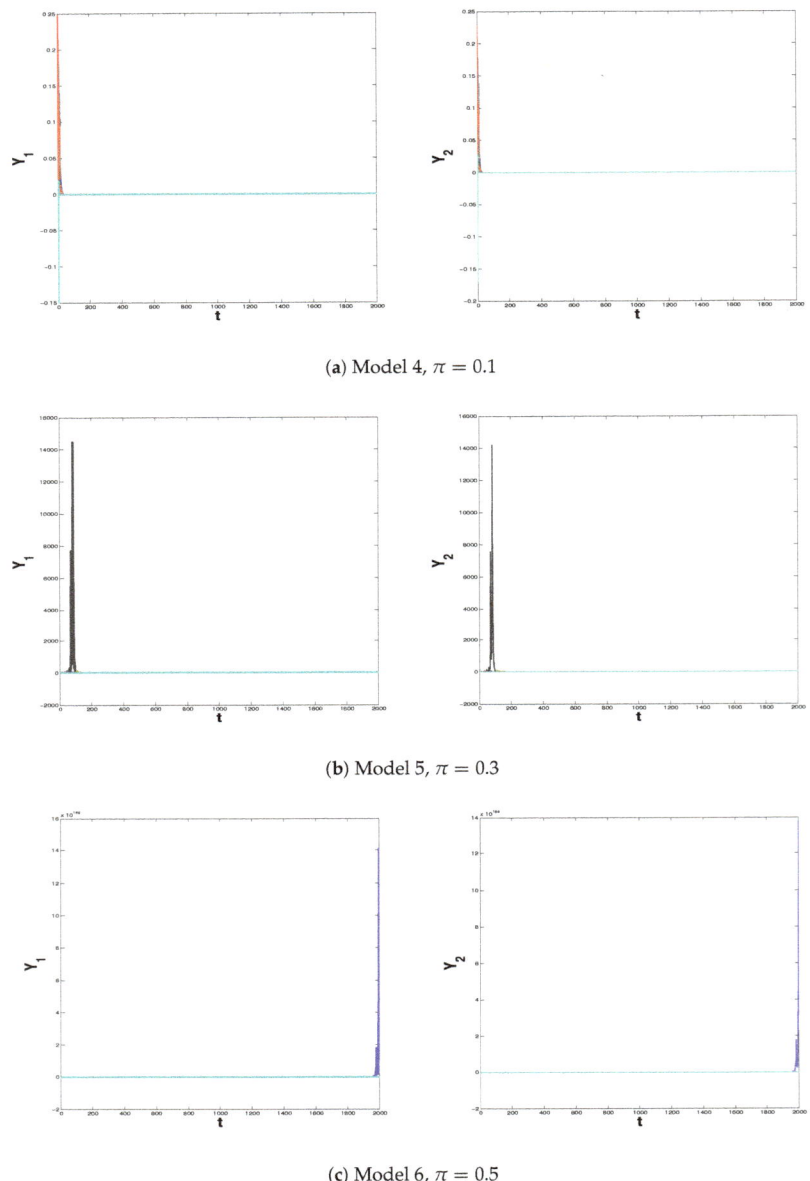

Figure A2. Simulated paths represented by different colors from models 4–6 for a different set of histories over a $n = 2000$ period using $m = 200$ simulated paths. The parameters are those from Table 1 and the probability to be in the explosive regime 2 is equal to π.

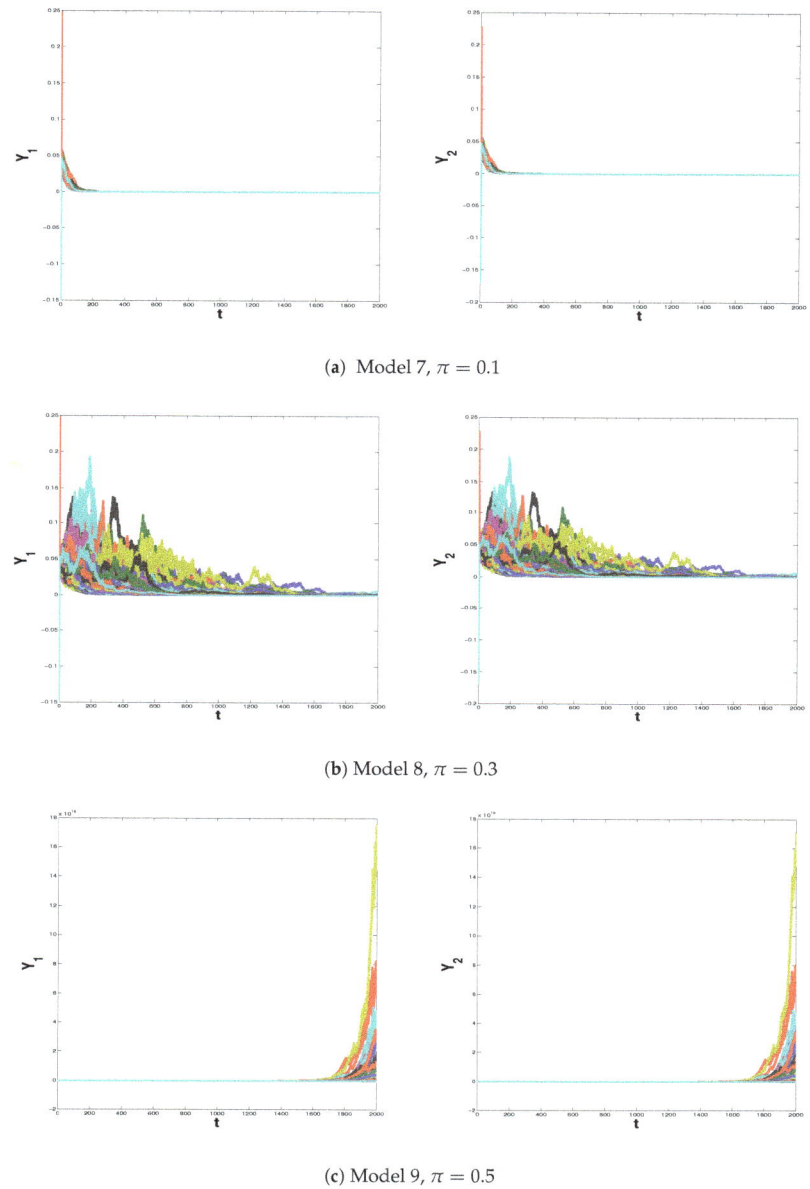

(a) Model 7, $\pi = 0.1$

(b) Model 8, $\pi = 0.3$

(c) Model 9, $\pi = 0.5$

Figure A3. Simulated paths represented by different colors from models 7–9 for a different set of histories over a $n = 2000$ period using $m = 200$ simulated paths. The parameters are those from Table 1 and the probability to be in the explosive regime 2 is equal to π.

References

Ahmed, Muhammad Farid, and Stephen Satchell. 2018. What Proportion of Time Is a Particular Market Inefficient? ... A Method for Analysing the Frequency of Market. Efficiency when Equity Prices Follow Threshold Autoregressions. *Journal of Time Series Econometrics* 10: 1–22.

Altissimo, Filippo, and Giovanni L. Violante. 2001. The nonlinear dynamics of output and unemployment in the U.S. *Journal of Applied Econometrics* 16: 461–86. [CrossRef]

Amihud, Yakov, and Haim Mendelson. 1986. Asset pricing and the bid-ask spread. *Journal of Financial Economics* 17: 223–49. [CrossRef]

Balke, Nathan. 2000. Credit and economic activity: Credit regimes and nonlinear propagation of shocks. *Review of Economics and Statistics* 82: 344–49. [CrossRef]

Barnes, Michelle. 1999. Inflation and returns revisted: A TAR approach. *Journal of Multinational Financial Management* 9: 233–45. [CrossRef]

Barnett, Stephen, and Colin Storey. 1970. *Matrix Methods in Stability Theory*. New York: Barnes and Noble.

Brockwell, Peter J., Jian Liu, and Richard L. Tweedie. 1992. On the existence of stationary threshold autoregressive moving-average processes. *Journal of Time Series Analysis* 13: 95–107. [CrossRef]

Calza, Alessandro, and Joao Sousa. 2006. Output and Inflation Responses to Credit Shocks: Are There Threshold Effects in the Euro Area? *Studies in Nonlinear Dynamics & Econometrics* 10: 1–19.

Chan, Kung S., and Howell Tong. 1985. On the use of the deterministic Lyapunov function for the ergodicity of stochastic difference equations. *Advances in Applied Probability* 17: 666–78. [CrossRef]

Chen, Cathy W. S., Mike K. P. So, and Feng-Chi Liu. 2011. A review of threshold time series models in finance. *Statistics and Its Interface* 4: 167–81. [CrossRef]

Conlisk, John. 1974. Stability in a random coefficient model. *International Economic Review* 15: 529–33. [CrossRef]

Conlisk, John. 1976. A further note on stability in a random coefficient model. *International Economic Review* 17: 759–64. [CrossRef]

Engle, Robert F., and Jose Gonzalo Rangel. 2008. The spline-garch model for low-frequency volatility and its global macroeconomic causes. *Review of Financial Studies* 21: 1187–222. [CrossRef]

Evans, George. 1991. Pitfalls in testing for explosive bubbles in asset prices. *American Economic Review* 81: 922–30.

Fazzari, Steven M., James Morley, and Irina Panovska. 2015. State dependent effects of fiscal policy. *Studies in Nonlinear Dynamics and Econometrics* 19: 285–315. [CrossRef]

Feigin, Paul D., and Richard L. Tweedie. 1985. Random coefficient autoregressive processes: A Markov chain analysis of stationarity and finiteness of moments. *Journal of Time Series Analysis* 6: 1–14. [CrossRef]

Griffin, John M., Federico Nardari, and René M. Stulz. 2007. Do investors trade more when stocks have performed well? *Review of Financial Studies* 20: 905–51. [CrossRef]

Hansen, Bruce. 1996. Inference when a nuisance parameter is not identified under the null hypothesis. *Econometrica* 64: 413–30. [CrossRef]

Hansen, Bruce. 2000. Sample splitting and threshold estimation. *Econometrica* 68: 575–603. [CrossRef]

Hansen, Bruce. 2011. Threshold autoregression in economics. *Statistics and Its Interface* 4: 123–27. [CrossRef]

Huang, Bwo-Nung, Ming-Jeng Hwang, and Hsiao-Ping Peng. 2005. The asymmetry of the impact of oil price shocks on economic activities: An application of the multivariate threshold model. *Energy Economics* 27: 455–76. [CrossRef]

Hubrich, Kirstin, and Timo Teräsvirta. 2013. Thresholds and smooth transitions in vector autoregressive models. *Advances in Eonometrics* 32: 273–326.

Jagannathan, Ravi, Ellen R. McGrattan, and Anna Scherbina. 2000. The declining U.S. equity premium. *Quarterly Review, Federal Reserve Bank of Minneapolis* 24: 3–19.

Knight, John, and Stephen Satchell. 2011. Some new results for threshold AR(1) models. *Journal of Time Series Econometrics* 3. [CrossRef]

Knight, John, Stephen Satchell, and Nandini Srivastava. 2014. Steady state distributions for models of locally explosive regimes: Existence and econometric implications. *Economic Modelling* 41: 281–88. [CrossRef]

Koop, Gary, and Simon M. Potter. 1999. Dynamic asymmetries in U.S. unemployment. *Journal of Business and Economic Statistics* 17: 298–312.

Koop, Gary, M. Hashem Pesaran, and Simon M. Potter. 1996. Impulse response analysis in nonlinear multivariate models. *Journal of Econometrics* 74: 119–47. [CrossRef]

Li, Fuchun, and Pierre St-Amant. 2010. *Financial Stress, Monetary Policy, and Economic Activity*. Working Paper. Ottawa: Bank of Canada.

Li, Johnny Siu-Hang, Andrew C. Y. Ng, and Wai-Sum Chan. 2015. Managing financial risk in chinese stockmarkets: Option pricing and modeling under a multivariate threshold autoregression. *International Review of Economics and Finance* 40: 217–30. [CrossRef]

Nicholls, Desmond F., and Barry Quinn. 1981. The stability of random coefficient autoregressive models. *International Economic Review* 22: 741–44.

Nicholls, Des F., and Barry G. Quinn. 1982. *Random Coefficient Autoregressive Models: An Introduction*. Lecture Notes in Statistics. New York, Berlin/Heidelberg: Springer, vol. 11, pp. 1–154.

Niglio, Marcella, Francesco Giordano, and Cosimo Damiano Vitale. 2012. *On the Stationarity of the Threshold Autoregressive Process: The Two Regimes Case*. Working Paper. Rome: Italian Statistical Society.

Peel, David A., and Alan E. H. Speight. 1998. Modelling business cycle nonlinearity in conditional mean and conditional variance: Some international and sectoral evidence. *Economica* 65: 211–29.

Petruccelli, Joseph D., and Samuel W. Woolford. 1984. A threshold AR(1) model. *Journal of Applied Probability* 21: 270–86. [CrossRef]

Phillips, Peter, and Jun Yu. 2009. *Limit Theory for Dating the Origination and Collapse of Mildly Explosive Periods in Time Series Data*. Working Paper. Singapore: Singapore Management University.

Phillips, Peter, and Jun Yu. 2011. Dating the timeline of financial bubbles during the subprime crisis. *Quantitative Economics* 2: 455–91. [CrossRef]

Phillips, Peter, Yangru Wu, and Jun Yu. 2011. Explosive behavior in the 1990's NASDAQ: When did exuberance escalate asset values? *International Economic Review* 52: 201–26. [CrossRef]

Phillips, Peter, Shuping Shi, and Jun Yu. 2015. Testing for multiple bubbles: Historical episodes of exuberance and collapse in the S&P 500. *International Economic Review* 56: 1043–78.

Potter, Simon. 1995. A nonlinear approach to US GNP. *Journal of Applied Econometrics* 10: 109–25. [CrossRef]

Rabemananjara, Roger, and Jean-Michel Zakoian. 1993. Threshold ARCH models and asymmetries in volatility. *Journal of Applied Econometrics* 8: 31–49. [CrossRef]

Saikkonen, Pentti. 2007. Stability of mixtures of vector autoregressions with autoregressive conditional heteroskedasticity. *Statistica Sinica* 17: 221–39.

Shen, Chung-Hua, and Thomas Chi-Nan Chiang. 1999. Retrieving the vanishing liquidity effect—A threshold vector autoregressive model. *Journal of Economics and Business* 51: 259–277. [CrossRef]

Tsay, Ruey. 1998. Testing and modeling multivariate threshold models. *Journal of the American Statistical Association* 93: 1188–202. [CrossRef]

Wang, George, and Jot Yau. 2000. Trading volume, bid-ask spread, and price volatility in futures markets. *Journal of Futures Markets* 20: 943–70. [CrossRef]

Yadav, Pradeep K., Peter F. Pope, and Krishna Paudyal. 1994. Threshold autoregressive models in finance: The price differences of equivalent assets. *Mathematical Finance* 4: 205–21.

© 2018 by the authors. Licensee MDPI, Basel, Switzerland. This article is an open access article distributed under the terms and conditions of the Creative Commons Attribution (CC BY) license (http://creativecommons.org/licenses/by/4.0/).

MDPI
St. Alban-Anlage 66
4052 Basel
Switzerland
Tel. +41 61 683 77 34
Fax +41 61 302 89 18
www.mdpi.com

Journal of Risk and Financial Management Editorial Office
E-mail: jrfm@mdpi.com
www.mdpi.com/journal/jrfm

www.ingramcontent.com/pod-product-compliance
Lightning Source LLC
LaVergne TN
LVHW071957080526
838202LV00064B/6771